Towards a Political Education Through Environmental Issues

Education Set

coordinated by
Angela Barthes and Anne-Laure Le Guern

Volume 8

Towards a Political Education Through Environmental Issues

Melki Slimani

iSTE

WILEY

First published 2021 in Great Britain and the United States by ISTE Ltd and John Wiley & Sons, Inc.

ISTE Ltd
27-37 St George's Road
London SW19 4EU
UK

www.iste.co.uk

John Wiley & Sons, Inc.
111 River Street
Hoboken, NJ 07030
USA

www.wiley.com

Library of Congress Control Number: 2020951823

British Library Cataloguing-in-Publication Data
A CIP record for this book is available from the British Library
ISBN 978-1-78630-588-6

MIX
Paper from responsible sources
FSC www.fsc.org FSC® C013604

Contents

Foreword

Laying Down the Principles of Intentional Political Curricula for the Anthropocene World

Proposed in the early 2000s to researchers in the life sciences and geosciences by the geochemist Paul Crutzen, the notion of the Anthropocene seeks to emphasize the idea of anthropogenic changes, which affect all the outer layers of the planet (gases, liquids and solids) and profoundly modify its biogeophysical dynamics. Climate and biodiversity issues would be good examples of this. Such modifications would come to characterize this new geological era and thus replace the previous one, the Holocene. From a natural sciences perspective, the matter would prove controversial and be discussed within the International Commission on Stratigraphy. Nonetheless, it has paved the way for a new account of the interface between the social history of humans and the natural history of the planet (Beau and Larrère 2018).

The questions that subsequently arise are not straightforward and require an ability to master systematic thought and make a collective decision in an uncertain situation: what should be done about tipping points, the irreversibility of climate change, the erosion of biodiversity, profound changes in biogeochemical cycles and the limits of the planet (Rockström *et al.* 2009a, 2009b)? Based on proposed theories, how can we date and ascertain the origin of this new era, that is, the beginning of agriculture, the conquest of America, the invention of the steam engine and the edging towards overconsumption during the second wave of globalization? The answers to these questions require that we develop new theories and appropriate new knowledge, but they also concern fundamental issues. Anthropological answers include the links between culture and nature which condition our capacity to address the challenges posed at the risk of relegating humanity to one of its constituent areas (the North, the West, etc.; see Descola 2019). Yet there are also sociological answers, which refer to the relations of domination in production systems and the sharing of resources.

It is therefore a question of metanarratives and politics: a metanarrative because the idea of great acceleration and planetary limits is imposed on the whole of humanity by mixing scientific data and studies with mediatized discourses that stir up fears as well as hopes of another world and is therefore conceived as a mobilizer for the whole of humanity; and political because it tends to make people forget that these environmental and resource issues were historically rooted in 18th-century Europe (Fressoz 2012; Bonneuil and Fressoz 2013) and resulted from political choices that confirmed to the market the environmental risk in view and in favor of "extractivist" development. However, the contrary is true: the dissociation of time from nature, politics and social issues is at the root of the globalized environmental and social crises we are collectively facing (Theys 2015, 2019). Our way of living and thinking about the world is not fit for purpose (Lussault 2018).

It subsequently becomes an educational issue, too. As Fressoz demonstrates, the school has been a major player in this historical process by disqualifying local knowledge, for example, in favor of scholarly knowledge alone, which is put at the service of a narrative of progress. It has also been a source of standardization, of a colonization of curricula, which Descarpentries (2018) describes as covertly epistemicidal and extractivist. Moreover, the school and the world of education, taken in their broadest sense, are also a means of collectively constructing another relationship with the world. Citizen groups, associations, activists, neighborhood committees and spontaneous youth movements have understood this. The United Nations General Assembly has also made this point strongly by voting in its plenary session on the role of education as a catalyst (SDG 4) for all the goals it adopted in 2015. We will add to this the issue of training and skills development for societal responsibilities (Barthes and Lange 2018).

However, in the media and in formal education, environmental development issues are most often considered purely from a technical and economic angle. There is therefore a need to put education at the service of the collective development geared towards a new way of inhabiting the world, which implies changing our relationship to crises, uncertainty, resilience and, therefore, to the highly hierarchical productive worlds and forms of knowledge transmission in our societies. These desirable transformations lead us to focus our attention on a certain number of key and determining points in terms of content. The questions of scales (in terms of time, space and complexity), the relationship with others (otherness, multiculturalism, multi-referentiality) and the relationship with nature, resources and production are all benchmarks and values to be discussed as part of education for sustainable development.

Not excluding questions of health, citizenship, environment and territories, all types of education (Barthes *et al.* 2017) are generally designed as a means of conceiving the future insofar as it forms a continuum with the present and the past rather than being disconnected from them (Vergnolle-Mainar 2011; Julien 2018). They are a means of thinking about duration not as a linear dynamic but as a time limit, which implies a retroactive conception of the future with a consideration for the occurrence of possible but unquantifiable disasters and the avoidance of naive catastrophism that inhibits commitment (Lange and Martinand 2014). They enable us to think about the question of the local and the global as a whole in terms of the contextualizations that facilitate the appropriation of the issues at stake. Moreover, they are a way of rethinking enabling environments (Janner-Raimondi 2017); considering the values of solidarity, fraternity, sharing and cooperation as support tools rather than obstacles to change and commitment in tomorrow's world; conceiving scales of organization in terms of complexity (Morin 2015), which implies thresholds, disruptions and beginnings; and thinking about systems in terms of societal responsibilities, among other things (Lange and Martinand 2014).

The changes implied by taking the educational project seriously in the Anthropocene era are therefore considerable. To this end, there is a need to lay the groundwork for intentional curricular development principles that serve political education through environmental and developmental issues. This is what this book serves to provide.

Jean-Marc LANGE
University Professor of Education Sciences
and Training, University of Montpellier

Angela BARTHES
University Professor of Education Sciences
and Training, Aix-Marseille University

January 2021

Introduction

Environmental and development issues (EDIs) have emerged as a matter of public interest through a new type of political mobilization that has characterized contemporary human societies: ecological mobilization (Zaccai and Orban 2017). These mobilizations, which act as alerts for a global ecological crisis, reflect an awareness of the potentially catastrophic effect of human activity on the ecological functioning of the planet (Little 2017). EDIs have thus appeared as indicators of a turning point in political life in the Anthropocene.

Ecological mobilizations have been brought to life in the form of popular movements at the global/international level, such as the Cities in Transition[1] movement, and at the regional level, such as the Climate Justice Action[2] movement in Europe. While the first proposed alternatives for a more resilient urban life to economic and climate crises (Krauz 2014), the second demanded a democratization of the climate discourse and a broadening of the scope of climate change action through a confrontation with the dominant capitalist system in order to break it with acts of disobedience. A recent analysis of the discourse of transitions shows that it is becoming heterogeneous and divided between two trends: a "localist" and politicized discourse in citizen and public policy initiatives on the one hand, and a mainly economic technocentric discourse (Audet 2016) on the other.

1 The urban transition movement initially originated in Great Britain in 2006 with Rob Hopkins who, along with his students, proposed a transition model for a city. Today, there are several other transition initiatives in several countries around the world, which form an international transition network.

2 In Europe, Climate Justice Action is a network of European grassroots movements that came into being in October 2014 at a time when COP21 symbolized the collective struggle for climate and social justice.

Comparing the conceptions of "political community" in these two movements also makes it possible to illustrate other trends running through them. In fact, actors in the Cities in Transition movement tend to see themselves as a harmonious geographical community linked to similar local communities (depoliticized conception), whereas actors in the Climate Justice Action movement conceive society explicitly in conflictual terms and consciously integrate themselves into this explicitly politicized context of contestation (Kenis 2016).

Parallel to these popular movements, the international political scene also has a movement aimed at institutionalizing these mobilizations. The first wave of institutionalization took place within the framework of the 1972 *United Nations Conference on the Human Environment* in Stockholm, which was aimed at formulating expectations surrounding the link between environmental problems (resulting from the ecological crisis) and the development of human societies (Boutaud 2005). The second wave took shape within the World Commission on Environment and Development (1983–1987) leading to the "Brundtland Report[3]". This report made it possible to reformulate the environmental issue in the light of the interests and expectations of various stakeholders. The third was within the framework of the *United Nations Conference on Environment and Development* (UNCED) in Rio de Janeiro in 1992, leading to declarations and thematic conventions (the Framework Convention on Climate Change, the Convention on Biological Diversity, the Declaration on Forests and the Convention to Combat Desertification), Agenda 21 and the Millennium Development Goals (MDGs). The most recent wave gives rise to the Agenda 2030 in the form of 17 goals (with their targets and indicators) for sustainable development by 2030. This agenda, developed by UN expert groups, is reviewed by the Economic and Social Council (the body responsible for coordination and dialogue on economic, social and environmental issues) and then approved by the UN General Assembly (the deliberative and decision-making body).

In fact, in the international arena, several EDIs – such as those arising from agroecology – constitute "contested" territory between institutionalization movements and social movements. There are two camps of actors in the field of agroecology: the camp of the World Bank and its "allies" (agricultural universities, governments, private sector, etc.) on the one hand, and the camp of social movements (Latin American agroecology movement, Latin American Scientific Society of Agroecology, International Planning Committee for Food Sovereignty, etc.) on the other. These two types of actors mobilize two opposing visions: one that sees agroecology as a set of tools to perfect the technical procedures of modern agriculture, and another that sees it as an alternative which provides tools to transform agricultural policy monocultures (Giraldo and Rosset 2018).

3 This report is entitled "Our Common Future".

In Tunisia, environmental struggles re-emerged in the period following the events of 2011. In fact, the context of political change which was triggered has been accompanied by the emergence of environmental social movements in a way that makes it difficult to characterize such movements, even in general terms (Vernin 2017). However, the frankly political imprint of these movements remains salient. It is also noteworthy that the political management of conflicts over state land shows a trend towards institutionalizing this type of mobilization in Tunisia. This institutionalization has taken the form of a project called "Promotion of Organizations and Mechanisms of the Social and Solidarity Economy" (PROMESS). The project, advanced by the Tunisian government in its cooperation with the International Labour Organization (ILO) and funded by the Netherlands, was spread over a four-year period from 2016 to 2019 (Mokadem 2018). The creation of a legal and institutional framework specific to the social and solidarity economy is one of the main axes within this project. A draft law[4] on the social and solidarity economy was already being finalized by the Ministry of Social Affairs by May 2018.

Field studies of environmental mobilizations show that these practices are part of an informal[5] political education through the learning that develops among the actors who take part in it (Seguin 2015). These civic apprenticeships (Biesta 2011) on conflict and the construction of collective agreements through participation and deliberation form an informal educational process of socialization for a democratic citizenship. According to Kluttz and Walter (2018), these mobilizations involve three interconnected levels of informal political learning:

– the first level, which is microscopic, corresponds to learning that takes place in self-directed situations (individual study of environmental issues, for example), in situations where activists observe and experiment, or in situations where activists participate in conversations during workshops organized by non-governmental organizations;

– the second level, which is mesoscopic, includes the learning that takes place when activists, in elaborating their strategies to combat an issue, consider their experiences in a broader context that integrates the experiences of other activists;

– the third level, which is macroscopic, corresponds to the political learning that takes place when activists interact with their allies or opponents (police, government institutions, businesses, etc.) in forming their petitions.

4 Accessible online on the Tunisian legislative portal: http://www.legislation.tn/sites/default/files/files/textes_soumis_avis/texte/mshrw_qnwn_lqtsd_ljtmy_wltdmny_1.pdf.

5 Informal education corresponds to learning that takes place in daily activities outside the academic framework of formal education and all other organized educational processes, such as those of non-formal education and its devices, including popular education or literacy (Brougère and Bézille 2007).

In non-formal education, Eco-Schools are one of the pioneering schemes (founded in 1994 in Denmark) that have been implemented around EDIs. In several countries[6] around the world, this initiative has been developed in primary, middle and high schools (eco-schools) and universities (eco-campuses). It consists of learning support on six priority topics (food, biodiversity, waste, water, energy, social support) for the concrete implementation of sustainable development in educational institutions in partnership with the local community and the students' parents.

Non-formal education around EDIs is also affected by international educational policies. Historically, the latter shows two successive cycles of "educational institutionalization" taking the form of two recommended mechanisms that have succeeded one another over time: the Decade of Education for Sustainable Development (2005–2014) and Education for Sustainable Development Goals.

In formal education, EDIs are covered by disciplinary curricula. In France, three school and/or academic disciplines deal with these questions: life and earth sciences, which take on the environmental dimension; economics, which takes on the economic dimension; and geography, which takes on the social dimension (Simonneaux 2011). Vergnolle Mainar (2008, 2009) notes that geography and life and earth sciences are the two disciplines that overlap the most with the environmental approach. This author also identifies areas of interdisciplinarity in the school disciplines concerned with the environment, which she differentiates into two groups: disciplines which have a significant overlap with environmental topics (life sciences, earth sciences and geography) and disciplines which are fairly unrelated to environmental topics (physics, chemistry, mathematics, technology, physical education and sport, history, civic education, economic and social sciences, French, philosophy, artistic disciplines and languages). The Tunisian context presents almost the same characteristics when it comes to school disciplines involving environmental issues.

The two international educational policy cycles mentioned above, as well as the disciplinary curricula, constitute inflections allowing the passage from informal education in ecological mobilizations to non-formal education or to formal education. Moreover, aspects in this educational trilogy can be hybridized as the line between formal, non-formal and informal becomes increasingly blurred (Barthes and Alpe 2018).

Several research programs on the links between the political and content involving EDIs in formal and non-formal education are being implemented around the world. Research in the Americas has focused on the interactions of formal and

6 These non-formal education mechanisms are absent in Tunisia. No Tunisian school is registered on the network of eco-schools website: http://www.ecoschools.global/national-offices/.

non-formal environmental education (e.g. for adults) with the dominant neoliberal political and economic context (Hursh *et al.* 2015; Stahelin *et al.* 2015). They open up a discussion of pedagogical practices and content that teachers can use to help learners develop forms of environmental citizenship that actively challenge the neoliberal privatization of environmental responsibility (Dimick 2015).

Other programs follow the French tradition of didactic research: that of the didactics of socially acute questions (SAQs) and that of the didactics of the curriculum of education for sustainable development (ESD). In these two programs, the political is presented according to a double register: strategic and tactical (Lange 2011). Indeed, the work of Lange (2011, 2013, 2015) on the didactics of the ESD curriculum puts forward the political as a strategic purpose of this education on the one hand and as an organizing (tactical) principle of educational situations on the other. This research has enabled proposing an analytical model of the functioning of an educational situation for sustainable development as a social academic practice of democracy. Furthermore, the work of Simonneaux (2013b) and his team (Simonneaux 2011; Bérard *et al.* 2016) presents the political according to the strategic register of education geared towards scientific citizenship and according to a tactical register as organizers of situations of debate and deliberation on problematic environmental issues. Such scientific citizenship can be the aim of non-formal education for the political (action research aimed at popular education in politics).

Another program borrows from the Nordic tradition (Håkansson *et al.* 2017) whereby the political dimension of EDIs is identified in four aspects of the political as:

- generating inclusion and consensus;
- containing cognitive and emotional elements;
- involving power;
- representing a decision-making process.

The researchers involved in that program aim to transpose the idea of the political dimension practice of teaching and research to educational situations involving EDIs. Indeed, the work of Håkansson *et al.* (2017) proposes a categorization of these situations according to the political trend running through them. This trend may take the form of "democratic participation", "political reflection", "political deliberation" or a "political moment". More recently, these researchers (Håkansson and Östman 2018) have proposed an analytical model integrating four phases of the "political moment" in these educational situations. The work of Van Poeck and Vandenabeele (2012) and Van Poeck *et al.* (2014) underline the importance of analyzing the democratic character of educational practices in terms of enriching the discussion on the democratic paradox in environmental education and sustainable development. Subsequently, these researchers set out to develop a method for analyzing "political movement" to study how teachers' actions facilitate or hinder the opening of space for the political in educational situations (Van Poeck and Östman 2017). The work of Sund and Öhman (2014) and Sund (2016) proposes a reconsideration of the political in environmental education and sustainable development according to several guidelines (unmasking the political dimension, repoliticizing education, seeing beyond the relativistic and objectivistic divide and using emotion as a driving force).

Curricula are objects of formal schooling that privileges the universalization of its contents and strives to prohibit the unexpected and heterogeneous (Ardoino and Berger 2010). Non-formal education systems are also formalizations of the informal with normative drifts (Barthes 2017). Taking these two facts into account leads to the problem of the "fate" of the political in the EDIs when it comes to its inflections in non-formal and formal education.

This book aims to build a model in order to structure the political in educational content involving EDIs. The components of this model serve as didactic guidelines for the elaboration of the content of a possible curriculum for a political education through these questions. The book consists of six chapters.

Chapter 1, which follows the introduction, suggests that EDIs should be categorized into metathemes: environmental policies and environmental change, environmental ethics, sustainable development, agri-food issues, environmental technology and environmental management and, finally, the issue of transitions. This chapter also proposes a differentiation of the constitutive themes of these metathemes according to their anti-political or political trend. This thematic categorization refers to a historical analysis of human political thought.

Chapter 2 focuses on the development of a conceptual and analytical framework for the political potential of EDIs. This analysis identifies this potential in four components: environmental literacy, environmental deliberation, ecological citizenship and collective environmental action.

Chapter 3 presents a conceptual elaboration of political learning in educational content involving EDIs in relation to the socialization process. This learning is categorized according to four areas: learning about ecoliteracy in relation to disciplinary cognitive socialization, learning about citizenship in relation to political socialization, learning about deliberation in relation to critical cognitive socialization and learning in action regimes in relation to democratic socialization.

Chapter 4 presents the methodology for data collection and analysis. This chapter introduces the empirical research by justifying the choice of two case studies and sources of evidence considered in this study: analyses of official documents, guided interviews for teachers and learners, and observations of classroom sessions using observation grids.

Chapter 5 presents the results of analyses of educational content in a first case study chosen in non-formal education: that of learning content in the UNESCO document entitled "Education for the Sustainable Development Goals".

Chapter 6 presents the results of the analysis of in the case of formal education: that of content involving EDIs in Tunisian secondary and undergraduate curricula.

1

The Political Trend in Environmental Issues

1.1. Politics, the political and depoliticization

To characterize the political field that intersects with EDIs, we have drawn on Gachkov's (2012) advanced reading of the main concepts of the French philosopher Lefort[1] (politics, democracy, revolution and human rights). In this reading, the author proposes a conceptual distinction between "politics" and "the political", where the first term is conceived as a more niche sphere of social phenomena that exists among others (religion, law, civil society, etc.). Politics is seen as an institutionalization of the political (a symbolic field), actualizing it through the participatory civic form of radical democracy as "a democratic order in which the irreducibility of the plurality of understandings of the common good, the necessity of openness and transparency, an acceptance of fundamental uncertainty and the impossibility of ending the democratic quest are central" (Blokker 2014, p. 379).

According to Gachkov's reading of Lefort, paradoxically, liberal politics through its insistence on individual liberties cannot provide decent protection for them because most of the people involved (the bourgeois) are depoliticized. This depoliticization, which is the consequence of the refusal of the bourgeoisie to participate in political debates because "their will is to take care only of their families and their advancement" (Gachkov 2012, p. 385; author's translation), can provoke the appearance of totalitarian power sacrificing the lives of citizens based on a logic that "consciously confuses political power and civil society" (Gachkov 2012, p. 384; author's translation). Thus, liberal politics (of which representative

1 Claude Lefort (1924–2010) was a major figure in contemporary French political philosophy. He was the co-founder, with Cornelius Castoriadis (1922–1997), of the group "*Socialisme ou barbarie*" in 1949.

democracy is a component) makes democracy vulnerable to totalitarianism. In democratic society, where politics as an activity that questions the entire social domain, political power and civil society must coexist without domination in a social field where "power, law, knowledge are tested by a radical indeterminacy" (Gashkov 2012, p. 383; author's translation). In contrast to a totalitarian society that wants to be certain of its future, political freedom in democratic society corresponds to the capacity of such a society to open up to uncertainty.

1.2. The political and the anti-political

According to Howard (2010), the history of human political thought can be traced back to two trends that originated from the first political experience of human society: democratic Athenian city.

The first trend constitutes a descending line of Platonic thought, itself interpreted as a reaction to the defeat of Athenian democracy. It is an anti-political trend that took shape at different moments in human social history. Christian theological thought fed this current, with Augustine and Luther as outstanding examples in the 5th and 15th centuries. Hobbes' philosophy in the 17th century is representative of this trend in political philosophy, which culminated towards the end of the 18th century and during the 19th century in an anti-political project that reabsorbed politics into a logic of historical progression playing the role of a source of legitimacy anchored in a type of reasoning rooted in economics.

The second trend is a line of ideas descending from Aristotelian thought, itself based on the experience of Athenian democracy, which crossed Christian theological thought with Thomas in the 13th century and Calvin in the 16th century, as well as philosophical thought of the 17th century with Locke.

A third hybrid trend, exhausting its references from the experience of the Republic of Rome, manifested itself in the philosophical thought of Machiavelli (15th century) and Rousseau (18th century). It constituted a reference for the French Revolution and for the American Revolution. The latter invented the political form of a republican democracy, showing its resistance to the anti-political forms that quickly attenuated the French Democratic Republic by the institution of an anti-political project. The latter reigned during the 19th century until the outbreak of the war in 1914.

The 20th century was one of a new vitality of political thought through the installation of a conflict of interpretation of the democratic paradigm of political legitimacy. The debate was between new forms and orientations of totalitarian, liberal or social democracy.

In the remainder of this chapter, the political/anti-political trend in EDIs is explored through the following:

– a discussion of the conceptualization of the political field with its symbolic dimension (the political) and its formal dimension (politics) of Lefort by Gachkov and Blokker. This discussion makes it possible to specify a set of expressions covering the political field: "power", "depoliticization", "democracy", "participation", "citizenship", "domination", "justice" and "liberalism";

– the classification[2] of EDIs into six metathemes: "environmental politics and environmental change", "environmental ethics", "agrifood", "sustainable development", "environmental technologies and management" and "transitions", to explore their political content via the Internet;

– the association of EDI metathemes with expressions from political/anti-political or politicized/depoliticized discussions in French and English in order to collect a relevant corpus on the Internet;

– a thorough reading of the collected corpus.

This chapter will help us to identify and characterize the political/anti-political trend of EDIs.

1.3. Environmental and development issues (EDIs) between the political and anti-political or politics and depoliticization: what are the trends?

1.3.1. *Issues of environmental politics and environmental change*

Environmental politics generally address water and air pollution issues, waste and ecosystem management issues and biodiversity protection issues. These issues are addressed in terms of political-legal regimes (*polity*), public policy (*policy*) or political action (*politics*). They also address issues of environmental change, which are changes in the climate system, hydrological systems of freshwater supply and agricultural food production systems. These changes represent large-scale risks to the sustainability of these systems. Voß and Bornemann (2011) propose an analytical and political framework for environmental governance. In this model, the authors distinguish three dimensions: a first dimension referring to the substantive problems and solutions of policy; a second covering the structural side of polity such as norms,

2 The classification of industrial ecology contents in university programs proposed by Finlayson and his collaborators following an exploratory study conducted in 2012 and published in 2014 was the initial source of inspiration for categorizing the EDIs into six metathemes based on background reading.

procedures and political culture; and a third dimension of politics representing the actualized side of the policy process where actors with divergent views and interests interact.

1.3.1.1. *Environmental justice: a category which cuts across environmental politics*

Climate change is a contributor to environmental injustice. Indeed, the issue of climate change provides an opportunity to broaden the scope of environmental justice. The latter is not reduced to the issue of access to environmental resources nor to the problem of the unequal distribution of environmental costs. It involves a recognition of "plural modes of being in the environment" (Centemeri *et al.* 2016).

In the field of international environmental politics, several environmental issues seem to have become urgent, such as:

– the question of the degree of shared responsibility for climate change between rich and poor countries (Roberts and Parks 2007a, 2007b);

– the issue of ecological debt and the injustice of climate change combined with the effects of poverty and environmental degradation (Magrath 2010);

– the issue of intergenerational domination, which can stem from a violation of the freedom of future generations through climate change (Beckman 2016).

Environmental justice is also considered both as a category of collective action social movements (political action) and of action in public environmental policies as well as a political-legal category. The history of the idea of environmental justice is influenced by two contexts: the context of social mobilizations and the academic context (Fol and Pflieger 2010).

In the context of social mobilizations, the notion of environmental justice, which is derived from the concept of environmental racism, has given rise to a social movement that has adapted the frameworks of action of other social movements such as academics and political actors. The term "justice" has been preferable to "equity" by the social movements of environmentalists, which refers to broadly militant usage (Fol and Pflieger 2010). Related to this trend are:

– local and global environmental politics initiatives (Blanchon *et al.* 2009) in response to local social movements denouncing situations of environmental injustice, such as exposure to an environmental impact, as well as situations of unequal access to environmental resources and the marginalization of inhabitants around protected areas (Blowers and Leroy 1994; Dozzi 2008; Faburel 2008; Gobert 2008; Gardin 2012);

– other social movements of environmental politics are responses to global initiatives that introduce social equity into environmental protection. These movements use political ecology as a theoretical tool (Robbins 2012). Political ecology also provides a theoretical basis for discussing issues of "democratization of environmental explanation" in scientific practice between scientific expertise and public participation as a factor of environmental governance (Forsyth 2003).

Epistemologically, these two types of environmental politics initiatives demonstrate two conceptions of justice: justice as an essentially local struggle and fight characterized by the bottom-up approach deriving from the North American current; and justice as the governmental top-down approach illustrated mainly by increasingly less sectoral environmental public policies (Gardin 2012).

According to Fol and Pflieger (2010), in the academic context, debates on environmental justice have diverged into two main areas:

– distributive justice dealing with the identification of team beneficiaries and services with high environmental efficiency, such as public transport, sewage treatment plants and other infrastructure. It seeks to distribute justice in the light of environmental harm and effects according to social categories;

– corrective justice dealing with the correction of the effects of actions and policies causing harm.

These two dimensions appear complementary because this academic debate on distributive justice is geared towards the implementation of corrective environmental policies. According to the authors (Fol and Pflieger 2010), several criticisms are made on the uses of the notion of environmental justice. These criticisms reflect the debate between the political and anti-political realm within environmental politics.

1.3.1.2. *A risk of depoliticization*

Environmental governance has not escaped the risk of "depoliticization" through the claim that this type of social interaction on environmental issues is apolitical (McCarthy 2013).

Green economy and ecological modernization discourses are basically depoliticized (or post-politicized) environmental discourses because they advance a view by some dominant actors that certain issues of environmental degradation such as climate change cannot be a subject of debate nor democratic decision-making. The choice between certain mechanisms of political practices, such as market practices to avoid adverse environmental effects, constitutes a neoliberal mechanism for the depoliticization of environmental politics. This mechanism makes it possible to maintain power relations brought about by the market by trying to make them unquestionable by representing the environment as external to society (Felli 2015).

In the field of political theories, several authors agree that climate change discourses and research are "symptoms of a post-political condition" (Swyngedouw 2010; MacGregor 2014a; Pepermans and Maeseele 2014; Maeseele 2015). The post-political perspective, aimed at building social, rational and moral consensus on climate change problems and solutions, is criticized by a second politicized perspective that sees climate change as inherent to representations that are the result of conflicts and power struggles (Kenis and Mathijs 2014a, 2014b; Kenis 2016; Pepermans and Maeseele 2016). Moreover, these authors propose the urgent re-politicization of environmental issues, especially those related to climate change, as only the critical perspective is capable of providing tools for socio-ecological change.

1.3.2. *Environmental ethical issues*

Environmental ethics is a value system that aims to guide human action in the environmental field. In terms of power relations, while environmental ethics has focused on the relationship between humans and nature, this has mainly been by criticizing the vision of humans dominating nature (Ballet *et al.* 2013).

1.3.2.1. *Environmental ethics: a democratic deliberation rich in political teachings*

A meta-ethical analysis of environmental ethics (Létourneau 2010) shows the presence of two positions: principled positions and situational (contextual) positions.

Larrère (2010) identifies biocentrism and ecocentrism as the two main currents of principled position in environmental ethics:

– biocentric ethics is opposed to a position that recognizes moral dignity only for human beings (anthropocentrism). Its ambition is to show that natural entities possess intrinsic value, by substituting a multiplicity of individuality for the anthropocentric duality of the opposition between humans and things. It insists above all on the principle of the equal status of all living beings;

– ecocentric ethics considers that value should be given not to individual entities but to the biotic community as a whole by advancing the formula that "something is right when it tends to preserve integrity, the stability and beauty of the biotic community. It is unjust when it leans in the opposite direction" (Leopold, quoted by Larrère 2010, p. 408). Unlike biocentrism, ecocentric environmental ethics emphasizes the interdependence of elements in biotic communities: it is indeed a holistic ethics that opposes the individualism of biocentric ethics.

The main characteristics of biocentrism (intrinsic value) and ecocentrism (biotic community) are also at the origin of the criticisms put forward for these two trends in environmental ethics. For biocentrism, Larrère (2010) raises the question of the capacity of such an overly individualistic approach to respond to the needs of a nature protection policy that necessarily involves choices between several possible scenarios and where the protection of the environment is not a priority and where the protection of nature necessarily implies the consideration of complex entities such as populations, ecosystems and landscapes.

For ecocentrism, the consequentialism adopted, which measures the quality of an action by its effects on the biotic community, tends to sacrifice individuals to the common good of the community, whereby humans are doubly sacrificed as individuals and as a species.

Both of these trends in environmental ethics are based on the condemnation of anthropocentrism. They are opposed to a narrow vision of the conception of instrumental value that does not take into account the diversity of instrumental values.

The monistic vision of value is replaced among pragmatists by a pluralist and rational vision within a democratic framework defining a new position of environmental ethics: the pragmatist posture of applied ethics (Larrère 2010).

The contextual posture corresponds to the pragmatism of applied environmental ethics.

This pragmatic approach uses the democratic foundation of "value pluralism": the solution to an environmental moral problem corresponds to a hierarchy of values derived from public deliberation and debate for the justification of environmental action.

This ethical orientation has the advantage of going beyond the limits of the anthropocentric approach (instrumental value ethics), the biocentric approach (intrinsic value ethics condemning anthropocentrism and which is principally deontological) and the ecocentric approach (mainly consequentialist, where the value of action is measured by its effects on the biotic community). In fact, at the heart of ethical pragmatism are the democratic values of value pluralism that promote democratic deliberation on the "appropriateness" between certain moral positions and scientific positions (Larrère 2010). This ethical deliberation is modeled by Legault (2003), who assumes that any ethical decision is worked out in two stages. This has two inseparable aspects: the first consists of deciding on the end objectives, and the second on the means of achieving the desired objectives. This conception implies that the reasons for the decision must take into account both the ends and means by allowing for a pluralism of moral action in concrete decisions (Legault 2003). Ethical deliberation on the values of the environment, which makes it possible to go beyond the limits of deontology or consequentialism, is thus rich in political teachings.

1.3.2.2. *A risk of political impoverishment*

According to Kopnina (2012), the ethical discussion in environmental and sustainable development education programs has not escaped dominant political ideologies such as neoliberalism. These ideologies have played inhibiting roles in democratic deliberation to create a situational or contextual hierarchy of environmental values. They impose a communicative deliberation that is detrimental to pluralist ethical problematization in favor of an anthropocentric ethical approach at the expense of ecocentric or biocentric values. The sources of this depoliticization of the environmental ethical question are identified by Sauvé (2011), at the educational level, in an economic globalization program claiming a focal role for economic growth in resolving environmental and social problems. In this program, education is considered as “an engine of globalization” responding primarily to a mission of economic development through the development of human resources or human capital.

1.3.3. ***Sustainable development issues***

The prospect of sustainable development suggests the need to integrate environmental and equity issues with economic growth so as to preserve what is at stake with sustainable development. Hopwood *et al.* (2005) proposed an analytical framework for the different political positions taking place in debates on sustainable development. To do so, the authors used two analytical variables: justice on the one hand and environmental values on the other. They distinguish between two opposing approaches or points of view: the *status quo* and the transformative viewpoint and another intermediary, which is the reformist approach.

According to Hopwood *et al.* (2005), the *status quo* perspective assumes that sustainable development requires adjustments that do not require a genuine change to means of decision-making or power relations. Generally, positions that support this view (ecological modernization, green consumption, green economy, natural resource management, etc.) advocate the primordial role of the market in sustainable development. This is “green” capitalism practicing corporate citizenship.

The transformist viewpoint corresponds to a heterogeneous set of trends (social ecology, ecofeminism, ecosocialism, etc.) but share the same point of view, which assumes that environmental and social crises are interconnected and that social and environmental systems risk collapse crises in the absence of radical change (Hopwood *et al.* 2005).

Social ecology presupposes a dialectical relationship between humanity and nature. This leads to considering that environmental concerns must be rooted in social criticism by aiming to achieve radical social reconstruction.

Ecofeminism advances the relationship between environmental degradation and the subordination of women. This trend runs parallel to ecosocialism by assuming that capitalism attempts to detach social life from nature through its class and gender-dividing politics.

Based on the writings of Marx and Engels, ecosocialism establishes a link between environmental damage and capitalism‘s exploitation of people and the environment. Ecosocialists argue that changes in the material conditions and social structure of society are necessary to overcome both environmental crises and injustice.

The reformist point of view is supported by several government agencies and non-governmental organizations such as Greenpeace and Friends of the Earth. Reformers identify a key role for governments in sustainable development's assumption that reform of the political system, as an anchor for democracy and participation, plays a role in sustainable development (Hopwood *et al.* 2005).

This point of view is based on the observation that inequalities in development, which are a major cause of the crisis of sustainability facing the world at the beginning of the 21st century, are also at the root of ecological inequalities woven by economic power relations. Indeed, calculations of the ecological footprint show that "citizens of rich countries need an average of 4–10 global average hectares (10–25 acres) to support their lifestyles, whereas the poor get by on less than half a hectare (one acre)" (Rees 2008, p. 694). This issue of unequal development is further branched out to evoke territorial inequalities, inequalities in access to basic goods, inequalities in the face of risk and power inequalities (Chaumel and La Branche 2008). Inequalities in human development are considered causes that increase environmental degradation and consequently weaken ecosystems through deforestation and the loss of biodiversity resulting from the actions of the beneficiaries of their services (Laurent 2009).

1.3.4. *Agrifood issues*

Food systems are systems of social practices of food production and consumption that address several social, cultural, ethical and environmental aspects.

They are systems that are not immune to the impacts of the economic-social forces in perpetual dynamics in human society.

1.3.4.1. *Food literacy*

Wever (2015) puts forward the hypothesis that we can "read the world while eating". In this approach, agrifood issues are conceived as food literacy issues that the author conceptualizes as a set composed of the three knowledge domains identified by Habermas: empirical and analytical knowledge and skills, historical and hermeneutic knowledge and skills, and critical and emancipatory knowledge and skills. This author also proposes the development of a food literacy that goes beyond the consumerist approach (the ability of individuals to understand the origin and production of food and the application of this knowledge to make choices) towards a critical literacy aimed at unveiling the hidden power structures in food systems (Yamashita and Robinson 2016). This food literacy provides the foundation for a political literacy whereby people can exercise power to unlock and reshape the existing food system. According to this kind of literacy approach, food appears to be more than a "compilation of vitamins and nutrients; it is physical and social, personal and political, and inanimate yet animating entity" (Freedman 2011, p. 81).

1.3.4.2. *Food democracy*

The goal of food literacy is the development of an alternative democracy (Booth and Coveney 2015) that can support social movements for food justice, sovereignty or citizenship. These movements involve collective actions for the transition towards the sustainability of agrifood systems (Hassanein 2008). Booth and Coveney (2015) also propose a distinction between food sovereignty and food justice as alternative movements based on food democracy.

The two authors drew on the work of Renting *et al.* (2012) to conceptualize food democracy as a redistribution of power in the agrifood system where citizens increasingly claim their influence on the organization and functioning of food production. They thus move from the situation of passive consumers to that of active citizens by exploring new means of engagement.

The growing involvement of citizens leads to relationships with producers. The interfaces between the state, the market and civil society are generally fraught with tensions and contradictions. In the long term, this can lead to new alliances, institutional arrangements and the creation of organizational models for sustainable food systems (Booth and Coveney 2015).

These authors have also exploited the work of Hassanein (2008) to identify the following five dimensions of food democracy:

– collaboration for the sustainability of the food system, whereby democracy aims at bringing about collective action to address problems and increase the power of citizens;

– information about the food system based on a democratic theory that recognizes the importance of individuals with the knowledge to participate effectively;

– sharing ideas about the food system with others through ongoing discussion and deliberation that allows citizens to clarify food issues and discuss related values;

– developing the effectiveness of food systems in a political system which builds skills among citizens to determine a proper relationship with their food and resolve community food problems;

– orientation towards "community goods" by involving citizens who care about the public good and who are willing to look beyond their own interests and recognize the value of mutual support and interdependence.

1.3.5. *Issues concerning environmental technology and environmental management*

Environmental technologies are socio-technical systems. They correspond to the expansion of environmental concerns in technology products to socio-technical systems (Kanda *et al.* 2016).

Environmental technologies include:

– clean technologies such as renewable power generation and energy consumption technologies;

– recycling technologies;

– water, air or soil pollution control technologies;

– technologies developed with the specific objective of repairing damage caused by human activities through the application of biotechnology for the remediation of contaminated sites or through the application of innovative agricultural techniques to restore biodiversity (Smith and Stirling 2008, 2010).

There is a classification that proposes three categories of environmental technologies (Vachon 2007), where the term "technology" is broadly defined to include the design, equipment and operating procedures that limit or reduce the negative impacts of products and processes on the natural environment. In this classification, environmental technologies include:

– pollution prevention technologies, which are defined as structural investments that reduce or eliminate pollution at the source;

– pollution control technologies, which are structural investments that ensure proper waste disposal, reduce the release of pollutants or correct environmental damage;

– management systems, which are infrastructure investments that propose improvements to environmental performance through environmental impact assessment procedures when making investment decisions.

Additionally, environmental technologies have the characteristic of integrating a broad socio-political agenda of sustainability. This allows them to internalize, along with medical technologies and information communication technologies, the issue of desirable societal transformation. In fact, thanks to the idea of technological efficiency, environmental technologies that develop in the context of a sustainable development project make political content visible in the technological design (Valkenburg 2012).

Environmental management is a range of tools and procedures aimed at evaluating and subsequently reducing the impact of the activities of one or several businesses through environmental analyses or management control systems. Dohou-Renaud (2009) proposes a classification of environmental management approaches.

According to the same author (Dohou-Renaud 2009), environmental analyses and environmental management systems are based on two approaches: an environmental management approach called the "product approach" and another called the "organizational approach":

– the product approach includes life cycle analyses, which constitute a true environmental cost accounting system that enables an energy balance to be made by evaluating the impact of the production of goods or services on the environment;

– the organizational approach consists of designing or improving the design of products in order to minimize their impact on the environment by using life cycle analysis, resulting in the communication of environmental labels such as eco-labels.

Moreover, according to Dohou-Renaud, behind the adoption of these environmental management technologies, there are always institutional pressures from stakeholders such as environmental advocates, market players and organizational players (managers, shareholders, employees, etc.).

Reed (1996) discussed the issues and contexts that have historically guided theories in organizational science. According to this author, justice appears as a metanarrative framework for organizational analyses in the transitional context towards participatory democracy. In fact, this framework raises fundamental questions in organizational studies about the types of governance and control in contemporary organizations and their moral and political foundations regarding justice. It affirms the centrality of questions relating to the distribution of political, economic and cultural power. The emphasis on practices that cut across organizational structures and processes, such as the state, social class and professions, reveals the strategic role played by power struggles between institutional actors in shaping and reforming systems of rules that guide the political and economic actions of corporations and organizations in general (Reed 1996).

1.3.6. *Issues of transitioning to sustainability*

Transitions are processes of change from systems associated with social services such as housing, transportation, energy, food and water supply to more sustainable systems. They are

> processes of fundamental social change in response to societal challenges. They reflect a particular diagnosis of persistent social problems, in which persistence is attributed to the path dependency of dominant practices and structures (i.e. "regimes"), whose resolution requires long-term and structural change. By their very nature, transitions involve politics in the broadest sense of the word. (Avelino *et al.* 2016, p. 557)

According to Loorbach *et al.* (2017), the concept of regime, defined as a dominant and stable configuration in a societal system, is the most central notion in transition studies. This idea is at the heart of an original perspective in transition analyses: the multi-level perspective (MLP). The latter draws its origins from historical studies of system change on the one hand, and from the evolutionary economy on the other. It recognizes the co-evolutionary development of technologies, institutions and economic subsystems by putting forward the presence of three levels whose dynamics and interactions make it possible to understand transitions: the landscape or macro-level, the regimes or meso-level and the niches or micro-level.

The landscape (macro) level is composed of the overall socio-technical framework and macro-political developments that form the context of the transition. It is a kind of backdrop for the other two levels by stimulating and exerting pressure on the socio-technical regime.

The regime (meso) level comprises the structures that represent the practices and routines at stake, such as the rules and dominant technologies that ensure the stability and strengthening of the prevailing socio-technical systems. It can also be a barrier to change technological and social innovations.

The niche (micro) level is a designated space for experimentation and radical innovation. This level is loosely structured compared to the regime level. It is less influenced by the market and regulation. Coordination between niche actors is weaker than between regime actors. This allows the emergence of new interactions between actors that can support innovation (Loorbach *et al.* 2017).

Twomey and Gaziulusoy (2014), in a literature review on innovations and transition theories, note that "socio-technical transitions" is an umbrella term that includes two other perspectives in addition to the multi-level perspective (MLP): the transition management (TM) perspective and the strategic niche management (SNM) perspective. In fact, according to these authors, the latter two perspectives are derived from the former.

Research in the SNM perspective focuses on the niche level by emphasizing user participation in any early technological development. This approach has been inspired in part by historical studies showing that many successful innovations started as niche technologies and gradually overturned a dominant regime. The main concern of the SNM perspective is to establish processes by which innovative experiences can evolve into viable market niches to contribute to a shift towards a more sustainable socio-economic environment (Twomey *et al.* 2014).

Research in the TM perspective takes a broad system perspective that encompasses the three levels of the MPL perspective framework. It is concerned with the dynamics of structural change in society and the appropriate manner and timing for initiating, facilitating or shaping transformation. As in the MPL perspective, the importance of experimentation and learning is central. However, the starting point for the TM perspective is not a technological innovation but a societal challenge, such as how to meet the demand for energy, transportation or housing in a sustainable manner (Twomey *et al.* 2014).

1.3.6.1. *Approaches to transition research*

Loorbach *et al.* (2017) broaden the themes of transitions by proposing a distinction between three research approaches to study them: the socio-technical approach, the socio-institutional approach and the socio-ecological approach. This distinction is based on a comparison of their respective methodological focuses and objectives.

The socio-technical approach exhausts its references in scientific and technological studies. This approach relies on the MLP perspective as the main analytical tool with the technological innovation systems (TIS) framework.

The socio-institutional approach draws on the social sciences to understand systemic change in complex societal systems by drawing on economics, political science, sociology, governance studies and geography. It identifies institutionalized cultures, structures and practices as regimes in which transitional changes are taking place. The socio-institutional perspective applies especially to societal systems facing persistent environmental challenges such as mobility, waste management and energy (Loorbach *et al.* 2017).

The socio-ecological approach is based on knowledge from ecology, biology, the theory of complex adaptive systems and adaptive governance. It is rooted in ecology and resilience theory, seeking to understand instability in ecosystems, and has evolved to examine coupled socio-ecological systems (Loorbach *et al.* 2017).

1.3.6.2. *Power relations in transitions*

In the studies on transitions, Avelino and Wittmayer (2016) discuss four types of explicit treatments of the notion of power: a mechanistic perspective, a governance perspective, a horizontal perspective and an emancipatory perspective.

In the mechanistic perspective, power relations between collective actors (mainly industrial policy makers) constitute a causal mechanism of the targeted change. This type of change is perceived as a result of conflicts, power struggles, protests, lobbying, coalition building and negotiation between these actors and different social groups. Such a change thus results from a change in the power relations between the actors involved (Avelino and Wittmayer 2016).

From a governance perspective, transitions are conceptualized as changes in the dynamics of power relations and the struggle for dominance (Voß and Bornemann 2011) involving, in addition to individual actors, citizens and civil society (Geels and Schot 2007). Three levels of power are distinguished:

– the relational aspect related to the immediate interactions between the actors reflecting their interests;

– the dispositional aspect related to the rules and resources available and to the dominant representations of the actors;

– the structural linked to broader orders of signification and legitimization (Hofmann 2013; Geels 2014).

From this perspective, it is impossible to reduce the political character of socio-technical transitions to sustainability (Meadowcroft 2009; Voß *et al.* 2009).

The horizontal perspective is based on a qualitative typology of power relations. It asks how different actors (government, non-governmental organizations, citizens and scientists) manage to exercise power relations at different times (Avelino and Wittmayer 2016).

The empowerment perspective refers to emancipation in a broad sense as a process of empowerment (Avelino 2009, 2011). According to this perspective, the management of a transition is a kind of empowerment of niches by facilitating their grouping as well as the emergence of regimes that can eventually take over or replace regimes that are in place.

The management of socio-technical transitions constitutes a new concept of piloting the dynamics of this type of system which goes beyond the managerial conception generally associated with the idea of management control: the starting point of transition management is in fact "complexity and uncertainty", allowing a limited degree of steering with such societal dynamics (Rotmans 2005; Paredis 2013). Human geography criticizes the technocracy within the managerial perspective of socio-technical transitions for being "geographically naive" by conceptualizing space and transferability beyond a narrow range of case studies. Political ecology, a field of human geography, explicitly addresses the problematic power relations that underlie the production, transmission and sharing of knowledge and technology in socio-technical regimes (Lawhon and Murphy 2011).

The management of socio-technical transitions is also considered as a reflective and participatory mode of governance, which aims to orient socio-technical systems towards social goals by engaging actors at several levels and putting ideas to the test through experimentation, learning and adaptation as factors of change.

The transitions of socio-technical systems to sustainability have also taken the form of social movements such as the "cities in transition" movement in Belgium (Costa 2013; Kenis and Mathijs 2014). It represents a new culture that is developing: the culture of transition interpreted as a hybrid social and environmental movement (Neal 2013). Nevertheless, these social movements are not free from the pressures of depoliticization that can originate from different sources.

1.3.6.3. *The trend of depoliticization in transition issues*

There is a trend towards depoliticization in transition issues (Scrase and Smith 2009; Hess 2014; Kenis and Lievens 2017). Jhagroe (2016) identifies three origins of this trend in relation to different political frameworks.

The first origin is the conception of politics as a fundamentally institutionalized struggle that considers political institutions as the guarantor of any negotiation without taking into account the historical contingency of these institutions. The result is an institutionalized politics of transitions that does not take into consideration the ideological character of the institutions themselves (Jhagroe 2016).

The second stems from a liberal or neo-liberal conception of politics that assumes that political actors are free and equal individuals in a public debate specified in terms of economic (market) negotiation (deliberation). This conception favors market dynamics as well as economic procedures as the terrain of struggle (Jhagroe 2016).

The third stems from an anthropocentric conception of politics that introduces a segmentation between nature and culture and between physical and social systems. The underlying assumption in this conception is that human beings are fundamentally different and often superior to animals, plants and other materials. This "human supremacy" is often unchallenged (Jhagroe 2016).

1.4. Conclusion

The spectrum of thematic content of EDIs metathemes is broad. Background reading has enabled us to put forward six metathemes to characterize this content, namely: environmental politics, environmental ethics, agro-environmental ethics, sustainable development, environmental technologies and management, and transitions. In the same way, this research has allowed us to characterize the field of EDIs by the political/anti-political duality of their themes.

2

The Political Potential of Environmental Issues

2.1. The regulatory categories of political life

Political potential is defined as a set of principles organizing political life, which are supposedly regulatory categories. These categories have been characterized by different approaches: approaches rooted in political philosophy, approaches rooted in political science and others found in the educational field.

2.1.1. *Political philosophy approaches*

Morvan (2011) draws on presuppositions about the organizing categories of political life as criteria to group the work of several thinkers (Smith, Hobbes, Rousseau, Montesquieu, Kant, Arendt, Habermas, Weber, Machiavelli, Marx, Bourdieu, Rancière, Badiou, Abensour, Mouffe and Foucault) into families of thought. The author associates these families with four categories that these thinkers consider as potentially organizing political life in human society.

Smith's thinking is representative of the first family that the author associates with the category of "individual interest". Indeed, this thinker considers that it is the pre-established harmony of interests that constitutes the cause that allows the convergence of individualistic projects in which action obeys mainly an economic calculation.

The second family is represented by the political thought of Hobbes, Rousseau and Montesquieu. This family is associated with the category of "contract" as:

– a generator of a conventional political order against the state of nature dominated by the war of one against the other (Hobbes);

– an ideal regulating social life against natural inequalities and allowing the integration of the individual in the social group where humans become equal by convention and by law (Rousseau);

– the means allowing the defense of the individual against those who hold power and allowing the limitation and separation of powers (Montesquieu).

The third family brings together the works of Kant, Arendt and Habermas. It associates political life with community life or the *Polis*. The latter refers to:

– human freedom as the only legitimate goal that allows people who are naturally selfish to live both free and united (Kant);

– dialogue among citizens as a procedure for political choices and rational solutions to the problem of human coexistence (Habermas).

The fourth family includes the works of Weber, Machiavelli, Marx, Bourdieu, Rancière, Badiou, Abensour, Mouffe and Foucault. These thinkers assume that "conflict" is the regulatory category of political life. Indeed, conflict appears as:

– a divergence between the values that politically orient social activities in relation to a political grouping (Weber);

– a constitutive opposition of the social space generated by the opposition of the desires on which the political relationship and social existence itself are based (Machiavelli);

– a form of domination in the bourgeois state and formal democracy (Marx);

– competition for the constitutive power of the political field (Bourdieu);

– dissensus intersecting with human action and founding political life where democracy appears as the mode of subjectivation and the practice that wrenches from the governments the monopoly of this political life (Rancière);

– collective action aimed at developing in reality a new possibility suppressed by the dominant state of things (Badiou);

– constitutive agitation of the democratic revolution based on the law as a tool of resistance to power (Abensour);

– "agonal" confrontation conditioning the existence of democracy and giving a central role to passions and identities in political life (Mouffe);

– micro-sociological power relations structuring the political life and activities of men in society (Foucault).

2.1.2. *Political science approaches*

The most recent theorizations in the field of political science tend to consider the institution as a regulatory category (or the main organizational factor) of political life (March and Olsen 1984, 2006). In these so-called neo-institutionalist approaches, the institution is defined as follows:

> a relatively enduring collection of rules and organized practices, embedded in structures of meaning and resources that are relatively invariant in the face of turnover of individuals and relatively resilient to idiosyncratic individual preferences and expectations of individuals and changing external circumstances. (March and Olsen 2006, p. 3)

Lecours (2002) distinguishes three types of neo-institutionalism in a review of political science literature: historical neo-institutionalism, rational choice neo-institutionalism and sociological neo-institutionalism.

Historical neo-institutionalism advances the principle that it is contextual factors, exogenous to the actors and institutional in nature, that condition socio-political phenomena. According to this approach, these phenomena are thus the result of a macro-historical process of institutional development that underpins political life. This institutionalism also postulates that this life is under the effect of the accumulation of rules and social practices of mobilization, of which those that are crowned with relative success will constitute a repertoire of collective action (Palier and Surel 2005).

Rational choice neo-institutionalism is an institutionalism that focuses on the strategic importance of institutions. Institutions are considered according to the constraints and opportunities they offer to actors in decision-making without neglecting the ideas of rationality and the search for personal gain. According to this approach, the phenomena of political life are explained as products of individual and collective decisions that depend mainly on the institutional structures present.

Sociological neo-institutionalism develops the idea of institutions as the embodiment of cultural life (cultural norms, symbols and practices) shaping the perceptions and actions of actors. The political life of institutions is thus part of the evolutionary processes of cultural life marked out by the institutional forms themselves.

2.1.3. *Educational approaches*

2.1.3.1. *Education and democracy*

In the field of education, political life is considered as a form of civic engagement in a social transformation process. In fact, in this domain, the notion of citizenship intersects and overlaps with the notions of "the political" and "democracy" (Thésée *et al.* 2015). Democracy corresponds to an ideal based on the values of diversity, equity, social justice and peace. Citizenship is seen as a practice of democracy that supports commitment and participation. Carr and Thésée (2016) categorized the links between education and democracy using a four-dimensional space consisting of the following:

– "education about democracy", where there is deconstruction, reconstruction and construction of political facts while taking into account the different perspectives of social actors;

– "education through democracy", working towards an engagement in the practices of democratic action (dialogues, debates, deliberations, consultations, meetings and cooperation) and emancipatory social transformation;

– "education in relation to democracy", where there is a deconstruction, reconstruction and co-construction of knowledge and representations by different methods stemming from the epistemic currents of interdisciplinarity, feminism, anti-colonialism or indigenism;

– "education for democracy", working on a socio-critical awareness aiming to establish and pursue democratic values (social and environmental justice, peace, solidarity, diversity, equity, openness to others, radical love) with the help of a conscientizing citizenship. It corresponds to a spectrum of degrees of personal, citizen, community and human commitments.

According to this approach, the political potential for democracy in educational situations is dependent on the categories of critical engagement and participation and political literacy. Such literacy corresponds to an emancipatory political literacy, which goes beyond the ability to read and write and seeks a complex and meaningful engagement with society.

Critical engagement can take place through involving learners in actions on various issues or realities, outside the dominant media prism in society or discussions on controversial issues. This enables learners to learn to debate, criticize, listen and be open to various epistemological reflections; prepares them to engage actively in political life and complements experiences outside the school environment (Carr and Thésée 2017).

2.1.3.2. *The approach of education for political science*

Sloam (2010, 2011) proposes, with reference to Dewey and Kolb's models of experiential learning, a conceptual model of political learning in the context of educational research on the academic teaching of political science. This model predicts that such learning takes place in a multi-dimensional system where the different dimensions (literacy, participation, experiences and deliberation) are mutually reinforcing. These dimensions make up the regulatory categories of situations involving political life science education.

Engaging knowledge (literacy) on particular issues, such as youth participation rates in general elections, allows for the incorporation of a learner's personal "democratic experience" and civic and political activism into the learning process (Hildreth 2006). This process, evoking the participatory action of learners in society, is used by Bacon and Sloam (2010) as an indicator characterizing a "democratic education" that is identified as a mission for higher education in England from Dewey's experiential learning perspective. Because deliberation is such an important component of the political learning process, the author (Sloam 2011) adopts Habermas's theory of communicative action to link it to the other components of the process.

Participation refers to a set of activities through which citizens seek to intervene in the public decision-making process. It involves several examples of political actions (voting, activism in a political party or social group). In a broad sense, participation can include consultation such as public inquiries, distractive and financial information and association. It is interpreted as an extrajudicial conflict regulation mechanism that reflects the limits of institutions in the administration and orientation of public policies (Riel-Salvatore 2006).

Public consultation and meetings are participation tools or techniques that are part of a process of developing possible solutions. Consultation consists of making actors, individuals or representatives of groups express themselves separately on what they think of a situation or a project. The aim of consultation is to find an agreement or a solution to a problem that arises for stakeholders (Touzard 2006). If public consultation does not ensure the integration of the participants' points of view into decision-making, meetings are focused on partnership in a collective of actors whose interests are generally in opposition (Riel-Salvatore 2006).

In the following, this model, which brings together the four supposedly regulatory categories of political life in political science education situations, is adapted for use in characterizing political potential in situations involving EDIs.

2.2. The regulatory categories of political life in situations involving environmental and development issues

2.2.1. *Environmental literacy*

Environmental education began to emerge as a distinct field in the mid-1960s and has its roots in a variety of related fields, including conservation education, nature education, resource use education, outdoor education, geographic education and science education. It builds on several environmental literacy issues, such as the interrelationships between natural and social systems and humanity's unity with nature (Roth 1992).

Environmental literacy is an extension of scientific literacy to the EDIs. It is conceptualized by Roth (1992) as a *continuum* of three levels (elementary environmental literacy, functional environmental literacy and operational environmental literacy) that the author (Roth 1992) suggests should be operationalized in different types of components.

2.2.1.1. *Elementary environmental literacy*

A first level is qualified as elementary environmental literacy. It corresponds to rudimentary knowledge about the functioning of natural systems and their interactions with social systems by involving the following components:

– a component of knowledge that relates to the nature of the basic components of elementary systems (living and non-living, requirements of life), the types and examples of interactions between humans and nature, and the basic components of social systems;

– an emotional component involving an appreciation of nature and society, basic sensitivity and empathy towards nature and society, and basic perceptions of conflicts between nature and society;

– a component of problem identification and definition skills, recognition of the stakes in the problems identified or in the proposed solutions (latent and apparent conflicts);

– a behavioral component relating to activities of family or school organizations and habits aimed at maintaining the quality of the environment.

2.2.1.2. *Functional environmental literacy*

The second level, referred to as functional environmental literacy, corresponds to knowledge and natural systems. This level also has several components:

– a knowledge component of a number of ecological, economic, geographic, religious, educational and political processes, as well as an understanding of the actual impact of natural systems on human beings. This knowledge involves themes such as population dynamics, interactions, ecological limiting factors, energy transfers, biomass production, energy storage and degradation, biogeochemical cycles, living communities, ecosystems, succession, homeostasis, unequal distribution of resources on a global scale, dynamic relationships between science, technology and society, political ecological interdependence in urban and rural areas, human cultural activities affecting the environment, energy sources and uses, conservation of matter and energy, waste flows and recycling;

– a core competency component in analyzing problems and issues and investigating environmental problems and their historical contexts. These skills are based on such abilities as investigating environmental issues; evaluating information sources; analyzing environmental issues in various sectors of the economy; applying ecological concepts to probability prediction; identifying alternative solutions; evaluating alternatives; conducting basic risk analysis; identifying and clarifying value positions; examining local, national, regional issues and international perspectives; thinking in terms of systems; demonstrating the ability to anticipate and think ahead; thinking critically and creatively; distinguishing number, quantity, quality and value; working collaboratively with others; and playing, judging, valuing and articulating personal values;

– an emotional component involving basic affects, attitudes and values such as feelings of concern for society and the environment and a willingness to recognize and choose among different perspectives of values associated with environmental problems and issues;

– a behavioral component related to the lifestyle and community/organizational behaviors of individual and/or group position-taking and action such as persuasion and ecological management.

2.2.1.3. *Operational environmental literacy*

The third level, referred to as operational environmental literacy, includes broader and deeper knowledge than the previous level, as well as the ability to assess the impacts of human actions on the environment.

This level consists of the following components:

– a set of skills involved in assessing problems and issues based on available data and other personal information that can be used in planning, implementing and evaluating solutions, the ability to anticipate, plan, imagine, value, use primary and secondary sources of information, separate fact from opinion and determine the roles played by different human beliefs and values in environmental issues;

– an affective component involving affects and attitudes that indicate a valuing of nature and society with a sense of investment and responsibility in solving problems and issues, as well as respect for nature and society and a willingness to participate such as sensitivity to society and its programs, motivation to actively participate in the improvement and protection of the environment, concentration on current and potential environmental situations, awareness of the environment in our surroundings, balancing love of nature and love of humanity and showing respect for the diversity of human perceptions and their learning styles and value systems;

– a behavioral component relating to leadership skills in problem-solving and issue-based problem-solving in assessing actions for their impact on quality of life and the environment, making verbal commitments, acting to maintain biological and social diversity, continuously examining and re-examining cultural values and making decisions based on benevolence, justice, prudence, cooperation and compassion.

2.2.2. *Ecological citizenship*

Participation is the main category of political or democratic citizenship (Dalton 2014). According to Moore (2012), the original concept of "citizen" refers to a "category" of people actively involved in government, which was known in Athens as "the body of citizens". It is both a right and a duty to take part in decision-making in the city or town.

The development of modern citizenship began with the emergence of the nation-state in the 17th century and more precisely with the formation of the idea of popular sovereignty and the development of the theoretical foundations of liberalism. The revolutions of the 18th century such as the French and American revolutions integrated the idea of citizenship by allowing it to develop. During the 19th century, which was a period of intense political activity, the major challenge was to extend citizenship to the working class. It was primarily a liberal variant in which the rights claimed had to take precedence over the civic virtue that dominated. The 20th century saw the extension of civil rights to "social rights" such as rights to social and economic security. These rights were the subject of continued activism in the 1950s and 1960s by various civil, social and environmental groups (Moore 2012).

Ecological citizenship is a concept proposed in political theory to account for personal responsibility towards the environment (Jagers and Matti 2010). According to these authors, three aspects of this responsibility form the distinguishing characteristics of ecological citizenship:

– responsibility for the environment in the framework of ecological citizenship considers that the private activities and non-contractual relations between citizens have an impact on the public sphere (an inspiration that originates in the feminist political thought stream);

– responsibilities, rather than rights, are fundamental principles for the ecological citizen;

– the duties of the ecological citizen are non-reciprocal.

Historically, the first work dealing with the link between citizenship and EDIs began in the 1990s, paving the way for the conceptualization of a new type of citizenship: ecological citizenship.

MacGregor (2014b) identifies three streams of theoretical thinking that have shaped the development of the concept of ecological citizenship: the liberal stream defining a liberal environmental (or ecological) citizenship, the republican current defining a republican ecological citizenship and the post cosmopolitan current defining a global ecological citizenship.

2.2.2.1. *Liberal environmental citizenship*

Liberal environmental citizenship is primarily a citizenship of substantive rights to a clean and livable environment. It views the biophysical world merely as property in a liberal economy, advancing environmental citizenship as a result of adding an environmental dimension to the traditional framework of civil, political and social rights. According to this approach, environmental rights in fact constitute the virtue of the citizen's legal status conferred by the liberal state guaranteeing maximum individual freedom. Thus, political liberalism, anxious to maintain the neutrality of the state, avoids providing a substantial definition of the environment as a "common good" by keeping a definition open to "reasonable disagreement" through deliberation among citizens.

Fundamental environmental rights can be understood as resembling social rights (the state has a duty to provide citizens with the conditions for the exercise of their political and civil rights), arguing that environmental quality is a necessary condition for human life and should therefore be protected by law.

Liberal thinkers support the idea that treating environmental rights as social rights or limiting them to procedural rights is not enough. They must be binding in the same way as human rights, and they must be included in constitutions. In fact, environmental rights in many countries and communities[1] currently take the form of procedural rights, that is, rights to participate in environmental decision-making.

The arguments put forward in favor of ecological citizenship within liberal democracies are considered to be at the origin of a minimalist position on environmental issues. The liberal position in contemporary work on ecological citizenship faces great resistance targeting a liberalism that is seen as incompatible with environmentalism. The majority of theorists (republican and post-cosmopolitan) of ecological citizenship are moving towards emphasizing virtues, duties and responsibilities rather than the rights of individuals (MacGregor 2014b).

2.2.2.2. *Republican ecological citizenship*

Republican ecological citizenship defines an "eco-citizen" as an individual who identifies himself through his ecological virtues and recognizes his duties and responsibility towards the environment.

This second major current of the theory of eco-citizenship does not only propose the reform of liberal democratic institutions by including environmental protection and concerns about environmental issues. In fact, this political orientation assumes that a much more radical reorganization at the state level and a change in the personality of each citizen are necessary to achieve a sustainable society. This tradition emphasizes deliberative democracy as a culture that can frame a context in which eco-citizens can learn their social roles.

Civic participation constitutes an important pro-environmental behavior for republicans. Advocacy of a culture of active ecological citizenship in civil society is preferred to constraints that force citizens to follow rules designed by the state. Eco-citizens have a duty to demand the kinds of development that would ensure sustainability by opposing those that are environmentally destructive. Participation is therefore not only a right but also a civic duty. It ranges from participation in public consultations on environmentally risky proposals to participation in protest activities and direct action to try to stop environmentally damaging development processes.

Theorists of republican eco-citizenship go so far as to suggest including a "service of sustainability" similar to military service. Such a proposal is consistent with the view of republicanism that it is in active citizenship that human realizes his true potential (MacGregor 2014b).

---

1 An example is the Aarhus Convention, which came into force in the European Community in 2001 to give citizens the right to access to information and participate in the decision-making process on local, national and transnational environmental issues.

The idea of the common good occupies an important place in the republican conception of ecological citizenship (contrary to the liberal conception). This idea is based both on the individual duty to serve the common good (the health of the ecosystem) and on the need for a dynamic participatory politics that can challenge the forces of corruption in a capitalist state. In this way, ecological citizenship opens windows of hope for citizens to adopt the type of values allowing a radical transformation of society towards an inclusive relationship between nature and society. However, republican politics does not guarantee that the democratic process will lead to support for environmental sustainability. Indeed, citizens can democratically decide to continue to support a move away from sustainability (MacGregor 2014b).

2.2.2.3. *Post-cosmopolitan ecological citizenship*

The latest current of global ecological citizenship truly poses a fundamental challenge to the traditional conceptualization of citizenship by proposing an ecological citizenship that identifies global responsibilities that go beyond the nation-state and territory frameworks in which conceptualizations of citizenship have originated. It retains some aspects of global citizenship but rejects the pre-political notion of a "global community". According to MacGregor (2014b), post-cosmopolitan ecological citizenship must be politically interpreted as a position to resist neo-liberalism's claim to present individual choices and the pursuit of individual interests as natural and inevitable.

Post-cosmopolitan ecological citizenship is primarily conceptualized in the work of Dobson (2003) who rejects the notion of a "global community", which he considers pre-political, by proposing the idea of a "political community of post-cosmopolitan eco-citizens" emerging solely through the material conditions of the need to reduce the ecological footprint (MacGregor 2014b).

The first conceptions of post-cosmopolitan eco-citizenship were marked by an awareness of the transnational nature of environmental issues. This type of global ecological citizenship is defined as the right to an unpolluted environment, responsibility towards the environment and participation in its preservation. The awareness that local action alone will not solve environmental problems requires a global understanding of these problems. This approach is already being put into practice by non-governmental organizations (NGOs) that are moving towards the promotion of solidarity and international cooperation in the political. The Earth Charter can be seen as a global citizen initiative that supports a cosmopolitan environmental vision (MacGregor 2014b).

The notion of ecological citizenship supplants the idea of global community with that of ecological space, which brings together the metabolic and material relationships of individuals with their environment. A "good eco-citizen" takes responsibility for his or her own cause and that of those around him or her as driven by a belief in the equitable distribution of environmental resources and access to information.

Most theorists of post-cosmopolitan eco-citizenship focus on responsibilities and duties in terms of environmental protection and commitment to sustainable development. This can be seen as a response to the dominance of rights in other theories of citizenship over the last two centuries. Such rights and privileges are thought to be the cause of a breakdown in community ties and consequently the cause of a crisis of ecological unsustainability. Post-cosmopolitan eco-citizenship can thus be seen as a change in the way people understand their relationship with the state and with other inhabitants of the planet. This change is driven by the goal of moving towards a more sustainable society (MacGregor 2014b).

Criticizing Dobson's proposals, Machin (2012) argues that the very idea of eco-citizens voicing a political statement implicitly neutralizes any political debate by assuming a rational consensus on the responsibilities of eco-citizens. In the light of Chantal Mouffe's political philosophy, the author proposes the idea of a radical democratic ecological citizenship (also called agonistic).

2.2.2.4. *Radical democratic ecological citizenship (agonistic)*

Radical democratic ecological citizenship recognizes the inevitability of political debate supporting any collective action resulting from an EDI. According to this approach, environmental issues play an important role in the constitution of disagreement among humans by structuring a plurality of perspectives. The latter are the consequences of the physical embodiment of each human being in a unique environmental situation. Differences thus become inevitable. The recognition of human corporeality is the foundation of this approach to ecological citizenship: "beginning from an ontological perspective that envisions bodies as porous but resilient, plural, connected and inescapably embedded in both social and natural contexts" (Gabrielson and Parady 2010, cited by Machin 2012, p. 861). The environment is seen not only as a matter of concern and controversy but also primarily as a major source of political disagreement. Environmental sustainability is a dimension of citizenship as the origin of various conceptions of well-being among citizens. It recognizes the centrality of the environment in the production of "human subjectivity by acknowledging the variety of places that bodies inhabit and the diversity of human relationships with the natural world" (Gabrielson and Parady 2010, cited by Machin 2012, p. 861). Thus, this type of citizenship by its insistence on embodied differences appears particularly adapted to an agonistic framework that recognizes the inevitability of conflict.

Agonistic eco-citizenship is a model of citizenship that incorporates the environment as a ground for disagreement and affirms the responsibility to recognize that decisions are underpinned by such irreducible disagreement. Citizen responsibility, in this approach, corresponds to "a commitment to making and abiding a collective decision that incorporates its own lack of finality" (Machin 2012, p. 862).

For his part, Kenis (2016), by empirically studying two cases of social movements (Cities in Transition and Climate Action) and drawing on the theoretical work on "the political" put forward by the Belgian philosopher Chantal Mouffe, manages to characterize three perspectives of ecological citizenship: a liberationist perspective, a civic republicanist perspective (which includes communitarianism) and an agonistic perspective[2]. Through an analysis of these movements, the author focuses on the distinction between a communitarian "we" and an agonistic "we" that intersects them. The communitarian "we" is strongly depoliticized in the Cities in Transition movement while referring to a consensual deliberative vision involving the emotional and psychological dimensions of a depoliticized collective identity. The agonistic "we" in the Climate Action movement refers to a deliberative decision-making process based on political processes that advance a politicized vision of collective identity.

2.2.3. *Environmental deliberation*

Decision-making processes have not escaped the influence of the deliberative turn of contemporary democratic theory, which advances deliberation as a process of dialogue in which an exchange of reason is required to resolve a problematic situation (Zeleznik 2016).

According to Zeleznik (2016), although deliberative democracy has nowadays become an ideal, there is no generally accepted definition of this take on democracy. Indeed, it is seemingly diverse and complex, combining various ideologies (republicanism, liberalism socialism and multiculturalism) and various theories such as Rawls's Theory of Public Reason, Dahl's Pluralism, Arrow's Social Choice, Riker's Rational Choice Theory and Habermas's Communicative Action Theory.

The historical development of deliberative democracy has seen four generations of thought, each characterized by different orientations (Zeleznik 2016):

– the first generation focused on deliberations at the macro-economic level. The establishment of normative rationales and political institutions are the main contributions of deliberation this generation;

---

2 This is a post-Marxist perspective which, relying on poststructuralist authors such as Foucault, rejects rationalist approaches to deliberation such as those of Habermas or Rawls.

– the second generation broadens the scope of deliberation to complex civil society with the aim of institutionalizing it;

– the third generation is concerned with the institutionalization of deliberative practices at the societal level;

– the fourth generation focuses on the idea of deliberative systems. It involves the three levels of deliberation: micro, meso and macro. These levels of deliberation are taken separately in the first three generations by focusing on a particular sphere in which ideal deliberation takes place (individuals, civil society, state institutions).

In the field of environmental politics, Machin (2014) distinguishes three forms of deliberation on EDIs: environmental technocracy, ecological deliberation and embodied disagreement.

2.2.3.1. *Environmental technocracy*

The first form of environmental deliberation limits the democratic process of decision-making to the restricted circle of people possessing a particular form of scientific and technical knowledge. This is a Platonic form of expert authoritarianism. It is generally associated with a reaction to the inability of democratic institutions to act decisively in the face of environmental threats like climate change (Machin 2014). According to Machin (2014), technocracy can be the manifestation of two types of conceptions:

– the first is that of a trend to give more and more influence in political decision-making to those who possess particular forms of scientific and/or technological expertise;

– the second is that of a normative position whereby these experts themselves should make the relevant political decisions and where the democratic process is left to those who possess particular forms of scientific and technical knowledge.

Environmental technocracy theorists believe that it is too late to try to mitigate climate change, hence the urgent need for technological adaptation. They assume that democratic politics takes too long, and therefore,

> the only clear conclusion we can draw from the changing climate and people's response to it is that there is little time left to act [...]. In theory we could eat less and save energy but in practice we never will, unless made to do so. (Lovelock 2009, quoted by Machin 2014, p. 50)

Thus, the environmental situation generated by climate change appears to be a war whereby scientists should be called upon to serve their governments in an undemocratic framework of ecological or environmental authoritarianism. This is a Platonic form of authoritarianism based on expert opinion where democracy itself is seen as a problem because "democratic institutions are not suited to deal with crisis situations" (Shearman and Wayn 2007, quoted by Machin 2014, p. 51).

This category of technocracy is characterized by the growing influence of economists (especially neoclassical economists) with its focus on the natural sciences and engineering. This influence on the democratic process can be seen in publications in favor of a green economy at the end of the 1980s as well as in the privileged role of economists in the valuation of ecosystem services. In fact, it is not the presence of economic advisors that is undemocratic; it is the importance of their advice relative to other forms of knowledge that sets up environmental authoritarianism (Machin 2014).

2.2.3.2. *Ecological deliberation*

The second method of environmental deliberation advances a communicational rationality articulating the knowledge of experts and laymen as well as the values of the environment when making decisions on EDIs.

Three reasons are fundamental assumptions for using deliberative democracy in environmental issues (Machin 2014):

– first, deliberative democracy improves the flow of information and social learning needed to address complex environmental problems;

– second, it has an ethical value in its "moralizing effect on public discussion";

– third, deliberative democracy is inclusive. It ensures the participation of those who are often excluded and marginalized and who have direct local experience knowledge of their environment because it allows for the articulation of environmental knowledge and values between experts and lay people.

Ecological deliberation also gives importance to scientific and technological expertise. In fact, citizens generally do not have the time, capacity or willingness to constantly examine scientific developments, but the presence of a critical public such as public pressure groups to debate and question research programs is a condition for the formation of a democratic public space. Indeed, a deliberative system can manage the division of labor among citizens who are responsible for guiding social objectives and experts who bring their know-how to influence the development and implementation of political choices (Machin 2014).

In practice, in Denmark, for example, consensus conferences where a small group of (almost) randomly selected citizens meet for several days to debate a controversial scientific or technological issue are organized. Experts have the opportunity to make a presentation to the citizen body and are then subjected to questions. Citizens then deliberate among themselves and produce a report. The deliberation is thus made possible by the expertise yet the decisions are left in the hands of the citizens (Machin 2014).

2.2.3.3. *Embodied disagreement*

The third form of environmental deliberation is based on the theory put forward by Mouffe's political philosophy, which considers conflict as a constitutive dimension of the political by evoking the importance of passions ignored by the rationalism of ecological deliberation.

This approach suggests that environmental disagreements are significantly conditioned by the embodiment of political perspectives in different experiential and environmental situations. The political debate thus appears fundamentally "greened" from the outset because it is the environment that also conditions political perspectives (Machin 2014).

Environmental and physical differences generate conflicting perspectives which political stakeholders grasp and use to affect the world. This reaffirms the specificity of the meaning and values that flow from a particular form of ecological life such as those in urban metropolises, rural villages, polar expanses or arid deserts; these diverse environments are experienced and perceived in different ways across organisms. The recognition of an ontologically embodied human existence undermines the technocratic and ecological deliberation assumptions for which individuals are able to free themselves their life forms by putting their individual capacity for reason ahead of the daily conventions with which they live (Machin 2014).

Theorists of embodied disagreement recognize that democratic discussion can liberate individuals from their narrow conceptions through "intersubjective dialogues" through which participants "come to acquire and appreciate the cultural and biological diversity of our interdependent relationship to all relevant aspects of the web of life" (Tully 2001, cited by Machin 2014, p. 63).

According to this approach, listening is as important as speaking because it allows for a better understanding of the perspectives of others as well as the nature of difference and conflict, and it finally allows us to grasp the different alternative practices. The example of the interaction of Western and Indigenous perspectives on environmental issues is illustrative because "the purpose of these discussions is not to exchange Western and Indigenous world views of the environment, but to understand the different practices in which Western environmental knowledge and the traditional ecological knowledge of Indigenous peoples are embodied" (Tully 2001, cited by Machin 2014, p. 64).

2.2.4. *Environmental collective action*

Collective action is a concept developed in several fields of social sciences, philosophy and economics. In the context of social movement studies, the term refers to a type of joint action by a collective of individuals, such as a demonstration or strike. For many theorists in these fields, collective action is exclusively oriented towards the joint production of public goods (Duit 2010).

In the social sciences, collective action is identified from an epistemological position which draws on the logic of human action. According to Bréchet and Schieb-Bienfait (2009), this epistemology can be characterized by five entries: the model of individual rationality, the figure of coordination or integration of the collective, the problematic situation or entry into problematization, the status of the future and the theoretical position.

According to Duit (2010), collective action for the environment refers to efforts that involve a multitude of individual actors oriented towards the joint production of environmental public goods to make environmental conditions healthier. In fact, this author proposes a distinction between two forms of collective action by going back to the hypothesis put forward by Olson[3] concerning the importance of group size for the emergence of this type of action: environmental collective action within an intermediate group and environmental collective action within a latent group.

2.2.4.1. *Environmental collective action of an intermediate group*

The intermediate group is defined as follows:

> A group which no single member receives a share of the benefit sufficient to give him an incentive to provide the goods himself, but which does not have so many members that no one will notice whether any another member is or is not helping to provide the collective good. In such a group, a collective good may, or equally well may not, be obtained, but no collective good can ever be obtained without some group coordination or organization. (Olson 1965, quoted by Duit 2010, p. 905)

Operationally, the measures of environmental class action in an intermediary group are based on self-reported estimates of participation in class actions such as

3 Olson argues that the size of a group and collective actions are inextricably linked. The likelihood of free-riding increases as the group sizes increases, and more sizeable groups will find it increasingly difficult (if not impossible) to achieve collective action among their members (Olson 1965, pp. 22–43). In the majority of empirical research, group size has been identified as a key variable for the emergence of collective action.

joining environmental organizations, attending meetings and signing petitions for environmental causes and contributions to environmental organizations (Duit 2010).

2.2.4.2. *Environmental collective action of a latent group*

The latent group "is distinguished by the fact that, if one member does or does not help the collective good, no other member will be significantly affected, and therefore no one has any reason to react" (Olson 1965, quoted by Duit 2010, p. 905; author's translation).

Operationally, measures of environmental collective action in an intermediary group are based on self-reported estimates of environmental collective actions such as waste recycling, purchases of environmentally friendly products and efforts to conserve water for environmental purposes.

In fact, according to Duit (2010), the fundamental difference between latent groups and intermediary groups is not the actual size of the group (latent and intermediary groups can have a very large number of members), but whether or not collective action can be carried out in an organizational context. Indeed, this difference makes collective action very difficult in latent groups. In contrast, intermediary groups may be able to take collective action if the organization is effectively functional.

Both forms of environmental action ultimately aim to produce a public good: a better environment. In the case of group environmental action, this is done through individual contributions (membership, events and monetary donations) to some sort of organization that, in turn, works to produce the public good. This means that the individual decides to cooperate based on an assessment of the organization in question where it is likely that other members will show up at the event and make a donation to the organization. Thus, organizations appear to contain norms and encourage collective identities (Duit 2010).

On the other hand, a latent group does not have the equivalent of the organization as a focal point for collective action. An individual who decides to participate in latent group collective action will probably only have heuristic knowledge of the relevant collective of collaborators (recyclers, water savers), with imperfect information on the actions of the other individuals in this collective and with weak or non-existent collective norms and group identities. Thus, collective action in latent groups appears to be deprived of the psychological and cultural mechanisms identified by research as essential to overcome collective action dilemmas (Duit 2010).

According to Duit (2010), collective action in intermediary groups has stronger links than collective action of latent groups with levels of social capital[4] in a community. Large-scale collective action in an organizational context has strong links with indicators of social capital (i.e. widespread trust and participation in voluntary organizations). However, collective action in a latent group, because of its lack of organizational foundation, is more dependent on a society's institutional structure than in intermediate groups. Thus, in the case of weak institutional structures that are notable to guarantee the cooperation of a sufficient number of people, or in the case of the absence of an organizational structure mitigating the weakness of these structures, the potential for environmental impact of these groups diminishes rapidly as actors come to discover that their efforts will be wasted because they are not reinforced by similar efforts of others.

2.3. Conclusion

The political potential of EDIs appears in four categories supposedly organizing political life in situations involving these questions. These categories are derived from the work of Sloam (2010, 2011), which assumes that political life is played out in a system of four reinforcing dimensions: literacy, participation, deliberation and experiences. They correspond to environmental literacy, ecological citizenship, environmental deliberation and environmental collective action. Each of these categories shows analytical levels ranging from the most basic to the most complex.

4 A central tenet of social capital theory is the close link between widespread trust and participation in voluntary organizations and networks (Duit 2010).

3

Political Learning and Socialization in Teaching Environmental Issues[1]

3.1. Educational purposes and projects: sociological, pedagogical and didactic approaches

3.1.1. *Educational purposes and social functions of school: the sociological approach*

Lenoir *et al.* (2013) conceptualize educational purposes as options for the organization of an education system that are actualized through projects that are mainly strategic in nature, as well as ideological and political. The authors have identified, through the study of sociological research, seven readings of the purposes of education: social reproduction, self-realization, investment, repression of desire, resistance, preparation for the world of work and emancipation. These readings are summarized by centering them around their presuppositions related to the social functions of the school institution:

– the purpose of social reproduction, where the function of the school is to perpetuate the social structure by maintaining the social hierarchy that is in place;

– the purpose of self-realization, where the school constitutes a place allowing individual and autonomous socialization through the development of self-esteem and the affirmation of individuality;

– the purpose of investment, where the function of the school is to offer adequate preparation for entry into the world of work from the perspective of companies considering individuals as human capital;

1 This chapter was published in French as an article in issue 50 of the journal *Éducation et Socialisation* (Slimani *et al.* 2018).

– the purpose of repressing desire, in which the school constitutes a place of "training" to humanize individuals by developing human qualities and bringing them out of an initial amoral and asocial "nature";

– the purpose of resistance, where the school constitutes a place of contestation of unjust power relations conveyed by neocapitalism and its logic of primarily individualistic cultural and economic hegemony;

– the purpose of preparation for the world of work, where the school constitutes a place where a professionalizing know-how can be developed and is aimed at the development of useful skills to meet the expectations of society independently of the ideological weight of liberalism and the perspective of companies;

– the purpose of emancipation, where the school constitutes a place for the exercise of the responsibility of the nation-state by questioning the person under the guarantor of a relation to knowledge and disciplines as an instrument of truth (pupil participation in the construction of knowledge) and not of truth (knowledge is constructed by the scholars and transmitted to the pupils). This option thus facilitates the emancipation of individuals.

These conceptualizations of the purposes of education, in relation to social options, educational projects and the social functions of the school, are especially valid for teleological analyses on the broad scale of educational systems.

For praxeological analyses on the scale of educational situations, pedagogy and didactics propose conceptualizations linked to a common project, which is the teaching and learning process.

3.1.2. *Educational purposes and regulation of the teaching and learning process: the pedagogy of learning approach*

Altet (1997, 2002) proposes modeling pedagogical situations as a coupling between teaching and learning (T–L) in the classroom microsystem. This coupling is ensured by the field of pedagogical communication, whose educational purpose constitutes an independent variable. Indeed, in pedagogy of learning, a purpose is considered as a lever of functional regulation and dialectical articulation between the teaching and learning processes in an educational situation.

It thus constitutes a factor of interpersonal adjustment and adaptation during the cognitive, socio-cognitive and affective mediating interactional processes in information processing and its transformation into knowledge between the actors (learners and teachers) involved in these situations (Altet 1994).

However, this schematization is not exempt from a hierarchical structure that gives a privileged position to the pedagogical approach in the analysis of teaching and learning situations. Indeed, according to this perspective, the educational purpose appears as a variable that influences the teaching and learning process mainly through the input of pedagogical communication.

3.1.3. *Educational purposes and effectiveness of teaching and learning: the curricular didactic approach*

Curricular didactics, through the works of Coquidé (2000) and Lange (2006, 2011, 2013, 2015), among others, conceptualizes the purpose in a curriculum or educational situation as a variable constituting the criterion of effectiveness of teaching and learning.

Coquidé and Lange's works are based on Lebeaume's (1999) proposal of a scheme for the critical analysis of the coherence of the teaching of technology in secondary schools. This analysis questions the tasks (or activities) and references (or knowledge) related to the aims of technological education (Lebeaume 2006, 2011).

This praxeological conceptualization characterizes the educational purpose as a factor of consistency within the educational situations in terms of two indicators: on the one hand, its harmony with the school tasks carried out; on the other hand, its compatibility with the referents (reference knowledge and social practices). Such a characterization manifests the common project of didactics with pedagogy: that of teaching and learning situations viewed as situations of socialization in projects that make "tasks, products and manipulation of contents" succeed (Vial 2000).

Subsequently, discussions and conceptualizations of socialization will be presented drawing on approaches from the educational sciences[2], the philosophy of education, social history of education and education sociology.

3.1.4. *Educational purposes of socialization*

In education sciences, Charlot (2017) discusses the place of the purpose of socialization in the structuring of socialization and subjectivation. He thus identifies three configurations:

---

2 The grouping of educational research proposed by Charlot (2017) is used to differentiate between these domains. In this grouping, the author distinguishes between three units of research: the unit of research which is born out of disciplines (history, psychology, sociology), the unit of disciplinary didactics and the unit of educational sciences.

– a configuration where education is thought of mainly in terms of socialization/humanization, leaving little room for subjectivation. This configuration is found in traditional pedagogical practices;

– a second configuration that is actualized in the practices of the new (active, modern) pedagogy where education corresponds to a process of singularization (subjectivation)/humanization (in Ferrière and Freinet's work, for example) that is articulated with socialization (especially in Dewey's work);

– a third configuration, which appeared in the 1960s and became more radical in the 1980s and 1990s, where education is mainly interpreted as socialization in the sense of the conquest of a social position. Yet, in this conquest, "the subject is abandoned to itself: singularization is increasingly controlled as a trajectory and thought of less as subjectivation" (Charlot 2017, p. 25).

For his part, Marpeau (2013), a researcher in education sciences, distinguishes between three paradigms of educational goals:

– the paradigm of socialization, where education is understood as the internalization of knowledge, values and social norms;

– the paradigm of the construction of knowledge, where education is thought of as a guarantee for the child's access to rationality and equality (republican paradigm);

– the authorization paradigm, where the educational process is considered as a process leading to us becoming a leader.

In educational philosophy, socialization is conceptualized by Biesta (2014) as a goal of civic learning. In fact, for these civic learning processes, the author distinguishes between a conception of socialization and a conception of subjectivation that he links to two categories of citizenship that can be targeted: "Whereas a socialization conception of civic learning is about learning for future citizenship, the subjectivation conception of civic learning is about learning from the current citizenship, from current experiences with an engagement in the ongoing experience of democracy" (Biesta 2014, p. 6).

The same author (Biesta 2010) discusses the purposes of education in terms of the functions of qualification, socialization and subjectivation:

– in the function of subjectivation, education contributes to the emergence of the human subject;

– in the function of qualification, education contributes to the acquisition of knowledge, specific or general provisions and know-how;

– in the socialization function, education is seen as a means by which individuals integrate into the existing socio-cultural, political and moral order.

In educational sociology, Millet (2013) puts forward the theory that the theory of the school form elaborated by Vincent in 1980 allows us to highlight, thanks to its socio-historical perspective, a new mode of socialization that originated in Europe from the 17th century onwards: the school mode of socialization. In this form,

> school as a form of schooling in modern societies constitutes [...] the dominant form of socialization, both in that it has imposed its empire on an increasing number of individuals and for longer periods (generalized schooling process) and in that it is the matrix of this set of knowledge and processes which constitute pedagogy and whose development, somewhat monstrous, encourages us to think of social transformations in terms of pedagogical social relations. (Bernard 1984, quoted by Millet 2013, p. 15, author's translation)

According to Millet, this mode of socialization is characterized by the involvement of cognitive dimensions in the social phenomenon, because it requires a mobilization of rules of knowledge and a reflexivity about what is learned.

Vincent (2008) uses a socio-historical analysis approach to define democratic socialization as a new type of socialization (originating with the historical mutation of democracy) that can transform today's school. Indeed, according to this author, the orientation of the school towards a purpose of democratic socialization allows for the establishment of a new type of social relations through the construction of intra-generational and inter-generational power relations that welcome and preserve the indeterminacy of the future.

The conceptualizations of Vincent (2008) and Millet (2013) are used in a rereading of the discussions of Biesta, Charlot and Marpeau. In fact, a reclassification of these discussed purposes into two groups is proposed. The first is that of a cognitive socialization (moral, political, disciplinary, critical) as congruence between the purposes of humanization, qualification and construction of knowledge. The second is that of a democratic socialization[3] as congruence between the purposes of subjectivation, singularization and authorization.

3 Democratic socialization is differentiated from political socialization. The latter is conceived as the result of learning social roles in an existing political community. The former, however, is conceived as a learning outcome in collective action that takes into account creativity in human action and its openness to the future.

In the following section, this synthesis is used to highlight a certain evolution of the contributions of research in didactics, for the purposes of socialization.

3.2. Evolution of the contributions of didactic research for the educational purposes of socialization

3.2.1. *Sciences education and disciplinary cognitive socialization*

Within the framework of the didactics of learning about life and earth sciences (LES), Orange (2007) proposes the theory that, from the point of view of the didactic current of problematization, the question of learning is posed in terms of environment and adaptation. First of all, the author takes up Brousseau's theorizing, which itself borrows from Piaget's idea of learning as adaptation to an environment:

> Each piece of knowledge must be born from the adaptation to a specific situation... The student learns by adapting to an environment which is a factor of contradictions, difficulties and imbalances, much like human society does. This knowledge, the result of the pupil's adaptation, manifests itself through new responses which are proof of learning. (Brousseau 1986, quoted by Orange 2007, p. 39, author's translation).

Second of all, he adds to this vertical structuring of the educational situation, rooted in the theory of didactic situations (TDS) developed especially in mathematical didactics, a second structuring which he calls "horizontal", based on the physiological theory of the internal environment developed by the physiologist Claude Bernard. This new structuring corresponds to a triptych of the "external didactic environment" (EDE), "internal class didactic environment" (IcDE) and the "student's internal didactic environment" (sIDE).

According to the author, scientific learning can be achieved by adapting to TDS only if it goes through the IcDE. Indeed, the intermediate position of the IcDE between sIDE and EDE (essentially material) allows scientific learning to be interpreted as the construction of knowledge that is mainly explanatory, not aiming to eliminate problems by solving them but to construct them anew.

In fact, this idea of adaptation[4] constitutes a strong epistemological anchor for an educational purpose of socialization through disciplinary cognitive logics

4 Such an idea also guides other currents in the didactics of discipline learning, such as that of social representations and conceptions. The first presupposes a cognitive adaptation by modifying the social representation of a given phenomenon among learners. The second

(disciplinary matrices) by considering the teaching and learning of sciences not as a corpus of de-socialized factual content but as a cultural activity (Albe 2011). The educational situations involved thus become situations of acculturation to scientific problematization practices.

3.2.2. *Education for scientific uncertainty and critical cognitive socialization*

Simonneaux (2011) connects the didactics of socially acute questions related to globalization, GMOs, agricultural policy, agrofuels or food with the current of problematization in the didactics of the earth and life sciences discipline. Indeed, the author attributes the social vivacity of these questions to the uncertainties they convey. He identifies the reasoning on these questions as a socio-scientific reasoning reached by a specific problematization in teaching/learning situations involving this type of questions. The same author (Simonneaux 2013) characterizes these situations loaded with uncertainties with the help of seven inputs: contextualization of the situation, degree of interaction, role of values, degree of commitment of the actors involved, degree of neutrality of the educator, nature of knowledge and epistemological position.

In fact, the teaching methods proposed by the research in didactics on topical issues in society (debate situations, epistemological disturbances, case studies, etc.) are aimed at "warming up" these scientific questions, which have been qualified as post-normal because they have not stabilized, contrary to ordinary scientific questions, in an educational situation of scientific uncertainty. Epistemologically, this warming consists of taking into account a level of uncertainty[5] related to the diversity of perceptions of contexts and risks of using this knowledge (Morin 2013).

The debate, as a warm-up tool, constitutes a composite "place" for learning and socialization (Simonneaux and Legardez 2008). It favors reasoning and the development of exploratory discourses (Simonneaux 2013a) and allows us to go beyond the cultural consequences of instrumental rationality towards a model of collegial expertise. Such a model, based on the defense of different scientific theses,

---

proposes an allosteric model of learning that makes it possible to interpret learners' thinking logic as a modification of the structure of knowledge by moving from an initial state to a more stable one (Eastes 2013).

5 Morin (2013) distinguishes, in the epistemology of Post Normal Science (PNS), which he characterizes by the links it establishes between scientific knowledge and its socio-political contexts, two levels of uncertainty: "that linked to the processes of selecting information and controlling its validity during the production of knowledge" and "that of the relevance of the scientific knowledge produced in the context of its use".

does not block the controversy but rather opens it up to a field of possibilities (Morin 2013).

Collegial expertise, which is fundamentally open, exploratory and intercultural (guaranteeing a "distancing" from the human realities in which it is immersed) thus lays the epistemological foundations for critical cognitive socialization.

3.2.3. *Eco-citizenship education and political socialization*

Educational situations for eco-citizenship are defined as situations of "co-construction of knowledge and singular and supportive subjective identities towards a social, local and international division of labour that allows for real cohesion and universalized eco-citizenship" (Martinez 2010, p. 10, author's translation). Thus, eco-citizen identity operates in an "interlocutory and dialogical space" within the exchanges that take place through the processes of identification (conjugation of belonging and difference) in educational practice (Martinez and Poydenot 2009).

The types of learning targeted in educational situations are those of social roles (socialization) that characterize the status of the eco-citizen as a member of a political community (the community of eco-citizens[6]): this is political socialization.

3.2.4. *Education for sustainable development (ESD) and democratic socialization*

Within the framework of ESD didactics, Lange (2011 and 2015) proposes an analytical model of the functioning of an educational situation for sustainable development as an academic social practice of democracy. In this model and following the example of pragmatic sociology (Barthe *et al.* 2013), the author associates this social practice with a reflexive relationship that social actors at the school institution level maintain through their actions and those of others as part of collective action .

Reflexivity is conceptualized in the social sciences by Archer as a mediating process between the inner and outer world of people. It is a "regular exercise of the mental ability, shared by all normal people, to consider themselves in relation to their (social) contexts and *vice versa*" (Archer 2007, quoted by Vogler 2016, p. 71). Indeed, this idea, through its insistence on the role of individuals (as active agents who, by receiving heterogeneous and sometimes contradictory messages, define

6 The general condition for the emergence of such a political community is the generation of a "political duty" demanding justice under the conditions of a "limited ecological space" and through the material relations of the ecological footprint (Machin 2012).

their interests in a relational way), enables socialization to be reconceptualized as an ever-evolving and incomplete process (Caetano 2014) and as a factor of social change (Caetano 2015).

The reflexivity of social actors thus facilitates the construction of "provisions" (Lange 2011, 2015) translating the plural character of the action regime through a new vision of the identity of the social agents involved, as a construction resulting from a mode of socialization based on discussion: the democratic socialization.

This praxeological approach, which stems from an anthropo-pedagogical perspective of the didactics of educational situations involving the question of sustainable development, raises the urgency of a new challenge for schools: "the introduction of a non-partisan, democratic education for the political, which facilitates the emergence of and participates in the elaboration of societal orientations to be collectively imagined" (Lange 2015, p. 107, author's translation).

This issue of political education and development can be realized in educational situations involving different types of issues on the environment and development (in addition to the issue of sustainable development) in the form of learning moments[7] aimed at democratic socialization integrating moments aimed at cognitive socialization (disciplinary, critical, political).

3.3. Teaching of environmental and development issues and political learning: integrating socialization purposes

The content spectrum of Environmental and Development Issues (EDIs), which feeds into educational content in science education, education for scientific uncertainty, education for eco-citizenship and education for sustainable development, is very broad. The question of biodiversity is gaining more and more ground in scientific education. It is worth mentioning, among others, the work of Franc (2014) within the framework of conceptual change and that of Lhoste and Voisin (2013) within the framework of scientific problematization. Moreover, a recent study of scientific problematization has raised the question of climate change (Orange and Orange Ravachol 2017). This facet of thematic diversity is amplified by a second one relating to the duality of EDIs as questions that are easily depoliticized but can also be "excellent terrain for politicization" (Kenis and Lievens 2014). These two properties mean that the field of EDIs has great potential for political learning, political education and socialization.

7 The idea of learning moments is adapted from Bisault (2011). It seems appropriate in the context of political education because it goes beyond the disciplinary frameworks of sciences education by involving open and complex pedagogical modalities.

The work of Sloam (2010, 2011) predicts that political learning develops in a four-dimensional system (literacy, participation, experiences and deliberation, which are all mutually reinforcing). Both this perspective and that of Lange (2011, 2013) on the possible ESD curriculum are used to propose the structuring of a conceptual framework for political education through the EDIs.

This structuring takes a schematic form (Figure 3.1) in which political learning is organized in terms of four moments with different purposes. The first three curricular moments, disciplinary cognitive socialization, critical cognitive socialization and political socialization, are articulated thanks to the fourth type of learning moments, which occupies a pivotal position: moments of learning aimed at democratic socialization[8].

Disciplinary cognitive socialization moments are periods of technical, cultural and critical ecoliteracy learning (Huckle 2013) in scientific disciplines involving environmental literacy (Roth 1992), as an extension of scientific literacy to the EDIs.

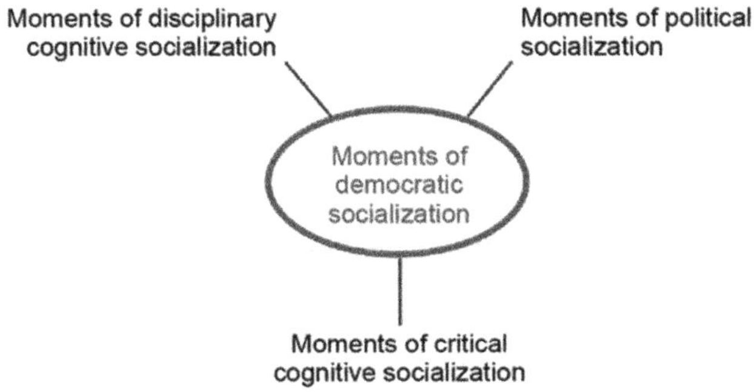

Figure 3.1. *Moments of socialization in political education through the EDIs. For a color version of this figure, see www.iste.co.uk/slimani/education.zip*

Moments of critical cognitive socialization are periods of learning about political debate on problematic environmental situations (Machin 2014; Håkansson *et al.* 2017) which are traversed by scientific uncertainty.

Moments of political socialization are periods in which social roles in a community of eco-citizens are learnt as a response to a requirement to reduce the ecological footprint (Dobson 2006; Machin 2012) in its various components (water footprint, energy footprint as examples).

8 This position is guaranteed by the fact that democratic socialization incorporates indetermination and discussion as a condition for the possibility of "living together".

Moments of democratic socialization are periods of learning with the help of political experiences based on collective environmental actions, as efforts involving a multitude of actors oriented towards the production of environmental goods (Duit 2010) at the level of the educational institution and its territory. These moments allow us to connect (Sloam 2010, 2011) the other moments of learning of the political (ecoliteracy, environmental deliberation, eco-citizenship) as well as their aims of cognitive (disciplinary and critical) and political socialization.

3.3.1. *Ecoliteracy learning*

Ecoliteracy is a conceptualization of literacy related to environmental issues that builds on the broader humanities by emphasizing the purpose of creating sustainable human communities requiring a reconstruction of the entire educational system. It differs from environmental literacy, which mainly refers to environmental sciences. McBride *et al.* (2013) refer to Wooltorton (2006) to summarize the six elements of environmental literacy:

– ecological self-reliance as a sense of interdependence with the life cycle based on care, compassion and respect for difference;

– sense of place and active citizen engagement with the culture, history, local traditions and biotic community of the ecosystem;

– systemic thinking with a sense of interdependence and contextuality;

– the ecological paradigm as the study of all components, relationships and networks with attention to processes;

– the pedagogy of education for sustainability as an experiential, participatory and multidisciplinary approach;

– cultural engagement with nature as early in life as possible.

In a critical approach to ecoliteracy, Code (2018) proposes a more in-depth study of the idea of ecoliteracy as the development of capacities that allow the reading of the "book of nature" considered as a text. Ecoliteracy thus appears to be dependent on the ability to read, decode and extract meaning from the events taking place in this book.

From a sustainability education perspective, Huckle (2013) distinguishes three complementary forms of ecoliteracy in society: a technical form, a cultural form and a critical form.

3.3.1.1. *Technical ecoliteracy learning*

Technical literacy initially evokes an understanding of fundamental sciences that regards their relevance in the treatment of societal questions, followed by the knowledge of the impact of human societies on ecological systems as well as an exploration of the co-evolution technologies linked to society and nature (Huckle 2013).

This form of ecoliteracy can be linked to an early conceptualization of literacy as a set of skills for accessing knowledge and information (UNESCO 2006). From UNESCO's perspective, the term literacy is used in a broad sense to refer to skills other than those that refer to literacy skills, such as "information literacy", "visual literacy", "media literacy" and "scientific literacy". For all of these concepts, the OECD proposes a conception of literacy as a set of essentially technical skills. In this conceptual landscape, the concept of multiple literacies has emerged, designating abilities for "reading the world" in different contexts: technological, health, informational, media, visual and scientific.

Thus, in this perspective, literacy fundamentally related to writing means the interpretation of signs (symbols, images, sounds) that vary according to the social context, not only the decoding and comprehension of words.

In short, technical ecoliteracy can be defined as a set of reading skills placed in the specific contexts of technical and scientific uses (Fraenkel and Mbodj-Pouye 2010).

3.3.1.2. *Cultural ecoliteracy learning*

Cultural ecoliteracy refers to comprehending the ways in which different cultures understand and value nature, recognizing a media discourse that values Indigenous, modern and postmodern cultural elements in support of environmental sustainability (Huckle 2013).

This form of literacy is related to a literacy defined by its applications, practice and context, thus going beyond the limits of a competency-based approach. It is based on the findings of ethnographic research from "new literacy studies" (Fraenkel and Mbodj-Pouye 2010) in that the application of literacy varies with the social and cultural context. In fact, this research falls within a school of thought that views literacy as a social practice within a social context rather than as a technical skill independent of context. This approach (new literacy studies) is primarily based on two concepts:

– "literacy events", defined as occasions in which a written word is a component of the nature of participants' interactions and interpretive processes;

– "literacy practices", which are social practices and conceptions of reading and writing.

This approach places undue emphasis on local factors. Such a focus fails to highlight the roles of forces such as colonial administrations, missionaries, international communication and economic globalization that have influenced the "local" experiences of communities. This limits the perspective of this approach for examining the potential of literacy, helping individuals move from their "local" position to broader political participation (UNESCO 2006).

3.3.1.3. *Critical ecoliteracy learning*

Critical literacy evokes an understanding of EDIs in the context of political economy and social production and reproduction. It also requires an assessment of existing forms and alternative forms of democracy on the part of the learners by considering the utopias advanced by the principles of international environmental charters and conventions. Critical literacy is primarily aimed at enabling learners to reflect on and act on the dominant type of political economy (modes of production, consumption and reproduction; Huckle 2013).

This form of ecoliteracy can be related to literacy seen as a learning process, as an active and broad learning process rather than the product of limited and targeted educational intervention (UNESCO 2006). In such a learning process, personal experience is seen as a central resource.

The concepts of collaborative learning, distributive learning, communities of practice and communities of learning place greater emphasis on social practices that build on the latest conceptions of critical literacy. Such literacy forms the basis of Paulo Freire's pedagogical project (Freire and Macedo 1987; Mayo 1995), which integrates notions of active learning in contexts that involve the socio-cultural realities of the learner in the learning process itself and then use the latter to challenge these social processes. In fact, at the heart of this pedagogy is the notion of critical literacy as a goal to be achieved by:

– "reading" books and other writings as interpretation, reflection, questioning, theorizing, research, exploration, study and questioning;

– writing as an action that has a bearing on the social world and its transformation.

These ideas of critical literacy have been used as pedagogical tools for the development of learners who have been oppressed, excluded or disadvantaged because of their gender, ethnicity or socio-economic status (UNESCO 2006).

3.3.2. *Deliberative learning*

Deliberative learning in the school environment is especially favored by the didactic modalities of socially acute environmental and development issues (debate situations, epistemological disturbances, case studies, etc.). These modalities can be interpreted in the light of the sociology of justification as didactic strategies for the development of justification regimes regarding these issues at the school education level. Indeed, according to Holden and Scerri (2015):

> Participatory, democratic deliberation oriented by the ideal of communicative rationality can induce truthfulness in the presentation of individual views and preferences, narrow the domain of preference profiles in a collective choice situation, and yield agreement on criteria for evaluation. (Holden and Scerri 2015, p. 369)

Håkansson *et al.* (2017) have proposed a categorization of educational situations involving the political dimension of environmental and sustainable development education according to the "political trend" that runs through them, which allows democratic values and attitudes to be socialized. This political trend can take the form of democratic participation, political reflection, political deliberation or an emotional political moment. Political deliberation is a reflection that takes the form of reasoning aimed at defending an opinion, a point of view or an alternative scenario. By exploiting the results of an empirical study, the authors have distinguished three categories of political deliberation: normative deliberation, consensual deliberation and conflictual deliberation.

3.3.2.1. *Normative deliberative learning*

Normative political deliberation is oriented towards the adoption of a point of view specified *a priori* by the teacher. It aims to prepare learners for different roles through the development of capacities to take care of their own health or that of their families to contribute to a more sustainable development through social participation in an active citizenship. It also seeks socialization through the internalization of norms, values, attitudes and world views which go hand in hand with the norm towards which deliberation is directed. Such a standard is seen as the only alternative or solution to the problem at hand. This approach assumes that the training of the person can be done by accepting the identity consistent with the standard and the proposed solution (Håkansson *et al.* 2017).

3.3.2.2. *Consensual deliberative learning*

Consensual political deliberation is oriented towards a consensus making it possible to overcome differences. It targets both preparation (learning negotiation and conflict resolution) and socialization (learning the values of social harmony, peace).

This approach assumes that the person's training can take place in the formation of an identity in line with the expectations that go hand in hand with consensus building (Håkansson *et al.* 2017).

3.3.2.3. *Conflict deliberative learning*

Conflicting deliberation is characterized by its openness to the defense of opposing perspectives that are in dispute. It is aimed at the construction of the subjectivity of learners in situations giving an explicit importance for the conflictual, the defense of opposing perspectives, antagonistic relations and strong emotional experiences. These situations are supposed to be capable of leading to subjectivation enabling the preparation of learners for social and political life through the acquisition of new knowledge and new perspectives and through the acquisition of the ability to debate. They also enable socialization by embracing the values of critical thinking when defending divergent points of view (Håkansson *et al.* 2017).

3.3.3. *Learning through social roles in a community of eco-citizens and political socialization*

Johnson and Morris (2010), in a synthesis of conceptions of the "ideal citizen" from the critical pedagogical perspective put forward by Veugelers and his colleagues and by Westheimer and Kahne, identify three conceptions of the political citizen: adaptive, individualistic and critical democratic (Figure 3.2). Eco-citizenship is seen as a form of political citizenship, which allows us to use the same analytical framework as that of Johnson and Morris.

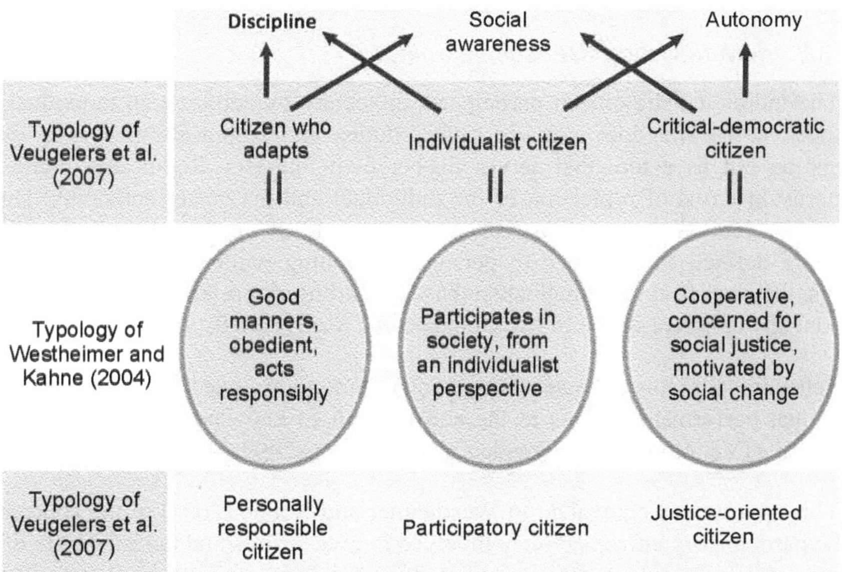

Figure 3.2. *Overview of citizen typologies (Johnson and Morris 2010, p. 85). For a color version of this figure, see www.iste.co.uk/slimani/education.zip*

3.3.3.1. *Adaptive citizenship learning*

A citizen who adapts is one who is obedient, who is well-mannered and who acts responsibly. According to this approach, the citizen is not seen as an autonomous individual who makes private choices but rather as a social and political person. The moral point of view is to fulfill our duties, which take priority over rights. This conception of adaptive citizenship is analogous to the concept of communitarian citizenship developed by political theories of citizenship. It is generally linked to an approach of value transmission in a pre-established pedagogical perspective (Johnson and Morris 2010).

Learners, therefore, do not have any opportunity to engage, to make judgments or to express their own values. In fact, values are conceived in a framework of social reproduction. Such educational approaches tend to hinder democratic participation by placing a high value on obedience (Veugelers 2007; Leenders and Veugelers 2009; Veugelers *et al.* 2017).

This conception corresponds, in the typology of Westheimer and Kahne (2004), to the personally responsible citizen who acts responsibly in his/her community (picks up litter, is a blood donor, is involved in recycling activities, obeys laws, etc.). Moreover, the values of honesty, integrity, self-discipline and hard work are among the aims of educational programs geared towards training responsible citizens (Johnson and Morris 2010).

3.3.3.2. *Individualistic citizenship learning*

The individualistic citizen participates in society by adopting an individualistic perspective. He/she does not see rights, duties and responsibilities as a moral obligation but as a tool that serves his/her own interests. Rights are interpreted primarily in terms of protection of the individual and his or her autonomy. Duties are undervalued as they entail a restriction of individual freedom. When educational aims are defined in reference to personal autonomy without reference to shared values, they can lead to individualism based on arbitrary preference and self-interest without any coherent vision of life (Johnson and Morris 2010).

Pedagogically, this approach, which values autonomy, selection, competition and individual performance, leads to the construction of knowledge without a societal perspective (Veugelers 2007; Leenders and Veugelers 2009; Veugelers *et al.* 2017).

This approach is equivalent in Westheimer and Kahne (2004) to the conception of the participatory citizen actively involved in civic affairs and the social life of the community. Educational programs aimed at training participatory citizens target activities to understand how communities function and train them to plan and participate in efforts to care for the poor or to guide school policies (Johnson and Morris 2010).

3.3.3.3. *Critical democratic citizenship learning*

The critical democratic citizen is cooperative, concerned with social justice and motivated by social change. Critical democratic citizenship is based on autonomy and social engagement. It aims at developing an attitude of critical questioning, courage and creativity to open new ways of thinking about social conventions and the power structures that support them. Critical democratic citizens try to combine individual and social development. They are people who are critically engaged in community transformation and the management of cultural differences (Johnson and Morris 2010).

Pedagogically, this approach is based on dialogue, diversity, critical analysis of power relations and social action. Cooperative, dialectical and reflective learning and knowledge building are central to this pedagogical approach (Veugelers 2007; Leenders and Veugelers 2009; Veugelers *et al.* 2017).

In the Westheimer and Kahne typology (2004), this approach is equivalent to the concept of the citizen motivated by justice which values collective work linked to the life and issues of the community (as in the case of the concept of the participatory citizen). Educational programs aimed at training citizens motivated by justice generally target a goal of social change. These programs are less likely to emphasize the need for charity and volunteering as ends in themselves and are more geared towards teachings about social movements and how to effectuate systemic change (Johnson and Morris 2010).

3.3.4. *Learning in collective educational action regimes*

Lange (2011, 2015), drawing on the work of organizational sociology, identifies a range of three types of action regimes: minimalist, intermediate and maximalist.

In the minimalist regime, coordination between social agents is merely a juxtaposition of interventions (where inter-comprehension would be instantaneous).

3.3.4.1. *Learning in an intermediate collective action regime*

In an intermediate regime, coordination may take the form of a community of practice as a learning arena where practice develops and continues and where the roles of members develop through various forms of engagement and participation. Indeed, the emergence of a community of practice is observable when the group of individuals engaged in an activity forms a "self-organized community, based on an area of common interest, a mutual, voluntary, free and almost invisible commitment, a collective memory based in particular on the capitalization of practices, and even a form of passion" (Bouchez 2014, p. 126).

Mutual engagement involves the sustained interaction of people in roles that flow from that interaction. Collective memory forms a common repertoire of signs, symbols, tools and language that are used as resources and have a specific meaning for the community. The learning process that takes place in such a community leads to the formation of community identity, which becomes a product of participation in the practice by simultaneously influencing it (Aguilar and Krasny 2011).

3.3.4.2. *Learning in a maximalist action regime*

In a maximalist regime, coordination among actors forms a learner community or learning community that can be defined as a collective of learners in a learning context that emphasizes social interaction and identity rather than individual action (Smith and Bath 2006). In fact, according to Orellana,

> [the] basic principle of the learning community is to highlight the importance of pooling the efforts, talents and skills of everyone and to value educational processes that integrate social dimensions, while being appropriate to the needs of individuals and communities and adapted to diverse and changing contexts. (Orellana 2002, quoted by Cristol 2017, p. 30, author's translation)

Cristol (2017) summarizes the conditions for the emergence of a learning community in eight dimensions:

– a common goal of the community;

– shared, meaningful and visible learning activities;

– a role of teacher, designer and facilitator of a learning space and learners responsible for carrying out their individual and collective learning and for their own evaluation;

– changes in the roles of participants according to their knowledge and skills, with each participant occasionally being a bearer or requestor of resources;

– members who are themselves considered as resources along with the community;

– a common language co-developed as members interact with each other;

– a consensus around knowledge by taking ideas further;

– a learner-led production of their own objects and ideas.

The concept of the learning community has limited use in the educational field. It refers to the practices of communities that bring together teachers, teachers and students, or more broadly teachers, students, parents and all stakeholders involved in educational success, or making the educational community a learning organization (Cristol 2017).

3.4. Conclusion

EDIs can take many forms, such as:

– the learning of ecoliteracy in sciences education which, for example, provides anchors for disciplinary cognitive socialization;

– deliberative learning in education for scientific uncertainty which, for example, provides anchors for critical cognitive socialization;

– citizenship learning in eco-citizenship education which, for example, provides anchors for political socialization;

– learning in collective action regimes in education for sustainable development which, for example, provides anchors for democratic socialization.

These anchors underpin the aims of a political education that integrates moments of learning about the political that target different types of socialization in educational situations involving EDIs. This opens up a didactics of political education in pursuit of a socialization project involving both pedagogy and didactics according to a new integrating configuration: that of democratic socialization.

4

Methodological Considerations

4.1. Case study methodology

Merriam (1998) conceives a case study as an intensive and holistic description and analysis of a delineated phenomenon such as a program, institution, person, process or social unit. The same author (Merriam 2009) defines this method by three characteristics; it is particularistic, descriptive and heuristic:

– particularistic because it focuses on a particular situation, event, program or phenomenon; hence, the importance of the case lies in what it reveals about the phenomenon. This characteristic makes this method particularly suitable for the study of issues in daily practice;

– descriptive because it leads to a detailed description (complete and literal) of the studied phenomenon by exploiting several sources of information;

– heuristic because it clarifies the understanding of a phenomenon by promoting the emergence of new meanings.

Hague and Harrop (2004) distinguish four types of case studies in the political field: the representative case, the prototypical case, the deviant case and the archetypal case:

– the representative case is the most used in political science research. Researchers often use their own country as a research site in the hope that the results will contribute to a broader, transnational debate;

– the prototypical case is chosen because the researcher expects it to become representative, that is, the study of a primary example can help forge an understanding of a phenomenon that is becoming increasingly important elsewhere;

– the deviant case seeks the exceptional and the atypical, rather than the norm. The deviant case study is often used to bring order and understanding to exceptions and anomalies;

– the archetypal case is a generator of a category taken as being representative.

4.2. Selection of case studies

4.2.1. *UNESCO's "Education for Sustainable Development Goals": a prototype case in non-formal education*

4.2.1.1. *Justification of the choice of case study*

An initial case study was selected in non-formal education and corresponds to the contents proposed for the "Education for Sustainable Development Goals" approach. This case study presents the structuring of the political within this content in relation to an international political educational context punctuated by tensions stemming from criticisms of works resulting in the approach entitled "Decade of Education for Sustainable Development 2005–2014", which was accused of being undemocratic and even neocolonial (Wals and Peters 2018). This context was also characterized by forms of resistance and acceptance (Charlier and Panait 2018) from the actors. These reactions ranged from total rejection (refusal to adopt and open opposition) to blind application (dissemination without adjustment). Intermediate positions included circumvention (refusal to implement with open disinterest and actions justified on the basis of other references and use of resources for other purposes), protest (denunciation of the effects generated), positive engagement (actions in line with what is expected) and negative engagement (negotiations and search for consensus in relation to the actor's experience during implementation that could lead to open conflict; Charlier and Panait 2018).

4.2.1.2. *Presentation of the institutional context*

Institutionally, the "Education for Sustainable Development Goals" approach was developed by UNESCO, a UN agency specializing in education, science and culture. The action of this institution is mainly driven by a vision for peace. This vision is centered on a set of actions and commitments in the cultural, educational and environmental fields: "It seeks to build peace through international cooperation in Education, the Sciences and Culture. UNESCO's programs contribute to the achievement of the Sustainable Development Goals defined in Agenda 2030, adopted by the UN General Assembly in 2015"[1].

1 https://en.unesco.org/about-us/introducing-unesco.

Thus, this approach is based on the international SDG Agenda 2030 developed by UN expert groups, examined by the Economic and Social Council (the organ responsible for coordination and dialogue on economic, social and environmental issues) and then approved by the UN General Assembly (the deliberative and decision-making organ). The UN's Sustainable Development Goals (SDGs) are designed to continue the work begun with the Millennium Development Goals (MDGs)[2]. These goals are summarized by Zhang and Alexander (2017) in a diagram called the 5Ps diagram: people, prosperity, peace, partnership and planet (Figure 4.1).

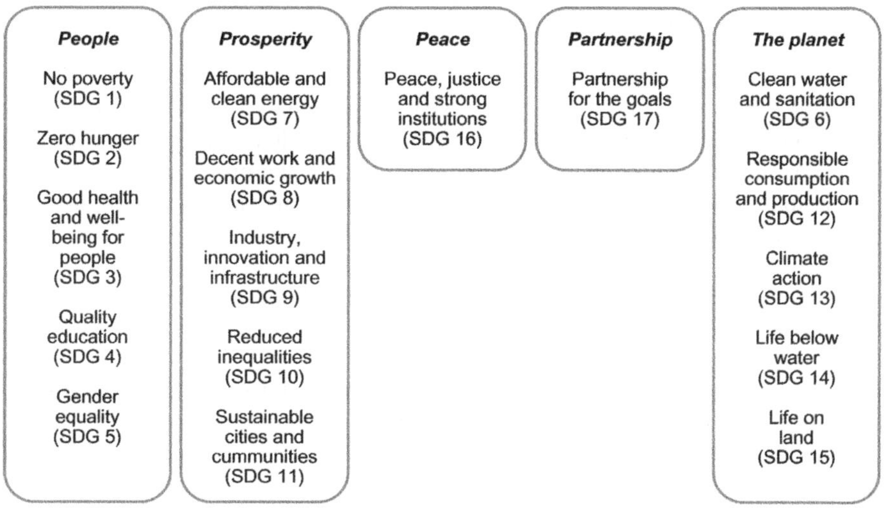

Figure 4.1. *The EDIs in the 2030 SDGs*

This case of the UNESCO approach is identified as a prototypical case of non-formal education based on a historical argument of the role of this international organization in the development of pioneering non-formal education mechanisms such as literacy: a field in which the notion of non-formal education originated and was developed (Brougère and Bézille 2007).

4.2.2. *EDIs in the Tunisian curriculum: a representative case in formal education*

4.2.2.1. *Justification for the choice of case study*

The second case was selected in formal education and corresponds to content involving EDIs in the Tunisian curriculum. This case makes it possible to present the

2 https://www.un.org/en/sections/what-we-do/promote-sustainable-development/index.html.

structuring of the political in a socio-political context, which has been taking place since 2011, stimulating debates and promoting the diversity of viewpoints (Poussel 2016). In this context, debates on the reform of the education system and the content of formal education fuel several controversies. The general curriculum for general education (primary education and the preparatory year of basic and secondary education) developed in 2017 explicitly involves the EDIs in the learning areas it specifies. Similarly, in higher education and since 2015, content reforms are being implemented in a context of controversies involving social protest movements.

4.2.2.2. *Presentation of the institutional context*

In Tunisia, schooling is structured in three major phases: basic education with two cycles (primary and preparatory years), secondary education, and higher education with three differentiated years in the undergraduate/postgraduate/doctorate system. An initial reading of the official curricula and the proposals of the sectoral commissions shows that EDIs (mainly the question of sustainable development) are very present in this course.

In the primary and preparatory years, the teaching is in Arabic, while in secondary and higher education, these issues are generally dealt with in French.

Basic education (primary and preparatory cycles) and secondary education are guided by educational politics summarized in the "Program of Programs" which is currently replaced by the "Tunisian General Curriculum". The latter is evidently oriented towards the "educations for" and the EDIs.

The secondary and higher education years of Tunisian education are differentiated by the fact that the teaching content in the former is unified because schools do not have the possibility of proposing specific educational content, while in the latter, sectorial commissions (in academic disciplines) give institutions the opportunity to propose content according to their specific characteristics. In thinking about strategies for validating the analyses, content taught in French has been subject to an initial selection process. A second selection is also necessary to pre-select content in higher education, given the dependencies of the establishments. This second selection is carried out at the university level[3] and then at establishments of the same university offering EDI courses within the framework of the "environmental protection degree"[4].

3 The Université Ez-zeitouna and the Université Virtuelle de Tunis (UVT) are excluded because of their restrictive specificities: the former dispense teaching in theology, while the latter work across other institutions (i.e. providing technical assistance for other universities).

4 A preliminary selection was made based on the work of the sectoral commissions, considering the presence of sustainable development terms or environmental protection in the title of a degree as criterion for selecting content.

The *Institut supérieur des sciences biologiques appliquées de Tunis* (ISSBAT) was selected as the institution at which data would be collected on potential curricula and produced curricula. Effectively, this establishment has set itself apart from other establishments through its announcement of a project to involve citizens in environmental protection.

The case of the Tunisian curriculum is considered a representative case in formal education with a provision that consists of an expectation of results contributing to comparative research on the structuring of the political within other national curricula.

4.3. Defining the analytical criteria

The criteria for the analyses carried out correspond to categories from the model of the political in EDIs already developed through the previous chapters (Chapters 1–3).

Categories (or codes) are thus defined with the aid of examples of indicators (in thematic analysis grids regarding textual content) with the aim of selecting educational content involving EDIs, analyzing the political/anti-political trend, analyzing the political potential and analyzing the potentialities for socialization in terms of political learning in these course contents.

4.3.1. *Criteria of the documentary analysis for selecting EDIs in prescribed curricula in Tunisia*

An initial analysis of the content of documents was carried out in order to select the contents involving EDIs in the Tunisian curriculum of secondary school and the undergraduate studies.

The categories of analysis used were taken from the conceptual framework developed in Chapter 1. These categories, of which there are six, correspond to the metathemes of EDIs: environmental politics, environmental ethics, agri-food, sustainable development, environmental technologies and management, and transitions (Table 4.1).

EDI indicators are mainly keywords indicating themes in the metathemes of these issues. They are also defined based on the literature review produced during the development of the conceptual framework in Chapter 1.

These indicators are sought in the prescribed curricula, which are the official curricula of the disciplines taught for secondary school, and in the work of the sectorial commissions for the undergraduate studies.

Categories	Examples of indicators
Environmental politics	Ecological modernization, green growth, green economy, environmental justice
Environmental ethics	Environmental values
Agri-food	Consumption
Sustainable development	Management of natural resources, green consumer, social ecology
Environmental technologies and management	Rationality, order, control, participation
Transitions	Technological innovations, resource management

Table 4.1. *Analytical categories and examples of EDI indicators in educational content*

4.3.2. *Criteria for analyzing the political trend*

To develop the categories of political/anti-political trend[5] analysis in EDIs and their indicators, the metathemes and themes are cross-referenced with both political and anti-political trends (Table 4.2).

EDIs	Example of anti-political trend indicators	Example of political trend indicators
Environmental politics	Ecological modernization, green growth, green economy	Environmental justice
Environmental ethics	Communicative deliberation on environmental values	Democratic deliberation on environmental values
Agri-food	Market oriented towards liberalization: consumption, passive role of consumers, farmers and citizens	Market oriented towards values: commitment of consumers and producers as active citizens
Sustainable development	Management of natural resources, green consumers	Social ecology, ecosocialism, ecofeminism
Environmental technologies and management	Rationality, order, control	Participation, business ethics, industrial democracy
Transitions	Technological innovations, adaptive management of resources	Political disturbances

Table 4.2. *Examples of indicators of the political/anti-political trend in EDIs*

5 This trend implies a dialectic of the political and the anti-political.

Indeed, the indicators of the political trend and those of the anti-political trend correspond to keywords from the EDI themes classified into two groups according to the trend that runs through them.

These indicators are sought in the Sustainable Development Goals 2030, in UNESCO's recommendations "Education for Sustainable Development Goals", in prescribed curricula (official programs and work of sectoral commissions), in potential curricula (secondary school textbooks), and in produced curricula (inferred through observations and interviews with teachers and learners).

4.3.3. *Criteria for analyzing the political potential of EDIs*

The categories for analyzing the political potential of EDIs are divided into four classes: environmental collective action, ecological citizenship, environmental deliberation and environmental literacy (Table 4.3).

Categories	Subcategories	Examples of indicators
Environmental collective action	Latent group	Recycling of waste, purchasing of environmentally friendly products, water conservation for environmental purposes
	Intermediate group	Membership of environmental associations, organizing gatherings and signing petitions
Ecological citizenship	Liberal	Substantive and procedural rights in a healthy and livable environment
	Republican	Duty to participate in challenges against any destructive aspect of development
	Post-cosmopolitan	Cosmopolitan justice reducing the ecological footprint
	Democratic-radical	Inevitable political challenges between opponents
Deliberation	Technocratic	Solutions in the framework of neoclassical economics of the environment
	Ecological	Consensus and conventions in the context of conferences and international declarations
	Disagreement stated	Conflict, importance of emotions
Environmental literacy	Elementary	Basic knowledge of the elementary components of natural systems
	Functional	Knowledge related to ecological processes
	Operational	The impact of beliefs and values regarding environmental issues

Table 4.3. *Categories and indicators of the political potential of EDIs*

The association of the subcategories with numerical values (Table 4.4) reflecting levels[6] in the same category allows the construction and visualization of an ideal type[7] of the political potential of EDIs (Figure 4.2), which acts as a referent allowing the comparison of these potentials during the analysis in the two case studies.

Categories	Subcategories	Associated numerical values
Environmental collective action	Latent group	1
	Intermediate group	2
Ecological citizenship	Liberal	1
	Republican	2
	Post-cosmopolitan	3
	Democratic-radical	4
Deliberation	Technocratic	1
	Ecological	2
	Disagreement stated	3
Environmental literacy	Elementary	1
	Functional	2
	Operational	3

Table 4.4. *Values associated with subcategories of the political potential of EDIs*

Indicators for these criteria are expressions that summarize ideas. These ideas are also sought in the Sustainable Development Goals 2030, in the UNESCO recommendations "Education Goals 2030", in the UNESCO recommendations "Education for Sustainable Development Goals 2030", in the prescribed curricula (official programs and the work of sectorial commissions), in potential curricula[8] (secondary school textbooks) and in the curricula produced (inferred through observations and interviews with teachers and learners).

6 The value 1 is associated with the first level (sub-criterion) in a criterion, the value 2 to the second level, and so on.

7 The idea of "ideal type" is borrowed from the field of sociology in its sense of ideal representation (acts, states of things, tendencies) which reality can deviate from or come closer to. An ideal type can thus serve as a criterion for the comparison of observable states of things (Coenen-Huther 2003).

8 It was impossible to obtain potential curriculum elements for the Environmental Protection degree at ISSBAT.

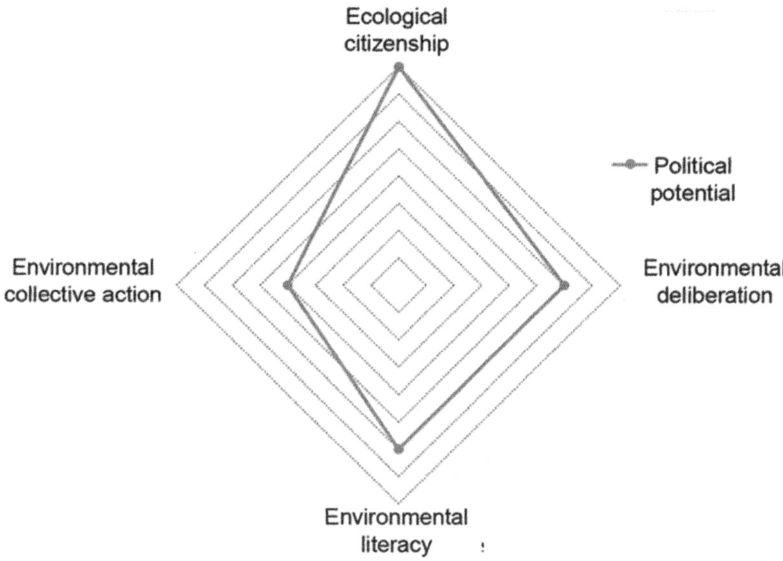

Figure 4.2. *Ideal type of political potential of EDIs. For a color version of this figure, see www.iste.co.uk/slimani/education.zip*

4.3.4. *Criteria for the analysis of potentialities for socialization in terms of political learning*

The categories for the analysis of the potentialities for socialization in terms of political learning are divided into four classes of isomorphs: learning in ecoliteracy and its isomorph (cognitive socialization in scientific disciplines), learning in citizenship and its isomorph (political socialization), deliberative learning and its isomorphic (critical cognitive socialization) and learning in regimes of action and its isomorphic (democratic socialization; Table 4.5).

In the same way, and with regard to the isomorphic potential socialization and political learning, it is possible to define an ideal type (Figure 4.3) using the same method of associating numerical values with the sub-criteria that have already been defined (Table 4.6).

The indicators for these criteria are representative of expressions that summarize ideas of political learning. These ideas are also sought in the Sustainable Development Goals 2030, in UNESCO's recommendations "Education for Sustainable Development Goals", in prescribed curricula (official curricula and the work of sectoral commissions), in potential curricula (secondary school textbooks) and in produced curricula (inferred through observations and interviews with teachers and learners).

Categories	Subcategories	Examples of indicators
Cognitive socialization in disciplines (ecoliteracy learning)	Technical	Basic sciences and their relevance for processing societal issues
	Cultural	Valuing nature depending on the culture
	Critical	Political economy, social reproduction
Political socialization (citizenship learning)	Adaptive	Good manners, obedience, responsible actions
	Individualist	Social participation with an individualistic perspective
	Critical democratic	Cooperation, social justice, motivation for social change
Critical cognitive socialization (deliberative learning)	Normative	*a priori* specified points of view
	Consensual	Consensus overcoming differences
	Conflictual	Defending opposing perspectives
Democratic socialization (learning through collective action regimes)	Minimalist	Separate interventions of social actors
	Intermediate	Community of practice
	Maximalist	Learning community

Table 4.5. *Categories and indicators for socialization in terms of political learning in educational content involving EDIs*

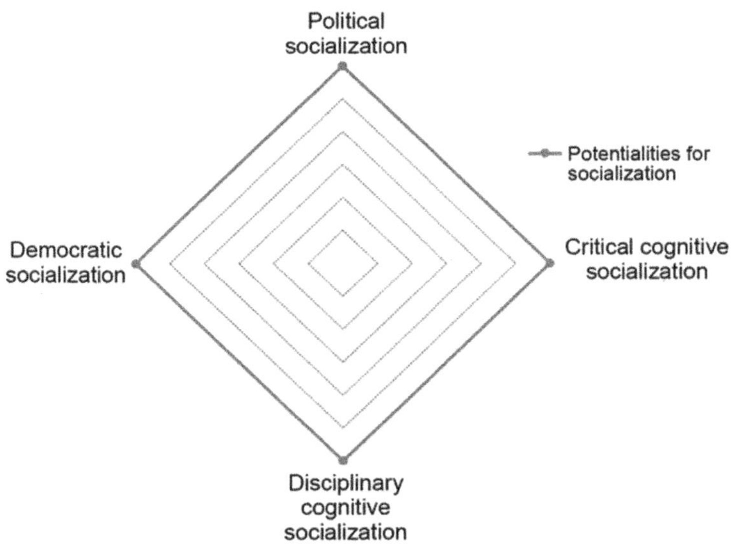

Figure 4.3. *Ideal type of potentialities for socialization in terms of political learning in educational content involving EDIs. For a color version of this figure, see www.iste.co.uk/slimani/education.zip*

Categories	Subcategories	Associated numerical values
Cognitive socialization in disciplines (ecoliteracy learning)	Technical	1
	Cultural	2
	Critical	3
Political socialization (citizenship learning)	Adaptive	1
	Individualist	2
	Democratic-critical	3
Critical cognitive socialization (deliberative learning)	Normative	1
	Consensual	2
	Conflictual	3
Democratic socialization (learning through collective action regimes)	Minimalist	1
	Intermediate	2
	Maximalist	3

Table 4.6. *Values associated with the subcategories of potentialities for socialization in terms of political learning*

4.4. Procedure for data collection and analysis

In the field of qualitative research, the case study approach is characterized by composite data collection strategies because it essentially corresponds to an approach that is very sensitive to the human phenomenon and its complexity. The instruments used may include interviews, direct observation and the use of documents (Anadon 2006).

Table 4.7 outlines the data collection tools and data sources used in this research.

Methods	Tools	Sources
Document analysis	Thematic content analysis grid	Official requirements Textbooks Tutorial booklets and practical work
Observations	Observation grid	Lectures, tutorials and practical sessions Student presentations
Interviews	Interview guides	Secondary school and higher education teachers Students

Table 4.7. *Data collection methods and tools*

4.4.1. *Thematic content analysis*

Thematic content analysis involves comparing elements in a text in order to find units of meaning that can be grouped into categories which are themselves grouped into themes. It concerns a "logical classification of content once the semantic value of the content has been clarified" (Mucchielli 2006, p. 36).

According to Vanoutrive, Derobertmasure and Friant (2012), there are three main methods for creating an inventory of textual data and classifying it. The first two are described by Mucchielli (2006):

– a so-called inductive content analysis method, which considers categories that are not fixed in advance by a theory but constitute themselves throughout the examination of the text where they develop as and when during the reading process;

– another, so-called deductive method, where the categories are posed *a priori* in a grid developed according to a theoretical model, whose approach consists of the application of these categories (Dany 2016).

The third, identified by Mukamurera *et al.* (2006), is known as mixed or iterative, where theory constitutes the reference point for the construction of an analytical grid that is enriched through an iterative process throughout the reading process.

For his part, Dany (2016) refers to Hsieh and Shannon (2005) to characterize three types of content analysis by comparing them in line with the temporality of the definition of categories (or codes) and their sources (Table 4.8).

Type of content analysis	**Time sequence of the definition of codes or categories**	**Source codes or categories**
Conventional content analysis	Codes/categories are defined during data analysis	The codes/categories are derived from the data
Directed content analysis	Codes/categories are defined before and during data analysis	Codes/categories are derived from theory and significant results
Summative content analysis	Keywords are identified before and during data analysis	Keywords are derived from the interest of the researcher or a literature review

Table 4.8. *Types of content analysis (Dany 2016, p. 101)*

In this study, thematic analysis is considered deductive. It also exhibits the characteristics of a directed content analysis because categories are defined before and during data analysis and derive from the conceptual and theoretical framework. It is initially used in the collection of data to identify EDIs in the case of formal education and then in the analysis of the political/anti-political trend, of the political potential and of the potentialities for socialization and political learning in the content collected in the two case studies.

4.4.1.1. *Thematic content analysis for identifying EDIs*

In the chosen case of non-formal education, the contents of the EDIs are available directly in the document prepared in 2017 by UNESCO. In fact, the corpus of collected content includes the following components:

– the final list of proposed objectives, targets and indicators for the UN's 2030 SDGs;

– learning objectives, themes and examples of models and learning methods for UN's 2030 SDGs in the UNESCO recommendations.

However, content involving EDIs in the Tunisian curriculum (in the case of formal education) should be extracted from disciplinary curricula.

In fact, in the Tunisian secondary school curriculum, the EDIs are initially collated on the basis of the prescribed curriculum in search of content that can be related to the following themes: agri-food, environmental politics, environmental ethics, sustainable development, environmental technologies, environmental management and socio-technical transitions. This is specified in a grid prepared for this purpose (Table 4.9).

Levels	Metathemes and contents
1	
2	
3	
4	

Table 4.9. *Grid of EDI collection in prescribed secondary education*

The content is then investigated in potential curricula (textbooks) and in the curricula produced (using other tools described below: interviews with teachers and learners and direct observation of teaching and learning sessions involving these issues).

The corpus collected therefore corresponds to prescribed content involving EDIs in two secondary education disciplines in Tunisia. The discipline of Life and Earth Sciences (*sciences de la vie et de la Terre*, SVT) addresses these issues in two classes entitled: "Concept of sustainable development" (2nd year secondary school – Science section – SVT2 – 17-year-old students) and "Food and sustainable development" (3rd year secondary – Mathematics section – SVT3 – 18-year-old students). The economics discipline evokes the issue of sustainable development in two lessons entitled: "The costs of growth" and "Sustainable development" (4th year secondary – Economics and Management section – EG4 – 19-year-old students). The corresponding content in the potential curriculum is selected from textbooks.

In the undergraduate curriculum, the corpus of the study corresponds to national undergraduate programs proposed or evaluated by the Sectorial Commission on Biological Sciences[9] and selected in two stages.

The first step consisted of the choice, in the work of the Sectoral Commission of Biological Sciences in 2009 (before the events leading to political change in Tunisia) and in the 2015[10] programs that mention the term "environment" in the title of the proposed degree. The contents selected are those of the applied environmental protection degree. These contents play the role of a prescribed curriculum.

The second step was the selection based on these prescriptions, content that can be related to the EDIs mentioned above: agri-food, environmental politics, environmental ethics, sustainable development, environmental technologies, environmental management and transitions, according to the political/anti-political perspective presented in Chapter 1. These EDIs constituted the categories of the data collection tool (Table 4.10).

9 In Tunisia, Sectorial Commissions are national commissions working within the Ministry of Higher Education and are in charge of evaluating the new courses in the undergraduate/postgraduate/doctorate system proposed by the institutions, as well as proposing new educational reforms. They are made up of higher education teachers. These teachers, all of whom were appointed by the Minister before 2011, are proposed by the country's universities following a consultation with the institutions in proportions that respect the number of teachers per institution.

10 The prescribed programs for the two semesters 1 and 2 were published in 2015 and restructured in 2016. The prescribed programs for semesters 3 and 4 were published in 2017. The requirements for semesters 5 and 6 are still unpublished (in 2019).

Semesters	Metathemes and contents
1	
2	
3	
4	
5	
6	

Table 4.10. *Grid of EDI collection in prescribed higher education*

4.4.1.2. *Thematic content analysis to identify the structuring of the political in non-formal education and in formal education*

In the case of non-formal education, an initial comparative thematic analysis is carried out on the political trend and political potential of EDIs in the UNESCO recommendations "Education for SDGs" and in the document on which the development of these recommendations was based, namely the UN's 2030 Agenda for SDGs.

This analysis provides a relative assessment of this political potential using the probable gaps between the two documents.

A second analysis is then carried out on the UNESCO's document to explore its potential for socialization and political learning (Figure 4.4).

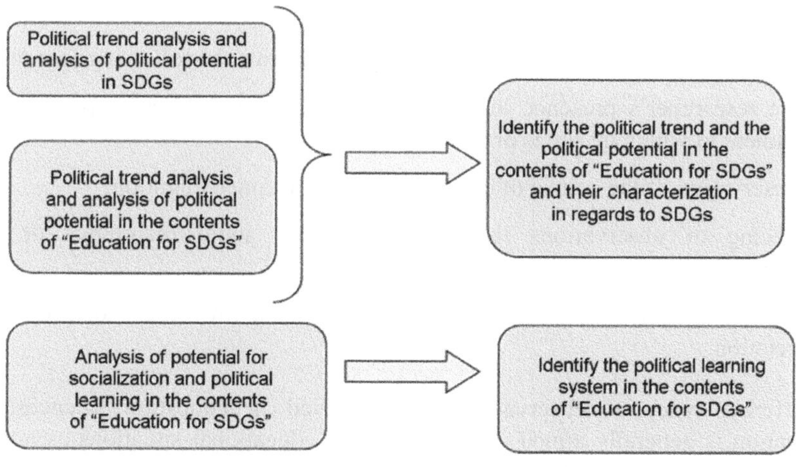

Figure 4.4. *Thematic analyses carried out regarding the contents of "Education for SDGs" in relation to their objectives*

In the case of formal education, three thematic analyses are carried out on the content selected from the Tunisian curriculum: an analysis of political trends, followed by a second analysis of political potentialities, and a third one of political learning and socialization (Figure 4.5).

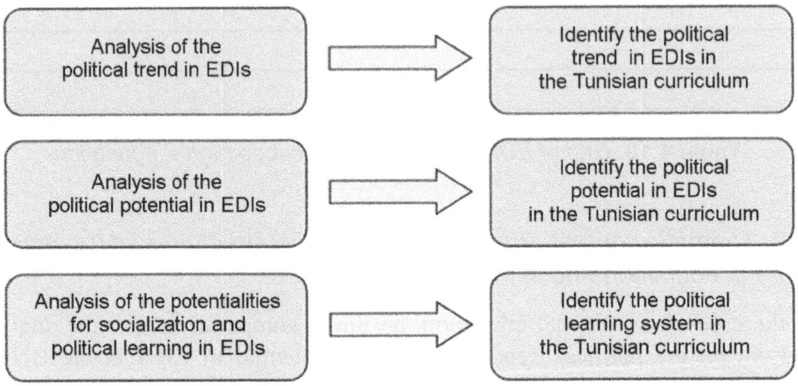

Figure 4.5. *Thematic analyses carried out on the content of the EDIs in the Tunisian curriculum in relation to their objectives*

4.4.2. *Direct observation*

Observation is "a data collection tool in which the researcher becomes a recorder of individual behaviors and practices within groups by residing in the very places where they take place" (Martineau 2005, p. 6).

According to this author, observation involves at least the following four tasks:

– the researcher's presence in the field of study and his/her adaptation to the environment in which he/she is present;

– observation of the course of events requiring sustained attention;

– tracing of observations through note-taking, audio recordings or video recordings;

– taking into account the observed phenomena in order to propose an interpretation.

Different types of observation are identified in education sciences. Free observation is generally aimed at understanding educational situations as a whole. Structured or directed observation focuses on phenomena previously selected, generally through the use of an observation grid.

Directed observation focuses more precisely on the selection of a phenomenon related to a question or its research questions.

In this research, a direct observation of the unfolding of teaching and learning situations is carried out. The main objective is the investigation of taught content involving EDIs in order to infer some aspects of the curriculum produced.

This observation is based on a grid which contains three components: presentation, content and pedagogical aspects (Figure 4.6).

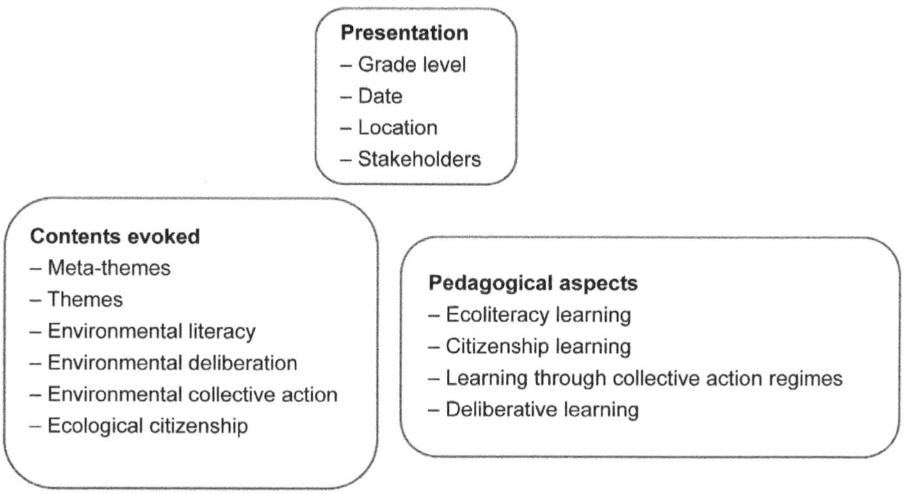

Figure 4.6. *Elements structuring the direct observation of sessions involving EDIs*

The observations considered and made (Table 4.11) are organized according to the EDIs involved and concern the issue of sustainable development (three sessions in secondary school and one session in the tertiary level) and other EDIs (two sessions in the tertiary cycle of which only one is observed).

EDIs	Secondary school		Undergraduate	
	Planned	Executed	Planned	Executed
Sustainable development	5	3	1	1
Other EDIs	0	0	2	1

Table 4.11. *Data on the number of observation sessions*

4.4.3. *Interviews*

De Ketele and Roegiers (2015) define interviews as a method of gathering information that can relate to a person's "actions, ideas and plans" as well as "objective facts". According to the authors, an interview can be free, semi-directed or directed:

– an interview is said to be free when the researcher follows the respondent's speech from a very general theme posed at the beginning;

– an interview is said to be directed when the respondent's speech corresponds to the answer to specific questions prepared in advance by the researcher;

– an interview is said to be semi-directed when it deals with a limited number of themes, leaving the respondent with the opportunity to develop his or her answers.

The function of an interview is thus determined by its structure: the open structure of an open-ended interview allows for a clinical function, the closed structure of a directed interview allows for an explanatory function, while the intermediate structure of a semi-structured interview allows for a research function.

This research exploits the method of directive interviews to collect data on the curriculum produced from the point of view of the actors involved (teachers and learners). It is based on interview guides prepared in advance. Five lists of aids are appended to these guides (Appendix 1) to help the actors in their responses[11].

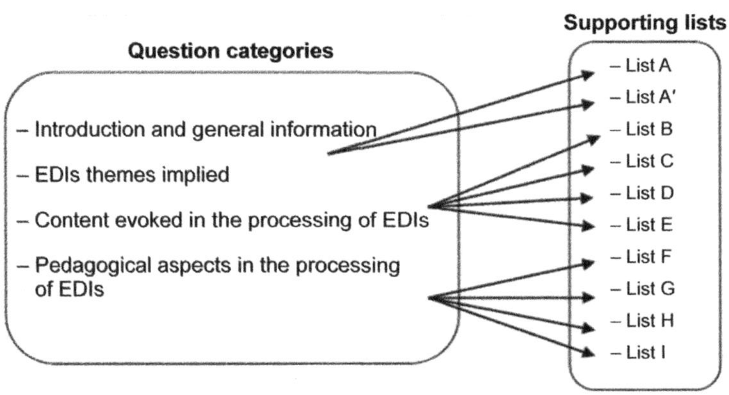

Figure 4.7. *Categories of interview questions and their supporting lists*

11 This method using supporting lists attached to interview guides is inspired by the work of Guerra (2014). It is suitable for conducting guided interviews to search for categories in the produced curricula.

Figure 4.7 summarizes the categories of questions and corresponding aids.

The interviews planned and conducted are organized according to the actors involved (Table 4.12).

Curricula		Secondary school		Undergraduate	
		Planned	**Executed**	**Planned**	**Executed**
Teachers	**Staff**	2	1	2	1
	Identifiers		(Te_2)		(Te_1)
Learners	**Staff**	6	2	6	6
	Identifiers		(St_1) (St_2)		(St_1), (St_2) (St_3), (St_4) (St_5), (St_6)

Table 4.12. *Data on the number of interviews planned and completed*

4.5. Defining the research quality criteria

The quality of qualitative research is discussed by several authors in terms of scientific legitimacy and validity.

Clénet (2007) supports the idea that the scientific legitimacy of qualitative research lies in researcher-driven "links" between the pragmatic epistemic and ethical dimensions of the research carried out. The scientific legitimacy of research thus develops in a systemic and dynamic manner involving the interaction between theory and practice, between the researcher and the stakeholders involved and between the researcher and the reader.

Yardley (2008, 2017) assumes that it is primarily the idea of validity which accounts for the quality of qualitative research and supports this idea by advancing four validity criteria: sensitivity to context, rigor and commitment, consistency and transparency, and impact and significance.

Yazan (2015) summarizes the quality criteria qualitative research advanced by Merriam in the field of education. These criteria correspond to strategies and techniques to guarantee the validity and reliability of the knowledge produced:

– six strategies to improve internal validity: triangulation, stakeholder review of data, long-term field observation, peer review, participatory research and the declaration of researcher preconceptions;

– three techniques to ensure reliability: explanation of the researcher's position in relation to the study, triangulation and use of an audit trail;

– three techniques to improve external validity: use of dense and detailed descriptions, different modal categories (epistemic, ontic, historical, axiological) and multi-site designs.

4.5.1. *Strategies for increasing internal validity*

Internal validity refers to the consistency of the knowledge produced by the research by way of its questions and objectives. It reflects the degree to which this knowledge is supported by the analysis conducted on the data, that is, the links between the data collected and the analyses conducted on the data.

Triangulation is considered the most effective strategy for achieving the validity of the results in the case study (Anadon 2006). It corresponds to the use of several data sources and the crossing of different points of view.

In this study, methodological triangulation is adopted for the formal education case study using three methods of data collection (Figure 4.8): document review, direct observation and individual interviews with teachers and learners (students and pupils).

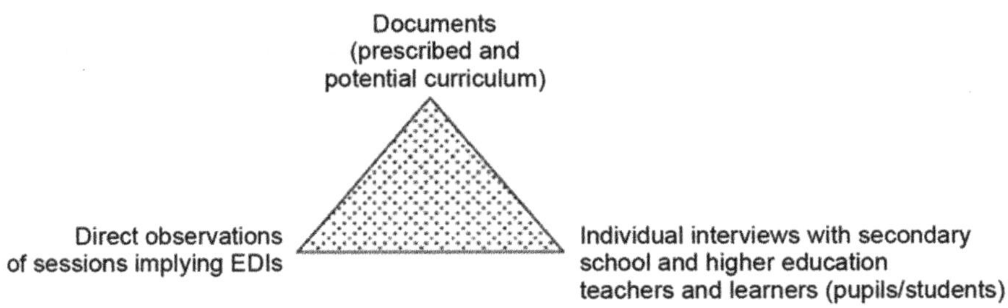

Figure 4.8. *Methodological triangulation of research*

The analysis of prescribed and potential curricula thus provides indications for the structuring of the political in the planned EDIs. Direct observations and interviews provide indicators about this structuring as a result of teachers' choices and decisions during the implementation of these programs.

4.5.2. *Techniques to ensure reliability*

Reliability or fidelity reflects the degree of stability of research results (Baribeau 2009). In qualitative research, it is linked to the validity of the study conducted (Guerra 2014). One of the strategies used is to organize the case study into phases (e.g. design, case selection and protocol, collection and analysis, reporting), which includes clear and systematic activities to achieve the case study objective. Another is the triangulation of data and multiple data sources.

The reliability of categories of thematic content analysis requires that "several coders record corpus units in the same categories. If one is alone, one must be able to justify choices by epistemological reflection or the presentation of indicators" (Dany 2016, p. 19).

For example, discussing with others to reach an agreement as to whether content placed in categories and themes is recognized by readers is one way to increase the reliability of qualitative research. However, for this study, finding French-speaking researchers who have worked on the political content of EDIs has proven very difficult.

To circumvent this difficulty, the use of computer tools can be considered a strategy to increase the reliability of the coding of the texts to be analyzed. In fact, Lejeune (2010) identifies five families of qualitative data analysis software that differ according to their functionalities: lexicometry, concordance, automata, reflexives, and dictionaries and registers.

Lexicometry (Lexico, spadT, Sato, etc.) corresponds to a lexical analysis allowing for a statistical exploration of the corpus of texts by assuming that the phenomena of word recurrence are relevant. Concordancers (Glossanet, Antconc, etc.) allow the corpus to be rearranged by focusing on an expression or a word to facilitate its investigation. Automata (Leximappe, Candide, etc.) use the distribution of words and their co-occurrences to propose a categorization in the corpus. Reflexivists (NVivo, Weft QDA, etc.) assist the researcher in reading and analyzing the textual corpus by helping him/her to annotate it in order to create categories. Dictionaries and registers (Tropes, Prospéro, etc.) allow textual corpora to be coded automatically by applying dictionary lists containing predefined keywords (Krief and Zardat 2013), which essentially include nouns (Lejeune 2008).

In this study, dictionaries associated with the Tropes software are used to increase the reliability of content categories identified by thematic analysis.

Indeed, Tropes corresponds to a semantic approach based on dictionaries containing hundreds of thousands of predefined semantic classifications. On these bases, the software initially provides, for the discourse to be studied, a "reference universe" analysis carried out on nouns and proper nouns, where each universe is composed of a set of "semantic equivalents", that is, groupings of semantically close terms, based on these predefined semantic classifications (Molette 2009).

In fact, this software also has the functionalities to perform co-occurrence analysis, chronological analysis and distribution analysis on verbs, adjectives and modalizers and connectors in a text. This enables researchers to identify relationships, regular expressions, remarkable propositions and general style in the analyzed textual corpus.

This research exploits the first functionality of this software (the universes of references). Indeed, the categories resulting from the thematic analysis are used (mainly as keywords[12]) for a semantic exploration of the textual corpus using this software. Any contradiction found between the two analyses (thematic and semantic) is interpreted as an ambiguity in the first one.

12 If the corresponding noun is not present in the corpus, another equivalent from the same corpus is used.

5

The Political within "Education for Sustainable Development Goals"[1]

5.1. Analysis of the Sustainable Development Goals (SDGs) 2030

5.1.1. *The political/anti-political trend*

Environmental politics referred to in the 2030 SDGs is oriented towards an analysis of poverty in terms of reducing vulnerability and ensuring resilience. These two properties are considered according to a mainly economic approach:

> By 2030, build the resilience of the poor and those in vulnerable situations and reduce their exposure and vulnerability to climate-related extreme events and other economic, social and environmental shocks and disasters. (Target 1.5 in the list of the proposed Sustainable Development Goal indicators)

> Achieve higher levels of economic productivity through diversification, technological upgrading and innovation, including through a focus on high-value added and labour-intensive sectors. (Target 8.2 in the list of proposed Sustainable Development Goal indicators)

Women are considered a vulnerable group for whom the issue of justice is also posed primarily in economic terms:

1 Appendix 2 is an uninterpreted report on the political in the 2030 SDGs and in the content of "Education for 2030 SDGs". This is an analysis of Appendix III of the UN document (2016) available at: https://unesdoc.unesco.org/ark:/48223/pf0000247444.

> Proportion of government recurrent and capital spending to sectors that disproportionately benefit women, the poor and vulnerable groups. (Indicator 1.b.1 in the list of proposed Sustainable Development Goal indicators)

The agri-food issue is oriented towards increasing agricultural productivity, especially that of specific social groups, with a view to adapting to environmental changes and providing equal access to environmental resources:

> By 2030, double the agricultural productivity and incomes of small-scale food producers, in particular women, indigenous peoples, family farmers, pastoralists and fishers, including through secure and equal access to land, other productive resources and inputs, knowledge, financial services, markets and opportunities for value addition and non-farm employment. (Target 2.3 in the list of proposed Sustainable Development Goal indicators)
>
> By 2030, ensure sustainable food production systems and implement resilient agricultural practices that increase productivity and production, that help maintain ecosystems, that strengthen capacity for adaptation to climate change, extreme weather, drought, flooding and other disasters and that progressively improve land and soil quality. (Target 2.4 in the list of proposed Sustainable Development Goal indicators)

The sustainability of development is posed in terms of the sustainability of consumption and production and the management of resources:

> Implement the 10-Year Framework of Programmes on Sustainable Consumption and Production Patterns, all countries taking action, with developed countries taking the lead, taking into account the development and capabilities of developing countries. (Target 12.1 in the list of proposed Sustainable Development Goal indicators)
>
> Support developing countries to strengthen their scientific and technological capacity to move towards more sustainable patterns of consumption and production. (Target 12.a in the list of proposed Sustainable Development Goal indicators)
>
> By 2030, achieve the sustainable management and efficient use of natural resources. (Target 12.2 in the list of proposed Sustainable Development Goal indicators)

The conception of environmental technology and management is oriented towards rationality and management control, but this conception also evokes the participatory management of social institutions as a condition for their sustainability targeted by the SDGs:

> Enhance scientific research, upgrade the technological capabilities of industrial sectors in all countries, in particular developing countries, including, by 2030, encouraging innovation and substantially increasing the number of research and development workers per 1 million people and public and private research and development spending. (Target 9.5 in the list of proposed Sustainable Development Goal indicators)
>
> By 2020, achieve the environmentally sound management of chemicals and all wastes throughout their life cycle, in accordance with agreed international frameworks, and significantly reduce their release to air, water and soil in order to minimize their adverse impacts on human health and the environment. (Target 12.4 in the list of proposed Sustainable Development Goal indicators)
>
> By 2030, enhance inclusive and sustainable urbanization and capacity for participatory, integrated and sustainable human settlement planning and management in all countries. (Target 11.3 in the list of proposed Sustainable Development Goal indicators)

The question of transitions is essentially based on technological innovations:

> Achieve higher levels of economic productivity through diversification, technological upgrading and innovation, including through a focus on high-value added and labour-intensive sectors. (Target 8.2 in the list of proposed Sustainable Development Goal indicators)

5.1.2. *Political potential*

In the SDG 2030 agenda, environmental collective action falls under the latent group type. It mainly refers to waste recycling and water conservation activities for environmental purposes:

> By 2030, improve water quality by reducing pollution, eliminating dumping and minimizing release of hazardous chemicals and

> materials, halving the proportion of untreated wastewater and substantially increasing recycling and safe reuse globally. (Target 6.3 in the list of proposed Sustainable Development Goal indicators)

> By 2030, substantially reduce waste generation through prevention, reduction, recycling and reuse. (Target 12.5 in the list of proposed Sustainable Development Goal indicators)

Ecological citizenship is a liberal type of citizenship that evokes the environment in terms of rights and access to environmental resources:

> By 2030, ensure that all men and women, in particular the poor and the vulnerable, have equal rights to economic resources, as well as access to basic services, ownership and control over land and other forms of property, inheritance, natural resources, appropriate new technology and financial services, including microfinance. (Target 1.4 in the list of proposed Sustainable Development Goal indicators)

Environmental deliberation is largely technocratic in the SDGs, mainly evoking adaptation to irreversibly committed environmental dynamics as well as solutions within the framework of neoclassical environmental economics in the green economy:

> Number of countries that have communicated the strengthening of institutional, systemic and individual capacity-building to implement adaptation, mitigation and technology transfer, and development actions. (Indicator 2 for Target 13.3 in the list of proposed Sustainable Development Goal indicators)

Environmental literacy, according to the SDGs, involves the first two dimensions only, that is, elementary and functional literacy:

> By 2030, ensure that all learners acquire the knowledge and skills needed to promote sustainable development, including, among others, through education for sustainable development and sustainable lifestyles, human rights, gender equality, promotion of a culture of peace and non-violence, global citizenship and appreciation of cultural diversity and of culture's contribution to sustainable development. (Target 4.7 in the list of proposed Sustainable Development Goal indicators)

> Enhance the Global Partnership for Sustainable Development, complemented by multi-stakeholder partnerships that mobilize and share knowledge, expertise, technology and financial resources, to support the achievement of the Sustainable Development Goals in all countries, in particular developing countries. (Target 17.16 in the list of proposed Sustainable Development Goal indicators)

Figure 5.1 visualizes the levels of political potential of EDIs in the SDGs compared to the ideal type.

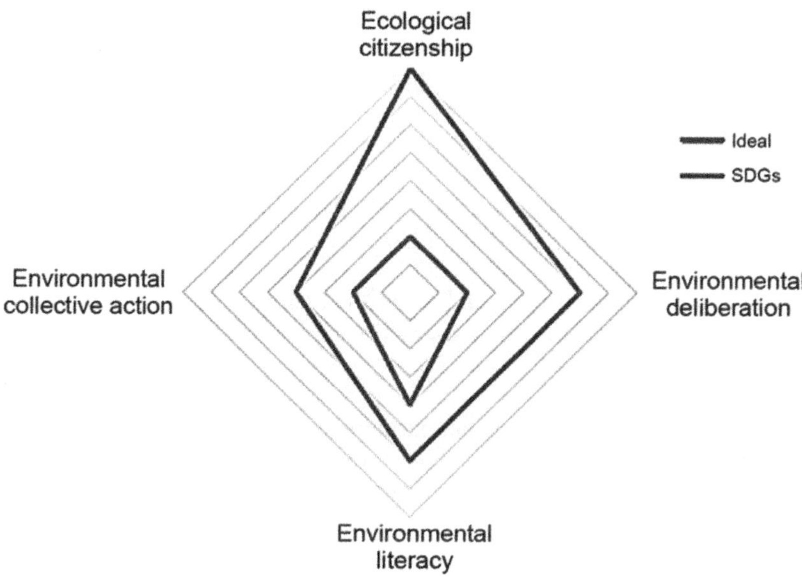

Figure 5.1. *The political potential of EDIs in the SDG 2030 agenda compared to the ideal type. For a color version of this figure, see www.iste.co.uk/slimani/education.zip*

5.1.3. *Conclusion*

In the SDGs, the anti-political trend appears to be dominant. This trend is related to limited political potential involving environmental literacy that does not go beyond the functional level, latent group-type environmental collective action, liberal ecological citizenship and technocratic environmental deliberation.

5.2. Analysis of the content of "Education for SDGs"

5.2.1. *The political/anti-political trend*

In "Education for Sustainable Development Goals", environmental politics involves the political trend of evoking environmental change in terms of inequality and justice and the anti-political trend of putting the green economy and green growth at the heart of environmental politics:

> The learner knows about causes and impacts of poverty such as unequal distribution of resources and power, colonization, conflicts, disasters caused by natural hazards and other climate change-induced impacts, environmental degradation and technological disasters, and the lack of social protection systems and measures. (Cognitive learning objective 3 for SDG 1)
>
> Green economy (cradle-to-cradle, circular economy, green growth, degrowth). (Themes proposed for SDG 12)

The agri-food issue is also dependent on the dialectics between a political trend referring to a conception of active citizenship and an anti-political trend dominated by consumption:

> The learner is able to evaluate, participate in and influence decision-making related to public policies concerning the combat against hunger and malnutrition and the promotion of sustainable agriculture. (Behavioural learning objective 2 for SDG 2)
>
> The learner is able to change their production and consumption practices in order to contribute to the combat against hunger and the promotion of sustainable agriculture. (Behavioural learning objective 5 for SDG 2)
>
> The learner is able to feel responsible for the environmental and social impacts of their own individual behaviour as a producer or consumer. (Socio-emotional learning objective 5 for SDG 12)

The sustainability of development is conceived according to the reformist point of view as well as by evoking an anti-political trend with the implication of natural resources management:

> The learner understands dilemmas/trade-offs related to and system changes necessary for achieving sustainable consumption and production. (Cognitive learning objective 5 for SDG 12)

The design of environmental technology and management is guided by pro-justice participation as well as managerial rationality of planning:

> The learner is able to develop criteria and make responsible consumption choices as a means to support fair working conditions and efforts to decouple production from the impact of natural hazards and environmental degradation. (Behavioural learning objective 5 for SDG 8)
>
> The learner is able to use their voice, to identify and use entry points for the public in the local planning systems, to call for the investment in sustainable infrastructure, buildings and parks in their area and to debate the merits of long-term planning. (Socio-emotional learning objective 1 for SDG 11)

The question of transitions is essentially based on technological innovations with the anti-political trend:

> The learner understands how innovation, entrepreneurship and new job creation can contribute to decent work and a sustainability-driven economy and to the decoupling of economic growth from the impacts of natural hazards and environmental degradation. (Cognitive learning objective 5 for SDG 8)

The ethical question is explicitly present in the cognitive and socio-emotional learning objectives. It evokes the negotiation (contextual posture) of rights as well as refers to principles (principled position):

> The learner understands ethical principles concerning equality and is aware of psychological processes that foster discriminative behaviour and decision making. (Cognitive learning objective 5 for SDG 10)
>
> The learner is able to negotiate the rights of different groups based on shared values and ethical principles. (Socio-emotional learning objective 3 for SDG 10)

5.2.2. *Political potential*

In "Education for SDGs", environmental collective action is broadened and mainly takes the form of the intermediary group (such as being a member of environmental associations, attending gatherings and signing petitions in favor of environmental causes, making financial contributions to environmental associations) in addition to that of the latent group:

> The learner is able to publicly demand and support the development and integration of policies that promote social and economic justice, risk reduction strategies and poverty eradication actions. (Behavioural learning objective 2 for SDG 1)

Ecological citizenship extends to a post-cosmopolitan citizenship where the environmental responsibility of the citizen refers above all to a cosmopolitan justice which explicitly mentions the requirement to reduce the ecological footprint:

> The learner is able to reduce their individual water footprint and to save water practicing their daily habits. (Behavioural learning objective 3 for SDG 6)
>
> Develop a business continuity plan for a local enterprise after the impact of a natural hazard. (Example of learning methods and models for SDG 9)

Environmental deliberation is broadened towards ecological deliberation referring to consensus and conventions elaborated in international conferences and declarations:

> The learner is able to identify and analyse different types of causes and reasons for inequalities. (Behavioural learning objective 3 for SDG 10)

Environmental literacy is broadened to include operational literacy, evoking the ability to distinguish between facts and opinions, to determine the impact of beliefs and values on environmental issues, to re-examine cultural values and to consider historical perspectives in dealing with issues of environmental awareness and sensitivity:

> The learner understands the concepts of extreme and relative poverty and is able to critically reflect on their underlying cultural and normative assumptions and practices. (Cognitive learning objective 1 for SDG 1)

Figure 5.2 visualizes the levels of political potential of the EDIs in the content of the learning objectives of "Education for SDGs" (LOSDGs) compared to the ideal type.

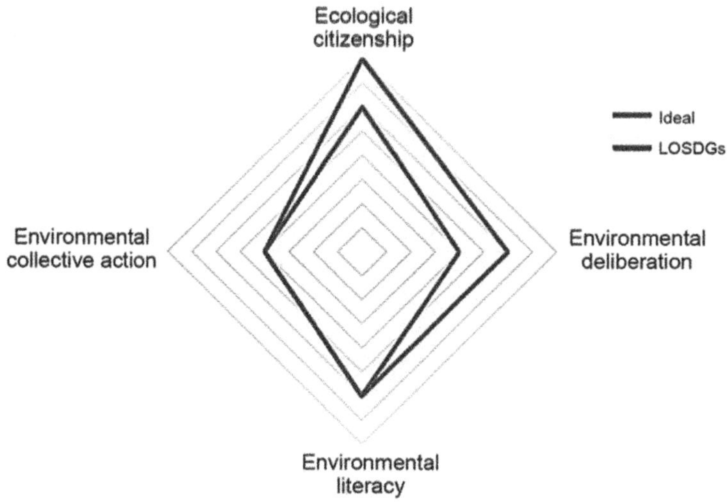

Figure 5.2. *The political potential of EDIs in UNESCO's recommendations compared to the ideal type. For a color version of this figure, see www.iste.co.uk/slimani/education.zip*

5.2.3. *The potentialities for socialization in terms of political learning*

The potentialities for socialization in terms of learning about the political in the contents of "Education for SDGs" imply a disciplinary cognitive socialization that is mainly based on learning technical ecoliteracy. Indicators of cultural ecoliteracy and critical ecoliteracy learning are also collected in these recommendations:

> The learner knows the main drivers and root causes for hunger at the individual, local, national and global level. (Cognitive learning objective 3 for SDG 2)

Political socialization is based on learning in adaptive citizenship and critical democratic citizenship:

> The learner is able to take on critically their role as an active global citizen in the challenge of combating hunger. (Behavioural learning objective 4 for SDG 2)

Critical cognitive socialization refers to teachings on consensual deliberation:

> Have interfaith dialogues in schools and college campuses about justice and equality. (Example of approaches and methods for SDG 16)

> Perform simulation games related to global conference negotiations (e.g. National Model United Nations). (Example of approaches and methods for SDG 17)

Democratic socialization is based on learning in three regimes of action (minimalist, intermediate and maximalist):

> Organize excursions and field trips to places where sustainable agriculture is practiced. (Example of learning approaches and methods for SDG 2)
>
> Plan and run a student company selling fair trade products. (Example of learning approaches and methods for SDG 1)
>
> Develop partnerships between schools and universities in different regions of the world (South and North; South and South). (Example of learning approaches and methods for SDG 1)

Figure 5.3 visualizes the potential for socialization in terms of the political impact of UNESCO's recommendations LOSDGs compared to the ideal type.

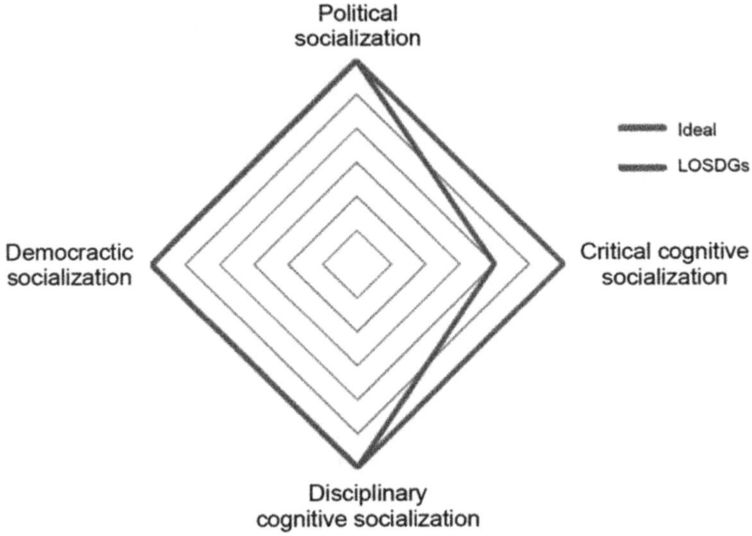

Figure 5.3. *The potentialities for socialization in terms of political learning in "Education for SDGs" compared to the ideal type. For a color version of this figure, see www.iste.co.uk/slimani/education.zip*

5.2.4. *Conclusion*

Within "Education for SDGs", the diverse range of EDI themes with anti-political and political trends is remarkable. This appears in connection with an important political potential involving an environmental literacy evoking different levels (elementary, functional and critical), environmental collective action as part of the latent group and intermediate group types, an ecological citizenship that reaches the post-cosmopolitan level and an ecological environmental deliberation. This political potential itself is in line with potentialities for socialization based on ecoliteracy learning which reaches the critical level, critical democratic citizenship learning, learning in a maximalist action regime and consensual deliberation learning.

6

The Political within the Tunisian Curriculum[1]

6.1. Secondary school curriculum analysis

In the secondary school curriculum, two EDI metathemes are identified: the agri-food issue and the issue of sustainable development. The contents of the prescribed curriculum, the potential curriculum and the produced curriculum relating to these two metathemes will be analyzed in the following section.

6.1.1. *The prescribed curriculum*

6.1.1.1. *The political/anti-political trend*

The agri-food issue presented in the 3rd year mathematics section of the curriculum is evoked from a consumerist perspective:

> Ingredients should be listed to identify their nutritional values and health benefits. The harmful effects of quick snacks ("fast food", fried foods, etc.), which are often harmful, should be pointed out.
>
> We will define organic agriculture and cite the virtues of the food that comes from this agricultural practice. (Earth and Life Sciences program, p. 35)

---

1 Appendix 3 is an uncommented report on the political in the Tunisian curriculum. This report summarizes the data collected to infer the composition of the prescribed, potential and produced curricula in the secondary cycle (secondary school) and the first cycle of higher education (undergraduate-level study).

The issue of sustainable development is identified in the Life and Earth Sciences curriculum for the 2nd-year Science section and in the Economics curriculum for the 4th-year Economics and Management section. This issue is addressed in the thematic form of rational management of ecosystems or management of a set of assets, including environmental capital:

> Towards a rational management of the ecosystem, notion of sustainable development. (Earth and Life Sciences program, p. 17)
>
> To show that the concept of development has evolved to integrate the human and environmental dimensions. (Economics program, p. 33)

6.1.1.2. *Political potential*

The environmental literacy targeted in the secondary involves both elementary and functional dimensions:

> To identify human development from the elements that constitute it. (Economics program, p. 33)
>
> To identify the factors that degrade the ecosystem; to propose appropriate solutions for the preservation of the environment. (Earth and Life Sciences program, p. 17)

Ecological citizenship can be interpreted as republican citizenship by evoking reflection on the following:

> a fundamental problem facing mankind, namely how to exploit the ecosystem without destroying it. (Earth and Life Sciences program, p. 17)

Environmental collective action is mainly of the latent group type because it evokes the two-fold importance of waste recycling:

> To show the importance of the recycling of matter in the functioning of the ecosystem.
>
> To carry out a project that focuses on an ecological problem of the region (waste recycling, biodiversity, dune fixation, reforestation, school garden ...). (Earth and Life Sciences program, p. 17)

Environmental deliberation is absent in these prescriptions.

Figure 6.1 summarizes the political potential of EDIs in Tunisian secondary school prescribed curricula, which appears to be weakened compared to the ideal type.

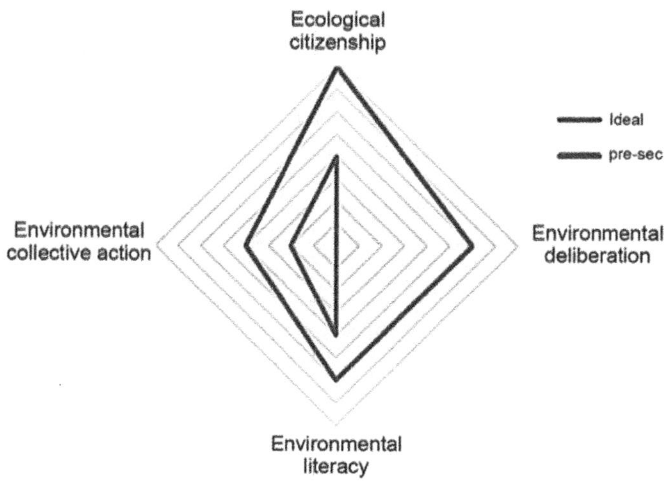

Figure 6.1. *The political potential of EDIs in the prescribed secondary school curriculum compared to the ideal type. For a color version of this figure, see www.iste.co.uk/slimani/education.zip*

6.1.1.3. *Political learning and the potential for socialization*

Disciplinary cognitive socialization refers to technical ecoliteracy learning involving contents of basic sciences (ecology and economy) and the repurposing of nature in different cultures:

> To identify the factors that degrade the ecosystem; [...] to value the traditional food of the region, we will present various traditional dishes and will mention their ingredients in order to identify their nutritional values and health benefits. (Earth and Life Sciences program, p. 35)

Political socialization is based on learning adaptive citizenship in the form of responsible actions:

> Propose solutions for the preservation or restoration of ecosystems and the protection of the environment, as part of a sustainable development strategy. (Earth and Life Sciences program, p. 17)

Critical cognitive socialization is absent because no learning of deliberation is evoked.

Democratic socialization is limited to learning in a minimalist action regime because the possible interventions of the learners remain separate. In fact, even if the term project is evoked, this does not go beyond a minimalist and generic conception by involving the pupil without specifying other stakeholders in the territorial sphere of the school and without discussing the school rhythms and times related to it:

> The theme of food and sustainable development in the form of a project. (Earth and Life Sciences program, p. 35)

Figure 6.2 summarizes the potential for socialization in terms of political learning in the prescribed curricula of the Tunisian secondary school compared to the ideal type.

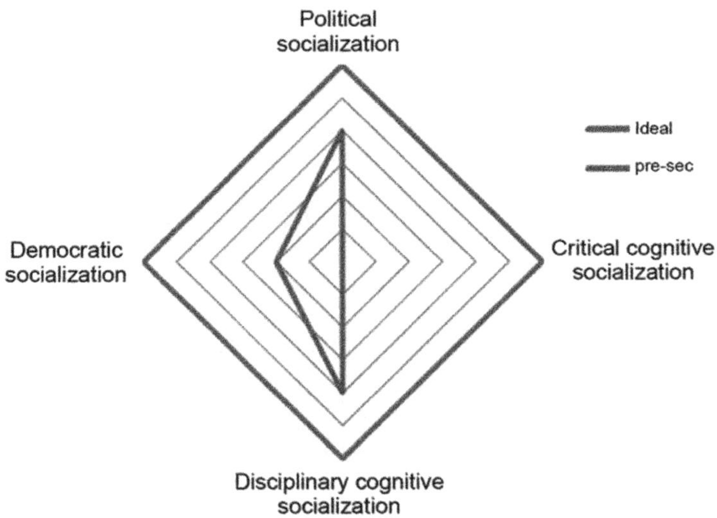

Figure 6.2. *The potential for socialization in terms of political learning in the prescribed secondary school curriculum compared to the ideal type. For a color version of this figure, see www.iste.co.uk/slimani/education.zip*

6.1.1.4. *Conclusion*

The prescribed curriculum of the Tunisian secondary school involves two EDI metathemes (the issue of sustainable development and the agri-food issue) which lean towards anti-political trends (consumption and management of natural resources). This appears in connection with political potential involving an environmental literacy evoking two levels (elementary, functional), an environmental collective action of the latent group type and intermediate group type and a republican ecological citizenship and the lack of involvement of environmental deliberation. This political potential itself is in connection with potentialities for socialization based on technical and cultural ecoliteracy learning, adaptive citizenship learning and learning in a minimalist action regime but without deliberative learning.

6.1.2. *Potential curriculum*

6.1.2.1. *The political/anti-political trend*

As in the prescribed curricula, the food issue in the 3rd-year textbook (Mathematics section) is also mentioned from a consumerist perspective:

> It produces food in smaller quantities but of better quality: richer in mineral salts, vitamins, organic matter with a natural taste. (3rd-year textbook, Mathematics section, p. 74)

The issue of sustainable development is identified in the Earth and Life Sciences for the 2nd-year Science section and in the Economics textbook for the 4th-year Economics and Management section. This issue is also mentioned, as in the prescribed curricula, in the thematic form of rational management of ecosystems or management of a set of capital, including environmental capital:

> Aware of the need to preserve ecosystems and manage natural resources rationally, mankind has put in place a set of strategies aimed at the sustainable use of resources in balance with economic development: this is the notion of sustainable development. (2nd-year textbook, Science section, p. 167).
>
> Natural capital: it is the totality of natural resources (soil, subsoil, fish resources, fauna, flora, etc.). Within the framework of sustainable development, their use must be compatible with the ecological balance (preservation of biodiversity) and must protect the interests of present and future generations. (4th-year textbook, Economics and Management section, p. 180)

6.1.2.2. *Political potential*

Environmental literacy in secondary school textbooks involves both elementary and functional dimensions:

> To know the environment and understand how it works, to use it reasonably, to reduce and especially to prevent factors that can sometimes lead to irreversible damage (2nd-year Science textbook, p. 79).

Ecological citizenship shows two aspects: a liberal aspect especially in the textbook of the Economics and Management section where the environment is perceived as a capital provider of basic needs for the population:

> Natural capital contributes to the production of goods and services, just like physical capital and the labour force. (4th-year Economics and Management textbook, p. 179)

The second aspect is republican. It is present in the textbook of the Science section, implying a duty to support the proper functioning of the ecosystem:

> The environment is therefore a fragile equilibrium which must be preserved through various actions. (2nd-year Science textbook, p. 155)

Environmental collective action is mainly of the latent group type because it evokes the preservation of natural resources for environmental purposes:

> Reforestation through the planting of forest trees helps regenerate the flora and fauna of an environment and reduce the effects of erosion. The creation of urban parks lowers the carbon dioxide content released by industrial activities and means of transportation. (2nd-year Science textbook, p. 167)

Environmental deliberation is absent in the textbooks.

Figure 6.3 visualizes the political potential of EDIs in Tunisian secondary school textbooks compared to the ideal type.

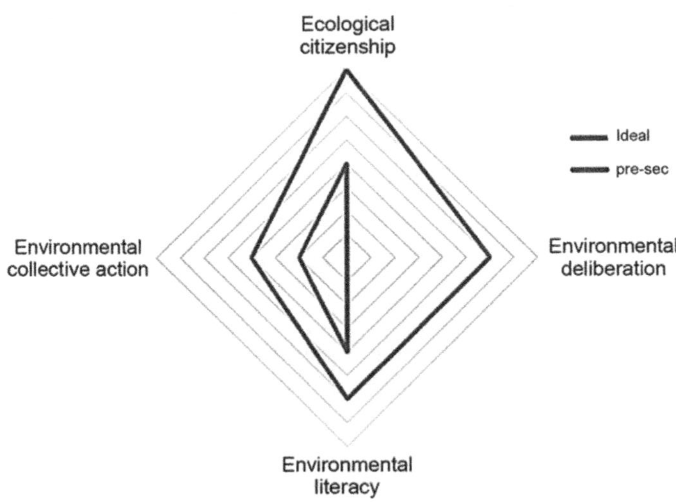

Figure 6.3. *The political potential of EDIs in the potential secondary school curriculum compared to the ideal type. For a color version of this figure, see www.iste.co.uk/slimani/education.zip*

6.1.2.3. *Political learning and the potential for socialization*

Cognitive disciplinary socialization refers to learning of technical ecoliteracy, as well as learning of cultural ecoliteracy mentioned in the Life and Earth sciences textbook for the 3rd year of secondary school (Mathematics section):

> In Tunisia, organic farming produces fruits (dates, almonds, table olives, prickly pears), vegetables (potatoes, tomatoes, …), olive oil, cereals, herbs and cinnamon. (3rd-year textbook, Mathematics section, p. 64)

Political socialization is based on learning about adaptive citizenship:

> Become aware of the need for sustainable development. (3rd-year textbook, Mathematics section, p. 63)

Democratic socialization is based on learning in a minimalist action regime:

> You plan to carry out an organic breeding of animals of a given species: rabbit, sheep, goat … What questions should you ask an expert who comes to advise you to carry out this project? (3rd-year textbook, Mathematics section, p. 71)

No indicators of deliberative learning are detected.

Figure 6.4 visualizes the potential for socialization in terms of political learning in the potential secondary curriculum compared to the ideal type.

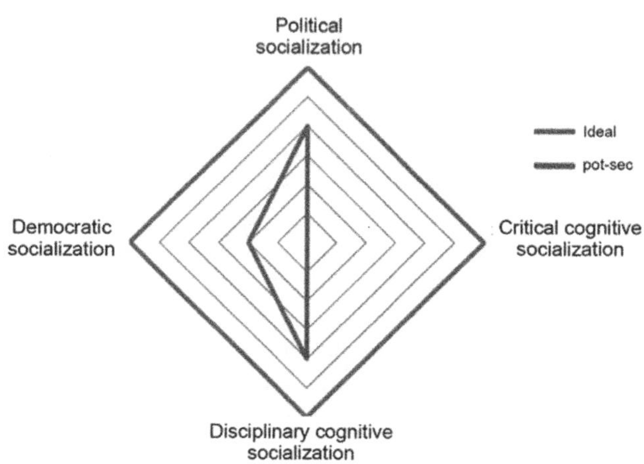

Figure 6.4. *Potential for socialization in terms of political learning in the potential curriculum of secondary school compared to the ideal type. For a color version of this figure, see www.iste.co.uk/slimani/education.zip*

6.1.2.4. *Conclusion*

The potential curriculum of Tunisian secondary schools involves, as in the prescribed curriculum, two EDI metathemes (sustainable development and agri-food) with the same anti-political trends.

This appears in connection with a political potential involving an environmental literacy evoking two levels (elementary and functional), an environmental collective action of the latent group type and a republican ecological citizenship and the lack of involvement of environmental deliberation. This political potential itself is in connection with potentialities for socialization based on technical and cultural ecoliteracy learning, adaptive citizenship learning and learning in a minimalist action regime but without deliberative learning.

6.1.3. *The produced curriculum*

6.1.3.1. *The political/anti-political trend*

Sustainable development appears under the aspect of natural resource management:

> Of course we need to have an idea about the management of natural resources to be able to talk about safeguarding them and the fight against the depletion and over-exploitation of these resources and the degradation of the environment. The student should be encouraged to think that these resources are essential to production and that future generations also have the right to use them. (Te_2, Table A3.4, Appendix 3)

6.1.3.2. *Political potential*

Environmental literacy addresses the basic components of natural and social systems and the interactions between humans and nature:

> For the elementary components of the natural and social systems, here it is clear that we consider the natural and social pillars as a starting point and this is important in the contents. Also, for the types of interactions between man and nature, it is obligatory to go through this idea. (Te_2, Table A3.4, Appendix 3).

> Human activity, whether production or consumption, regenerates pollution such as the discharge of household waste, which can cause

> water pollution by wastewater. Human over-exploitation of natural resources in industry pollutes the soil and the atmosphere and can cause diseases. (St_2, Table A3.4, Appendix 3)

Ecological citizenship appears to be more oriented towards a liberal trend:

> I remember that I mentioned the example of the demands of citizens in reaction to oil mill discharges or plant discharges in the region of Gabes. (Te_2, Table A3.4, Appendix 3)

> When you protect the environment, you get a healthy environment. This is a human right, such as the right to life and the right to health. (St_1, Table A3.4, Appendix 3)

Figure 6.5 presents the political potential of EDIs in the produced curriculum in the Economics and Management section in comparison with the ideal type.

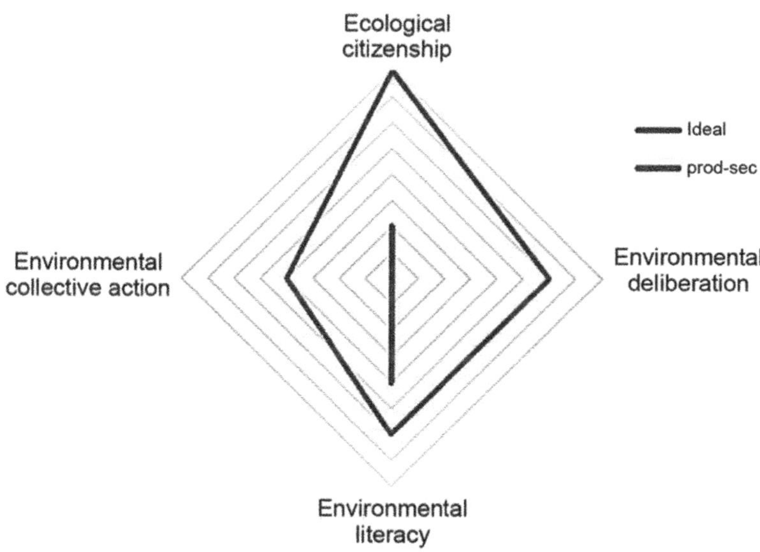

Figure 6.5. *The political potential of EDIs in the produced curriculum of the Economics and Management section in the secondary school compared to the ideal type. For a color version of this figure, see www.iste.co.uk/slimani/education.zip*

6.1.3.3. *Political learning and the potential for socialization*

Disciplinary cognitive socialization involves technical school learning focusing on the relevance of the economic concept of growth to found a type of human development based on safeguarding the environment:

> The notion of economic growth with basic needs is an essential concept to build the notion of sustainable development. (Te_2, Table A3.4, Appendix 3)

> Human development ensures well-being through health and education progress towards well-being. Sustainable development achieved without economic growth. (St_1, Table A3.4, Appendix 3)

Political socialization is oriented towards learning individualistic citizenship where social participation is encouraged with an individualistic perspective:

> Already in the general objectives of these programs the student must explore his or her environment. (Te_2, Table A3.4, Appendix 3)

> The voluntary commitment of the individual makes it possible to achieve development; the State, through its political and economic power, can intervene through laws to encourage this commitment. (St_1, Table A3.4, Appendix 3)

Democratic socialization is based on learning in a minimalist action regime where the interventions of the actors are supposed to be separate:

> The students' activity consisted in reading documents on the school textbook in response to the questions noted, which were oriented towards the objectives of constructing the concepts of development and sustainable development. (Te_2, Table A3.4, Appendix 3)

> We took note of the information the teacher said after reading about the book and answered the questions asked. (St_2, Table A3.4, Appendix 3)

Figure 6.6 summarizes the potentialities for socialization in terms of political learning in the studied produced curriculum, compared to the ideal type.

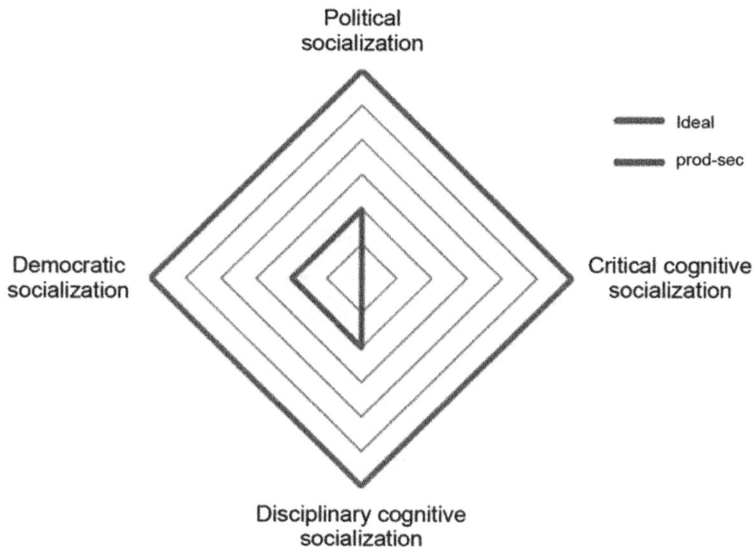

Figure 6.6. *The potential for socialization in terms of political learning in the produced secondary school curriculum compared to the ideal type. For a color version of this figure, see www.iste.co.uk/slimani/education.zip*

6.1.3.4. *Conclusion*

In the produced curriculum for the Economics and Managment section of the 4th year of secondary school, the metatheme of sustainable development is evoked in its anti-political trend of natural resource management.

This appears in connection with a political potential involving only elementary environmental literacy and liberal ecological citizenship. This political potential itself is connected with potentialities for reduced socialization which is based on ecoliteracy learning that not exceeding the technical level, citizenship learning not exceeding the individualist level and learning in an action regime not exceeding the minimalist level.

6.2. Analysis of the undergraduate curriculum: the bachelor's degree in environmental protection

6.2.1. *Prescribed curriculum*

6.2.1.1. *2009 requirements*

6.2.1.1.1. The political/anti-political trend

In the content proposed by the National Biology Sectorial Commission in 2009, four EDI metathemes were detected: environmental ethics, sustainable development, environmental politics and environmental technologies and management.

Environmental politics and changes are discussed in relation to a perspective that reflects a technical conception in the treatment of environmental degradation:

> Development and protection of the natural environment (coastal protection, fight against erosion and desertification, quarries, deposits, landfills, etc.). (2009 prescribed curricula, p. 59)

The question of environmental ethics is influenced by positions whereby environmental values are focused on the instrumental values of biodiversity and its roles in human development, well-being and biosecurity:

> Instrumental value. Goods and services. Scientific, socio-economic and cultural values. Aesthetic and recreational value (ecotourism). (2009 prescribed curricula, p. 40)

The issue of sustainable development appears to be closely linked to the management of biodiversity.

The question of technology and environmental management organizational rationality of management control:

> Environmental quality, standards for discharges into the receiving environment, ISO certification standards, labels, legislative aspects and international conventions. (2009 prescribed curricula, p. 54)

6.2.1.1.2. Political potential

Environmental literacy includes both basic and functional dimensions:

> To master the knowledge relating to the various sources of pollution and their consequences for living beings and the environment. (2009 prescribed curricula, p. 49)

Ecological citizenship is republican because it implies a vision that considers the maintenance of the ecosystem as a necessity:

> To make students acquire the notion of biodiversity, make them aware of its importance and the threats it faces, as well as the need to preserve it. (2009 prescribed curricula, p. 37)

Collective environmental action appears as a latent group action:

> Acquire know-how in the treatment of emissions and waste, and in environmental protection. (2009 prescribed curricula, p. 49)

Environmental deliberation is absent in this program.

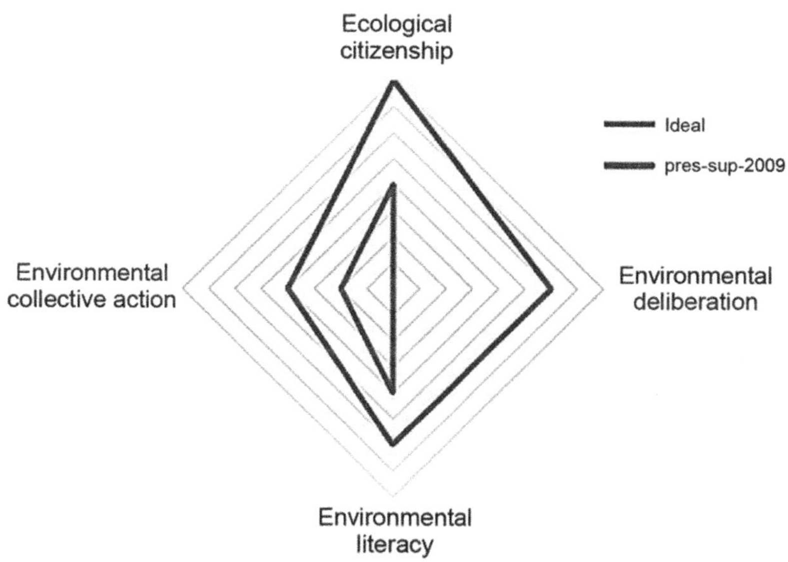

Figure 6.7. *The political potential of EDIs in the 2009 university prescribed curricula compared to the ideal type. For a color version of this figure, see www.iste.co.uk/slimani/education.zip*

Figure 6.7 summarizes the political potential of EDIs in the 2009 program compared to the ideal type.

6.2.1.1.3. Political learning and the potentialities for socialization

Disciplinary cognitive socialization is based on exclusive learning of technical ecoliteracy:

> To enable students to understand climatic phenomena, their changes and their impacts on the environment and to learn about data acquisition and storage tools using remote sensing and GIS. (2009 prescribed curricula, p. 41)
>
> To master the techniques of detection and measurement of the importance of pollution in the environment. (2009 prescribed curricula, p. 49)

Political socialization corresponds to the learning of adaptive citizenship:

> To make students acquire the notion of biodiversity, make them aware of its importance and the threats it faces, as well as the need to preserve it. (2009 prescribed curricula, p. 37)

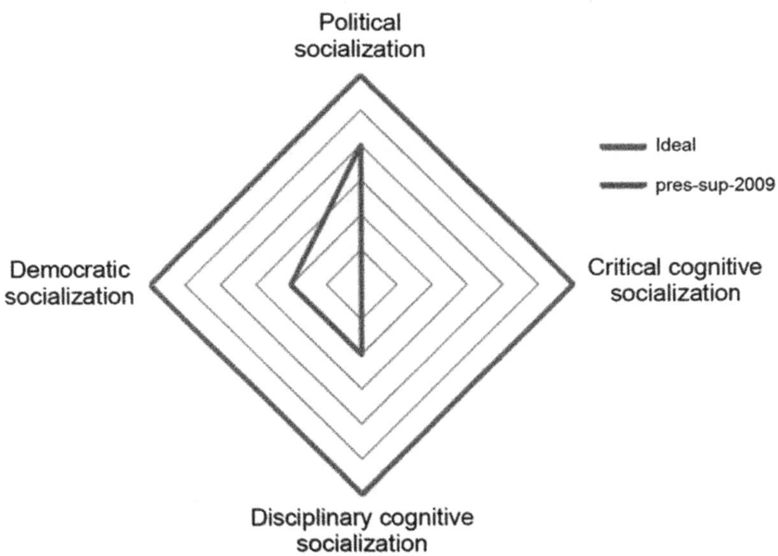

Figure 6.8. *The potential for socialization in terms of political learning in the 2009 university prescribed curricula compared to the ideal type. For a color version of this figure, see www.iste.co.uk/slimani/education.zip*

Democratic socialization refers to a minimalist action regime in the form of visits to places of activity oriented towards the protection of the environment:

> Visits to laboratories at specialized centers and wastewater treatment plants. (2009 prescribed curricula, p. 54)

Critical cognitive socialization is absent.

Figure 6.8 summarizes the potential for socialization in terms of political learning in the 2009 prescribed curricula compared to the ideal type.

6.2.1.1.4 Conclusion

In the 2009 academic prescribed curricula, several EDI metathemes (environmental politics and environmental change, environmental ethics, sustainable development and environmental technologies and management) are involved in their anti-political trends (ecological modernization, communicative deliberation, resource management and management control). This appears in connection with a political potential involving elementary and functional environmental literacy and ecological citizenship that reaches the level of republican citizenship and latent group-based collective action. Such political potential related to potentialities for socialization is based on the learning of ecoliteracy which does not go beyond the technical level, learning of citizenship that reaches the level of adaptive citizenship and learning in an action regime that does not go beyond the minimalist level.

6.2.1.2. *2015 prescribed curricula*

6.2.1.2.1. The political/anti-political trend

The EDIs evoked in the work of the sectorial commission of biology in 2015 can be related to the six metathemes: environmental ethics, sustainable development, environmental politics, agri-food issues, environmental technologies and management, and transitions.

Environmental politics issues are mainly related to the struggle against ecosystem degradation and the impact of climate change on the environment, but are not linked to environmental justice:

> The program provides basic training on the ecology and pollution present in the world and in Tunisia as well as the impact of this natural and essentially anthropogenic pollution on ecosystems. The program also provides important knowledge relating to environmental protection through the application of international conventions and legal and regulatory measures applied in Tunisia. (Objective of the Ecology and Environment unit)

The agri-food issue is oriented towards the improvement of production coupled with environmental protection:

> Food production and environmental protection: agri-ecosystems, comparison with natural ecosystems, global needs, the Tunisian issue, improving agricultural yield, crop processing, impact on health, solutions. (Tutorial program for the Ecology and Environment unit)

Environmental ethics is also determined by the role of socio-economic and cultural instrumental values in the design of the content offered:

> Scientific, socio-economic and cultural values. Aesthetic and recreational values (ecotourism). (Biodiversity and Conservation Biology course program)

Sustainable development is evoked in connection with the management of biodiversity as well as with the ecological footprint. The point of view supported in these contents is mainly a reformist one, which lies between the political and the anti-political.

Environmental technology is conceived as a rationality applicable to the management of pollution and ecosystem degradation:

> To understand the principles of environmental technologies and the potentialities of their application. (Environmental Technology program)

The question of transition is not mentioned explicitly but in the form of an example of a solution to the problem of the link between food production and environmental protection: permaculture. The solution of permaculture corresponds fundamentally to a depoliticization of the transition issue because it refers to a consensual vision involving the emotional and psychological dimensions of a collective identity that is depoliticized.

6.2.1.2.2. Political potential

Environmental literacy involves various elementary, functional and operational dimensions:

> Anthropogenic disturbances of biodiversity: introductions of non-native species and interactions with native species; characteristics of the geographical distribution of biodiversity (cosmopolitan, endemic, rare species, etc.); scientific, socio-economical and cultural values. (Biodiversity and Conservation Biology program)

Ecological citizenship implies reaching the level of a post cosmopolitan citizenship by evoking the ecological footprint through comparisons:

> Ecological footprint: individual calculation of the ecological – footprint according to a pre-established questionnaire + discussion of the results and comparisons between students and between the ecological footprints of different countries. (Practical work program of the Ecology and Environment unit)

Environmental collective action reaches the intermediate group type, evoking environmental associations:

> Associative activities (being responsible, ecological without doing too much). (Ecology and Environment course program unit)

Environmental deliberation reaches the level of ecological deliberation by referring to international conventions:

> Citation of the texts of conventions, laws, decrees, regulations, etc. (Practical work program of the Ecology and Environment unit)

Figure 6.9 summarizes the political potential of EDIs in the 2015 program compared to the ideal type.

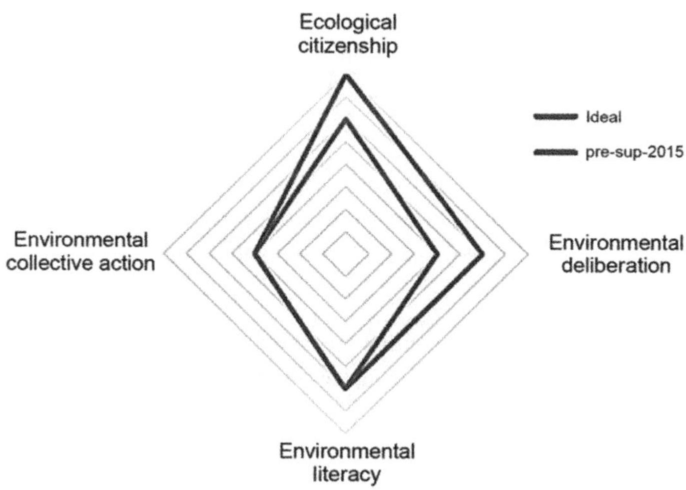

Figure 6.9. *The political potential of EDIs in the 2015 university prescribed curricula compared to the ideal type. For a color version of this figure, see www.iste.co.uk/slimani/education.zip*

6.2.1.2.3. Political learning and the potentialities for socialization

Disciplinary cognitive socialization is based on technical ecoliteracy learning:

> To establish a scientific basis for the actions necessary to protect and improve the conservation and sustainable use of ecosystems. (Ecology and Environment unit objective)

It also involves learning cultural ecoliteracy by posing the Tunisian problem of agricultural production and learning critical ecoliteracy involving a comparison of the ecological footprint.

Political socialization refers to content related to the learning of adaptive citizenship:

> Awareness-raising and associative activities (being responsible, ecological without going overboard, buying ecological, biodegradable, non-toxic products, etc.). (Ecology and Environment course unit)

Critical cognitive socialization is based on content involving a normative form of deliberation where points of view are *a priori* specified in relation to international conventions:

> The students, following the bibliography, develop the critical analysis in the general public concerning a current problem in pollution and the measures taken to protect ecosystems; citation of texts of conventions, laws, decrees, regulations, etc. (Practical work program in the Environment and Ecology unit)

Democratic socialization implies a minimalist form in a collective action regime where there is a mere juxtaposition of the interventions of the different actors involved such as students, teachers, environmental specialists and citizens on environmental politics issues:

> Presentation by an environmental specialist (teacher, researcher, expert, association, etc.). (Practical work program in the Ecology and Environment unit)

Figure 6.10 summarizes the potential for socialization in terms of political learning in the 2015 prescribed curricula compared to the ideal type.

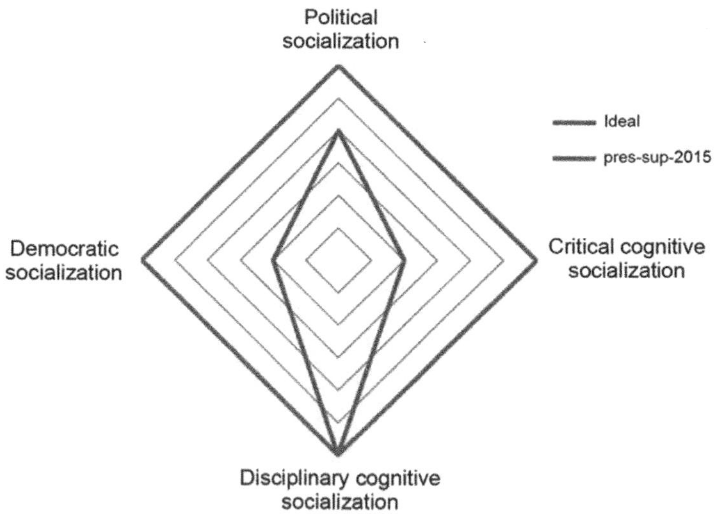

Figure 6.10. *The potential for socialization in terms of political learning in the 2015 university prescriptions compared to the ideal type. For a color version of this figure, see www.iste.co.uk/slimani/education.zip*

6.2.1.2.4 Conclusion

In the academic prescriptions of 2015, several EDI metathemes (environmental politics and environmental change, environmental ethics, agribusiness issues, sustainable development, environmental technologies and management, and transitions) are implicated in their anti-political trends (ecological modernization, communicative deliberation, consumption, resource management, management control and socio-technical approaches). This appears in connection with a political potential involving elementary, functional and operational environmental literacy, ecological citizenship reaching the level of post-cosmopolitan citizenship, latent and intermediate group collective action and environmental deliberation reaching the level of ecological deliberation. This political potential is connected with potentialities for socialization which are based on ecoliteracy learning (technical, cultural and critical), citizenship learning reaching the level of an adaptive citizenship, learning in an action regime not exceeding the minimalist level and learning of normative deliberation.

6.2.2. *The produced curriculum*

6.2.2.1. *The political/anti-political trend*

Sustainable development and environmental politics and environmental change are the two metathemes of the EDIs that are identified in the produced curriculum studied. These two themes are guided by anti-political trends in natural resource management and techno-scientific studies of the causes and effects of pollution:

> In my courses, I focus mainly on resource management and I have a module called wildlife management that I teach for the students of the GBR course. Even the consumption of products, I don't put too much emphasis on that. (Te_1, Table A3.10, Appendix 3)

> Generally, the focus is on global ecology and global changes, such as eutrophication. We define terms such as greenhouse gases, the ozone layer, aquatic pollution, biological pollution, etc., which are related to what we now call climate change. (Te_1, Table A3.10, Appendix 3)

6.2.2.2. *Political potential*

Environmental literacy involves mainly elementary knowledge, but reaches the functional level of analytical skills for environmental problems:

> First there are the elementary components [...]. Secondly, there are the types of interactions between man and nature because it is man who really manages this stock of resources. [...] Thirdly, the evaluation of the degradation of the state of nature, degraded or moderately degraded. In very few cases do I deal with cultural values. (Te_1, Table A3.10, Appendix 3)

Ecological citizenship is a liberal environmental citizenship; however, it also reaches the level of a post-cosmopolitan ecological citizenship by evoking the ecological footprint:

> For example, the right to clean air, because companies contribute to global warming with air pollution, deforestation and water pollution, that's why we need the right to protect the environment. (St_1, Table A3.10, Appendix 3)

> For example, the ecological footprint, they tell us that we would need four planets to ensure human food survival. That is to say we have to be aware of these global problems. But we don't talk about the political contestation behavior. The ecological principle is evoked just to justify why the international conventions have been developed: we think globally and act locally, that's what I try to make my students understand. (Te_1, Table A3.10, Appendix 3)

Collective environmental action mainly evokes latent group actions; however, it also evokes intermediate group actions:

> I insist on joining environmental associations because of their importance ... In fact, recycling waste, purchasing ecological products, all three can be considered as methods of environmental management. (Te_1, Table A3.10, Appendix 3)

> For example, how people deal with waste by following steps and studying the impact of projects to minimize discharges and their effects on the environment. (St_3, Table A3.10, Appendix 3)

The environmental deliberation mentioned is technocratic; it reaches the level of ecological deliberation by referring above all to international consensuses such as those drawn up following the Brundtland report:

> [...] apart from a simple reference to the Brundtland report, but it is only a reference. (Te_1, Table A3.10, Appendix 3)

> The example of the consensus developed during the COP meetings. (St_2, Table A3.10, Appendix 3)

Figure 6.11 summarizes the political potential of EDIs in the produced curriculum of the Environmental Protection degree program compared to the ideal type.

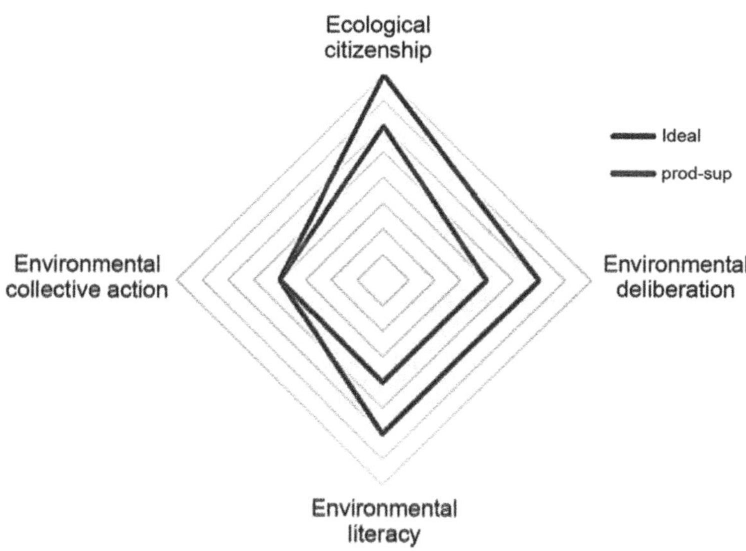

Figure 6.11. *The political potential of EDIs in the produced curriculum from the Environmental Protection degree program compared to the ideal type. For a color version of this figure, see www.iste.co.uk/slimani/education.zip*

6.2.2.3. *Political Learning and the potential for socialization*

Disciplinary cognitive socialization is based on ecoliteracy learning mainly at the technical level as well as at the cultural level:

> We are in the process of training technicians. The emphasis is on the management of bioresources; what interests us most is ecological, that is, the ecological functions of the environmental matrices are water, air and soil, which are sensitive to disturbances. (Te_1, Table A3.10, Appendix 3)

> There is the problem of pesticides that must be avoided because they damage. (St_2, Table A3.10, Appendix 3)

Political socialization is based on adaptive citizenship learning:

> [...] I encourage my students to participate in associations to be active in society. Students are taught that they are environmental physicians. I push them to be active mainly so that they can find work after university. (En_1, Table A3.10, Appendix 3)

> We can be protectors of the environment. (St_3, Table A3.10, Appendix 3)

Democratic socialization is based on learning in a minimalist action regime:

> Actually, the students didn't really do anything. In fact, I know that there was a small project that existed before, but the students dropped it for several reasons. (St_1, Table A3.10, Appendix 3)

> We studied this subject by hearing the teacher's words and noted the most important remarks by asking questions about the words that are difficult. (St_5, Table A3.10, Appendix 3)

Critical cognitive socialization is not targeted since no deliberative learning is involved in this produced curriculum.

> There was no discussion. In fact, the students don't have the training or skills to be involved in such a discussion. Usually, the students lean towards the teacher's point of view. They do not have a stance on environmental safety or conservation of environmental matrices. (Te_1, Table A3.10, Appendix 3)

No, there was no debate with different points of view. (St_6, Table A3.10, Appendix 3)

Figure 6.12 visualizes the potential for socialization in terms of political learning in the curriculum produced for the Environmental Protection degree program.

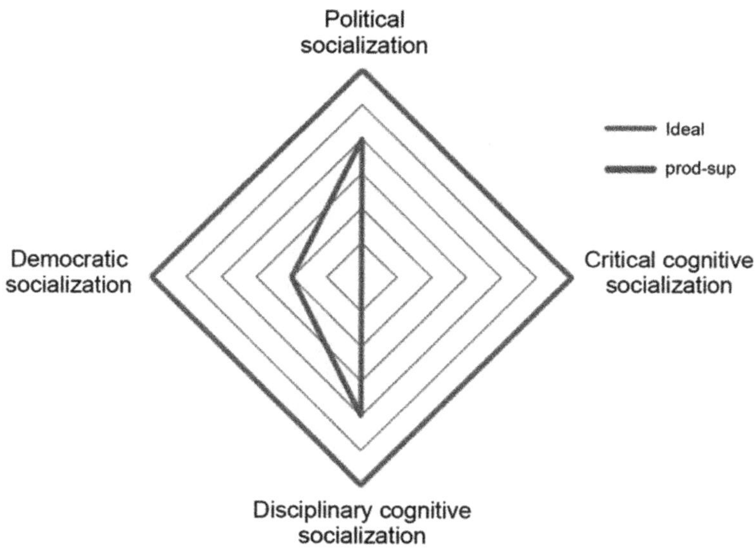

Figure 6.12. *The potential for socialization in terms of political learning in the produced curriculum for the Environmental Protection degree program. For a color version of this figure, see www.iste.co.uk/slimani/education.zip*

6.2.2.4. *Conclusion*

In the produced curriculum for the environmental protection degree, two EDI metathemes are involved: environmental politics and environmental changes evoked in their anti-political technicist trend, and sustainable development also evoked in its anti-political trend of natural resource management. This appears in connection with a political potential involving elementary and functional environmental literacy, and an ecological citizenship that reaches the level of post-cosmopolitan citizenship, an environmental deliberation that reaches the level of ecological deliberation and an environmental action of the latent group and of the intermediate group. This political potential is in connection with potentialities for socialization and is based on technical and cultural learning of ecoliteracy, learning of citizenship reaching the level of adaptive citizenship and learning in an action regime not exceeding the minimalist level.

Conclusion

In the educational content involving EDIs, the potential for democratic socialization, integrating cognitive (disciplinary and critical) and political socialization, is generated by a structuring of the political in this content. This structuring corresponds to a reality showing three levels forming an "onto-epistemological thickness" of the political sphere:

– a first "micro" level involving the political or anti-political trend that runs through these issues;

– a second "meso" level of the regulatory categories of political life in situations involving these issues, which corresponds to their political potential;

– a third "macro" level of policy learning in educational situations involving these issues.

C.1. The "micro" level of the political/anti-political trend of EDIs

At this level, EDIs appear to be intersected by two trends: a political (or politicized) trend and an anti-political (or depoliticized) trend.

The development of market practices in the processing of EDIs constitutes a trend of depoliticization which essentially promotes ecological modernization (or the green economy/green growth), an ethical type of anthropomorphism, a managerial approach to development (management of natural resources and transitions) or a consumerist approach in the treatment of agri-food issues.

In contrast, the politicization trend appears to be mainly oriented by justice as a political category valuing resistance to inequalities in the face of environmental changes, development inequalities and food inequalities.

C.2. The "meso" level of the political potential of EDIs

At this level, EDIs appear to carry a political potential generated by four categories supposedly regulating political life in situations involving this type of issue. These categories are environmental literacy, ecological citizenship, environmental deliberation and environmental collective action. The political potential of EDIs can take the form of environmental problem-solving skills, political contestation, political deliberation, and action and organization in collective identities.

C.3. The "macro" level of political learning in educational situations involving EDIs

At this level, the involvement of EDIs in educational situations allows for the development of political learning: ecoliteracy learning, deliberative learning, learning about social roles and learning in collective educational action regimes.

Pedagogically, political learning is based on tools and devices aimed at the development of learners. This fulfillment is encouraged by the development of an educational process of subjectivation, empowerment or authorization in experiences of political protest or commitment to social change or in learning communities that build knowledge and make it possible to reflect and act on dominant policies.

Also, this learning can be organized in the form of moments of democratic socialization articulating moments of disciplinary cognitive socialization, moments of political socialization and moments of critical cognitive socialization.

C.4. The political/anti-political trend and political potential of EDIs in the texts of the UN 2030 SDGs and the UNESCO "Education for SDGs 2030"

The great number of EDI themes manifesting an anti-political trend in the SDGs appears in connection with a relatively low political potential showing an environmental literacy that does not go beyond the functional level, an ecological liberal citizenship trend, an environmental action of the latent group level and an environmental deliberation technocratic level. However, the equally important presence of themes with an anti-political trend and others with a political trend within "Education for SDGs" is related to a higher political potential that implies operational environmental literacy, environmental collective action within an intermediate group, post-cosmopolitan ecological citizenship and ecological-type environmental deliberation (Figures C.1 and C.2).

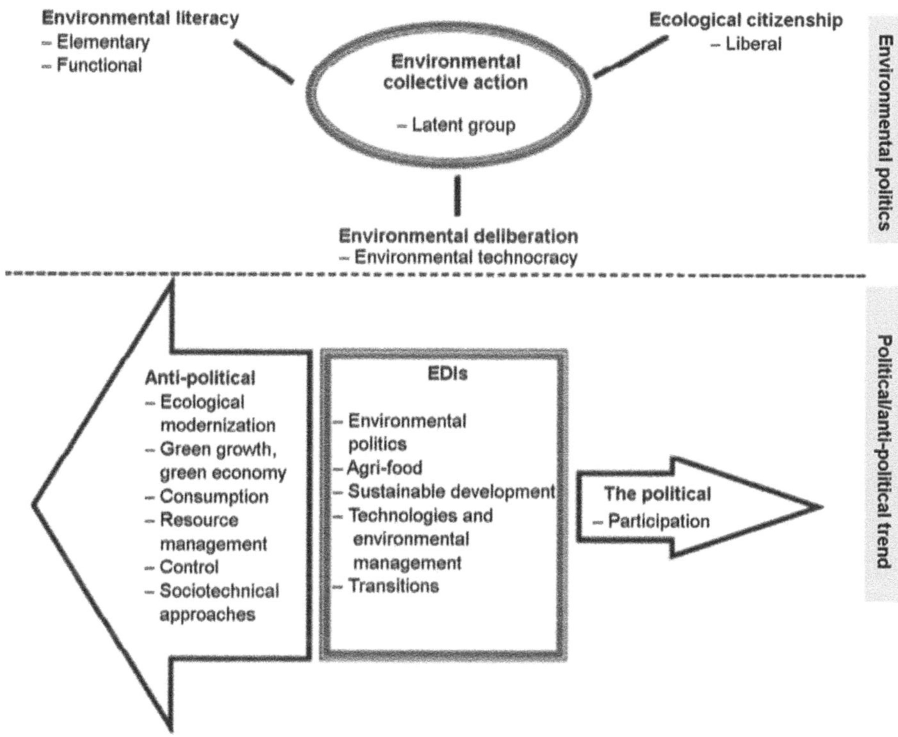

Figure C.1. *Political structuring in the SDGs. For a color version of this figure, see www.iste.co.uk/slimani/education.zip*

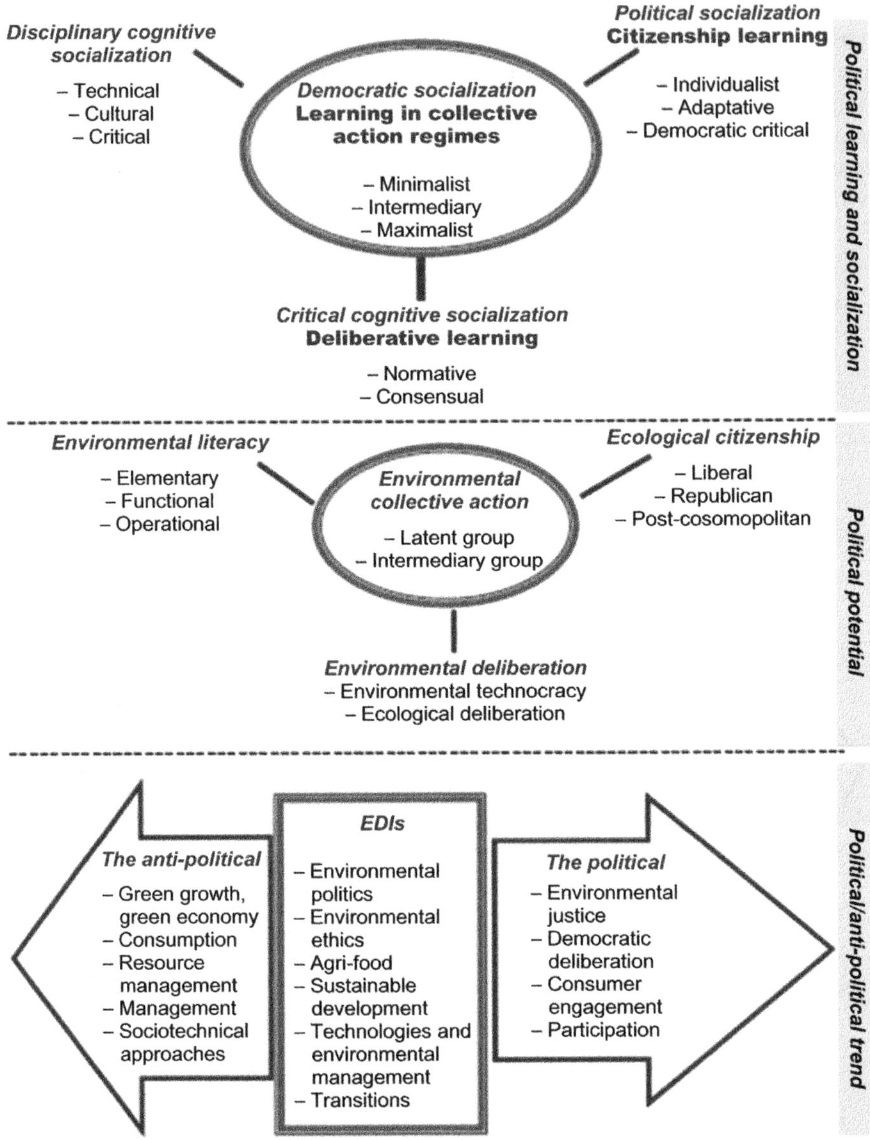

Figure C.2. *Political structuring in "Education for Sustainable Development Goals". For a color version of this figure, see www.iste.co.uk/slimani/education.zip*

This comparison thus highlights the pressure to neutralize the political potential of EDIs in the international SDG 2030 agenda (the objectives, targets and indicators).

This pressure limits this potential to the levels specified in the results described below. On the contrary, the political potential of EDIs in the UNESCO recommendations "Education for SDGs" appears to be much more important, although it does not reach, in its dimension of environmental deliberation, the "embodied disagreement".

C.5. The political/anti-political trend and political potential of EDIs between the prescribed curriculum, the potential curriculum and the produced secondary school curriculum

In these curricula, the EDI themes are not very diversified and tend to be anti-political. The political potential also appears low, with a functional level of environmental literacy, a republican level of ecological citizenship and environmental collective action that can reach the intermediate group level. This potential does not involve environmental deliberation (Figures C.3, C.4 and C.5).

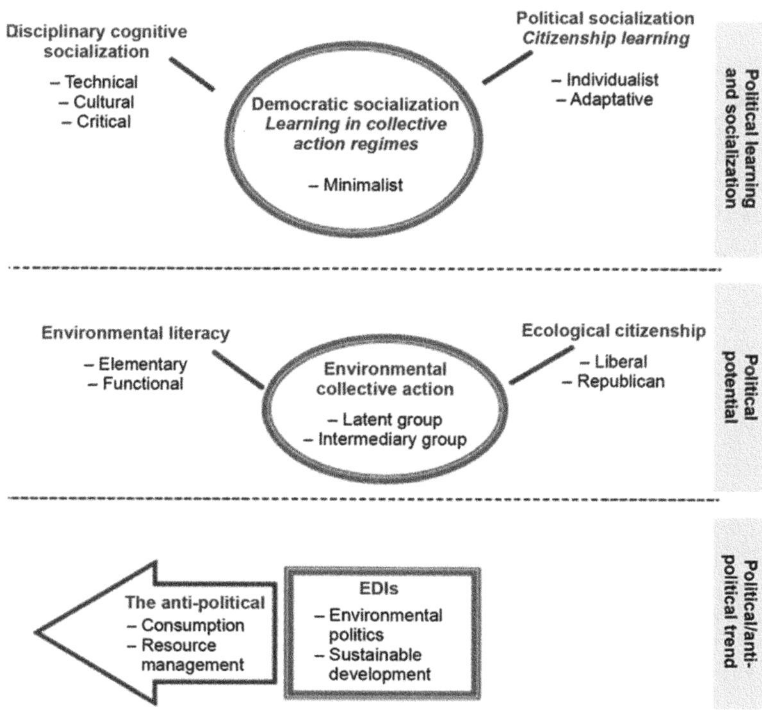

Figure C.3. *Political structuring in the prescribed Tunisian secondary school curriculum. For a color version of this figure, see www.iste.co.uk/slimani/education.zip*

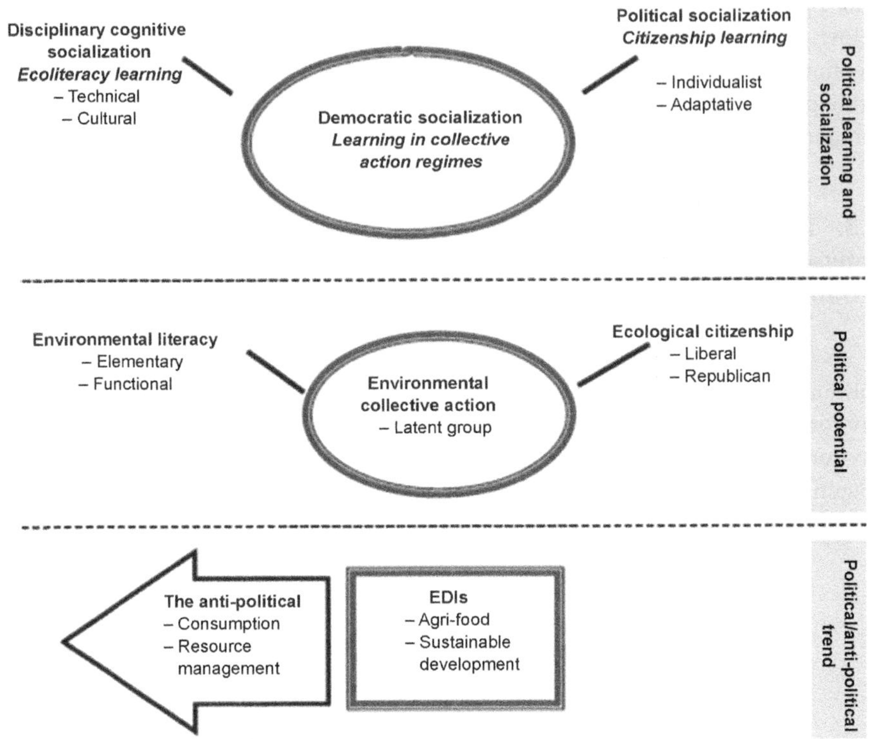

Figure C.4. *Political structuring in the potential curriculum of the Tunisian secondary school. For a color version of this figure, see www.iste.co.uk/slimani/education.zip*

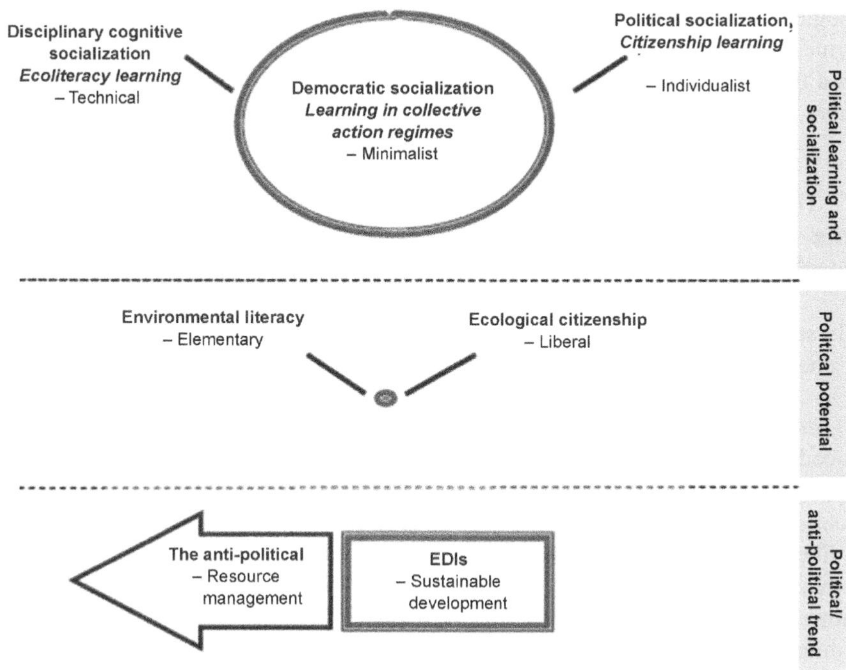

Figure C.5. *Political structuring in the produced curriculum of 4th-year Economics and Management in the secondary school. For a color version of this figure, see www.iste.co.uk/slimani/education.zip*

A single theme as in the curriculum produced for 4th year Economics and Management has very little political potential involving liberal ecological citizenship and basic environmental literacy without involving either environmental deliberation or environmental collective action.

C.6. The political/anti-political trend and political potential of EDIs between the 2009 prescribed university programs, the 2015 prescribed university programs and the produced curriculum for the environmental protection degree program

In the undergraduate curriculum (bachelor's degree in Environmental Protection), the richest potential appears in the 2015 requirements. This richness, amounting to elementary, functional and operational environmental literacy, a post-cosmopolitan ecological citizenship, a collective action of the latent group type and of the intermediate group type and an ecological environmental deliberation, is connected with a thematic diversity within EDIs, even with a single anti-political trend, which is more important compared to the 2009 prescribed and produced curricula.

C.7. The political potential and the potentialities for socialization in terms of political learning between the prescribed curriculum, the potential curriculum and the produced secondary school curriculum

In secondary school curricula, the political potential of EDIs is reduced to a level that does not involve environmental deliberation.

This potential is found in connection with political learning which is also reduced and does not involve deliberation. The apogee of the reduction is remarkable, especially in the produced curriculum for 4th year Economics and Management where this potential, not exceeding elementary environmental literacy and liberal ecological citizenship, is linked with much reduced political learning by involving learning of ecoliteracy not exceeding the technical level, learning in a minimalist action regime, learning of individualistic citizenship and no deliberative learning.

C.8. The political potential and the potentialities for socialization in terms of political learning between the 2009 university prescribed curricula, the 2015 prescribed curricula and the produced curriculum from the environmental protection degree

In the bachelor degree curriculum, the most important potentialities for socialization and political learning are also detected in the 2015 prescribed curricula compared to the 2009 prescribed curricula and the produced curriculum.

These potentialities, involving learning technical and cultural ecoliteracy, learning adaptive citizenship and learning in a minimalist action regime, are thus related to a relatively high political potential of EDIs (Figures C.6, C.7 and C.8).

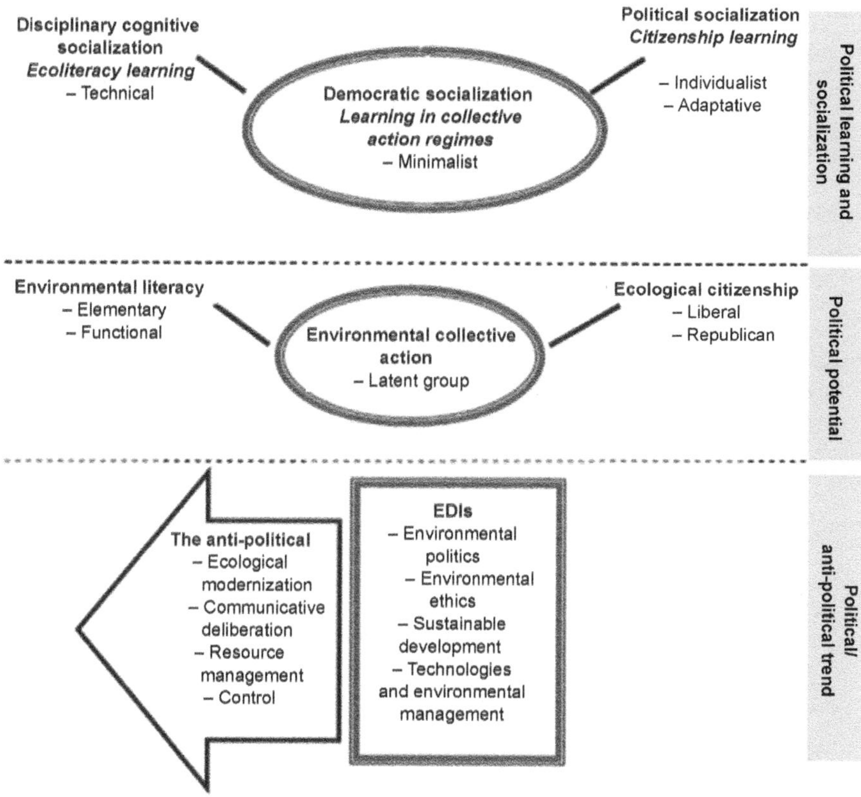

Figure C.6. *Political structuring in the 2009 academic prescribed curricula. For a color version of this figure, see www.iste.co.uk/slimani/education.zip*

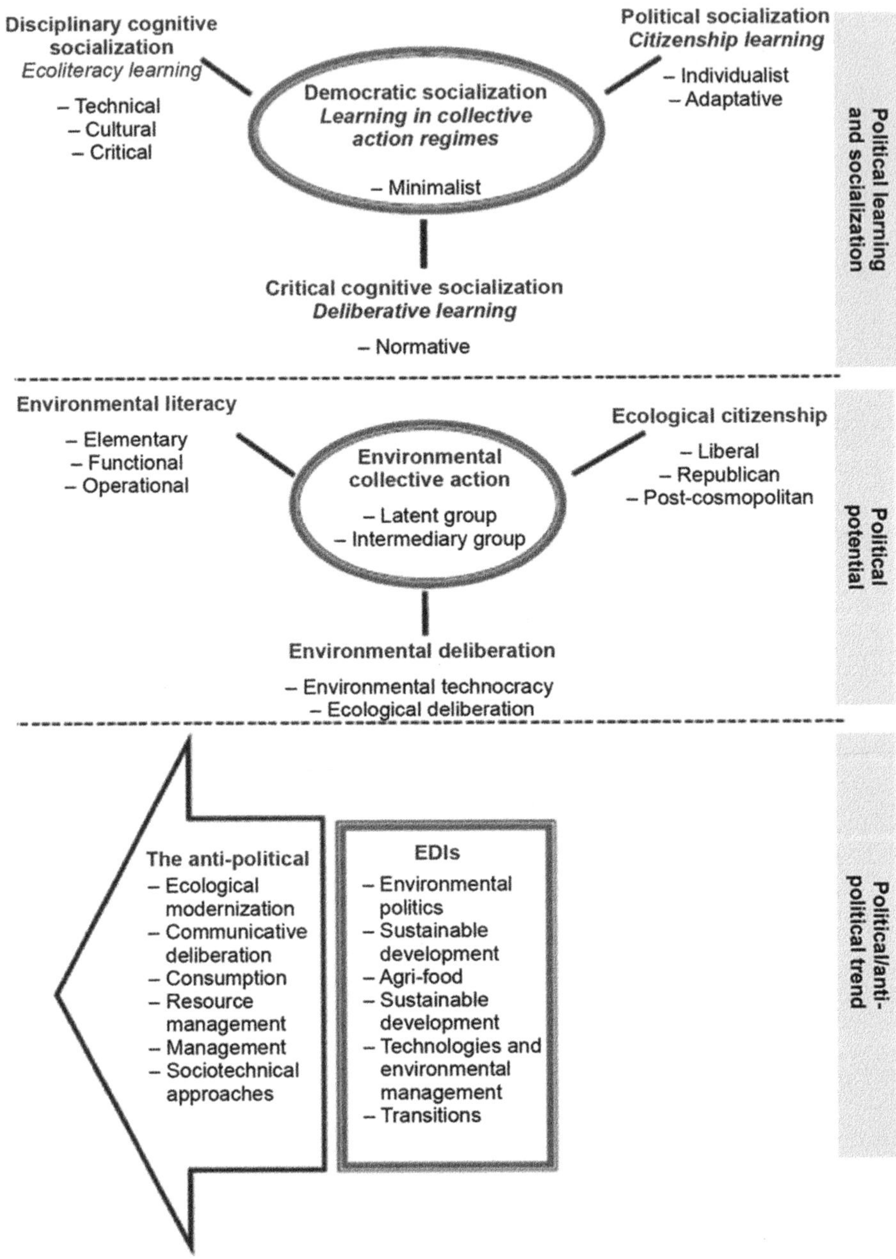

Figure C.7. *Political structuring in the 2015 academic prescribed curricula. For a color version of this figure, see www.iste.co.uk/slimani/education.zip*

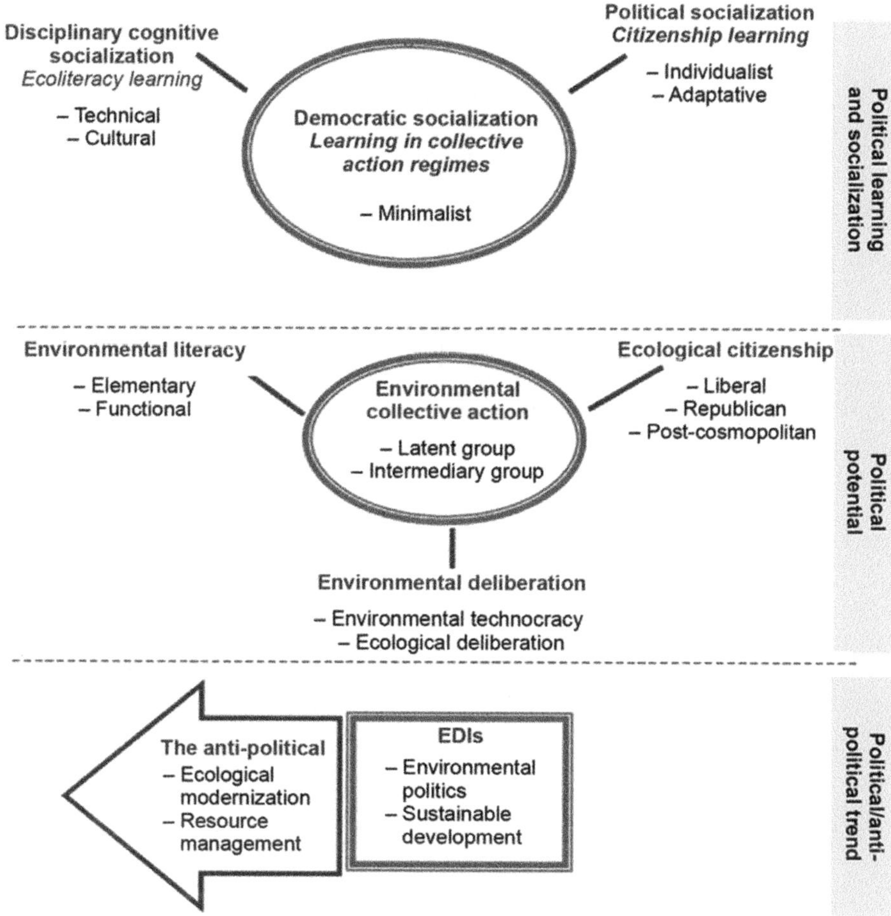

Figure C.8. *Political structuring in the produced curriculum of the Environmental Protection degree program. For a color version of this figure, see www.iste.co.uk/slimani/education.zip*

The confrontation between the conceptual elaborations and the reality of the elaboration of the educational content allows for the construction of didactic tags as well as tags to achieve political education through the EDIs. All of these tags can form mechanisms that generate potential for democratic socialization in educational content involving EDIs through an "onto-epistemological thickness" that structures the political of this content (Figure C.9).

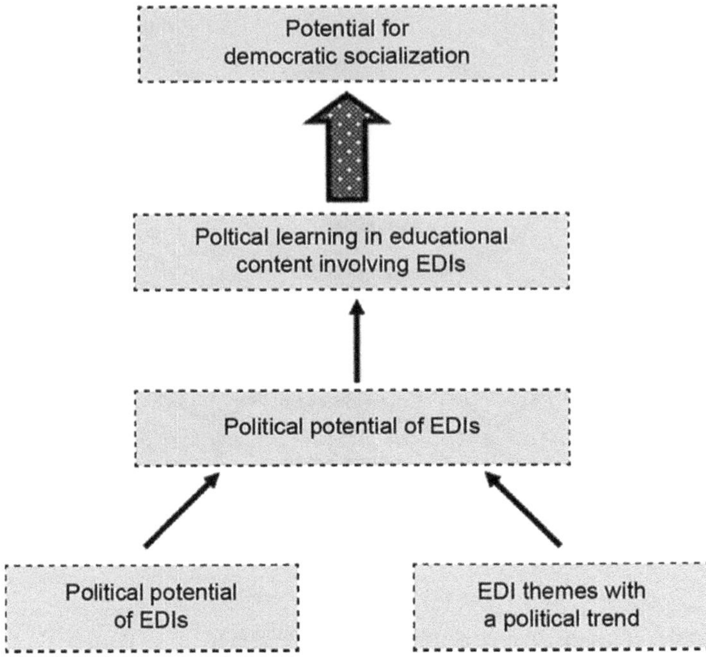

Figure C.9. *Generation of the potential for democratic socialization in educational content involving EDIs*

Appendices

Appendix 1

Interviews: Guides and Help Lists

Question guide	Objectives
Introduction and general information 1. Brief presentation of the researcher and the research project 2. Surname and first name, field of expertise, number of years working in education 3. How do you see the role of EDIs (or of an EDI) in the training of pupils or students?	Gather general information about the teacher involved and the teaching of EDIs
EDI themes involved 4. Can you please select the topics (from list A[1] or list A'[2] attached) that you feel are important in teaching EDIs? (sustainable development)? 5. Why do you consider them important? 6. Do you want to add a topic that you think is important? Why?	Identify the political/ anti-political trend in EDI teaching

1 The list that concerns the issue of sustainable development as a subject of teaching in secondary education and in a UCUE (biodiversity and sustainable development) for the environmental protection degree.

2 The list that concerns several EDIs as teaching topics in a unit (ecology and environment) for the environmental protection degree.

Question guide	Objectives
Content evoked in processing the EDIs 7.1. Can you please select the types of environmental knowledge evoked in the content you teach? (Use list B) 7.2. Could you explain your choices? 8.1. Can you please select the types of discussions referred to in the content you teach? (Use list C) 8.2. Could you explain your choices? 9.1. Can you please select the types of environmental actions discussed on the environmental issue(s) in the content you teach? (Use list D) 9.2. Could you explain your choices? 10.1. Can you please select the types of behaviors evoked in the content you teach? (Use list E) 10.2. Could you explain your choices?	Characterize the political potential in the EDIs involved
Pedagogical aspects in processing the EDIs 11.1. Can you please select the general objectives of your teaching? (Use list F) 11.2. Could you give us some examples? 12.1. Can you please select the specific objectives that your teaching aims to achieve in this (or these) question(s)? (Use list G) 12.2. Could you give us some examples? 13.1. Can you please select the types of discussions that took place during the teaching sessions of the EDIs? (Use list H) 13.2. Could you give us some examples? 14.1. Can you please select the types of actions carried out by the pupils or students? (Use list I) 14.2. Could you give us some examples?	Characterize the political learning system

Table A1.1. *Interview guide for teachers*

Question guide	Objectives
Introduction and general information 1. Brief presentation of the researcher and the research project 2. Surname and first name 3. How important is/are environmental issue(s) to you?	Gather general information about the learner
Themes of the EDIs involved 4. Can you please select the topic(s) (from list A[3] or list A′[4] attached) that you discussed in the session(s) devoted to addressing environmental issue(s)?	Identify the political/anti-political trend in EDI teaching
Content evoked in processing the EDIs 5.1. What types of environmental knowledge are discussed? (Use list B) 5.2. Could you give some examples? 6.1. What types of discussions are evoked on environmental issue(s)? (Use list C) 6.2. Could you give some examples? 7.1. What are the types of environmental actions? (Use list D) 7.2. Could you give some examples? 8.1. What types of behaviors are evoked? (Use list E) 8.2. Could you give some examples?	Characterize the political potential in the EDIs involved
Pedagogical aspects in the processing of EDIs 9.1. What behaviors are encouraged? (Use list F) 9.2. Could you give some examples? 10.1. What knowledge have you built up? (Use list G) 10.2. Could you give some examples? 11.1. How did you discuss these issues? (Use list H) 11.2. Could you give some examples? 12.1. What actions have you carried out? (Use list I) 12.2. Could you give some examples?	Characterize the political learning system Characterize the political learning system

Table A1.2. *Interview guide for learners (students)*

3 The list that concerns the issue of sustainable development as a subject of teaching in secondary education and in a teaching unit (biodiversity and sustainable development) for the environmental protection degree.

4 The list that concerns several EDIs as teaching objects in a teaching unit (ecology and environment) for the environmental protection degree.

List A: Sustainable development themes	
	Management of natural resources
	Consumption of products that do not harm (endanger) the environment
	Environmental problems as a consequence of power relations (domination)
	Collective ownership of production: a perspective for environmental sustainability
	Domination of nature and women by men as a root cause of environmental problems
List A′: EDI themes	
	Scientific study of global environmental changes (ecological modernization)
	Green growth
	Green economy
	Environmental justice
	Environmental services for human societies
	Ethical pragmatism (environmental values depend on the situation)
	Management of natural resources
	Consumption of products that do not harm the environment
	Environmental problems as a consequence of power relations
	Domination of nature and women by men as a root cause of environmental problems
	Consumption
	Consumer and food producer engagement
	Technological innovations for energy transition
	Decentralization of energy production
	Adaptive management of fossil energy resources
List B: Environmental knowledge mentioned	
	Elementary components of natural and social systems (living components, non-living components, etc.).
	Types and examples of interactions between human and nature

List B: Environmental knowledge mentioned	
	Appreciation of nature and society
	Empathy (benevolence, sympathy) for nature and society
	Ecological, economic, geographic, political, cultural and educational processes
	The impact of beliefs and values on environmental issues
	Cultural values and historical perspectives in dealing with environmental issues
	Environmental awareness and sensitivity
List C: Environmental discussions mentioned	
	Adaptation to irreversibly engaged environmental dynamics
	Consensus (agreements) and conventions developed at conferences and international declarations
	Dialogues involving experts and citizens in direct experiences and local knowledge
List D: Environmental actions mentioned	
	Recycling of waste
	Purchase of ecological products
	Membership of environmental associations
	Attending gatherings and signing petitions (requests, complaints) for environmental causes
List E: Environmental behaviors mentioned	
	Claim (demand, require, request) rights to a healthy environment
	Recognize the duties of participation in challenges (disputes) against any destructive aspect of development
	Recognize environmental responsibility as a requirement of cosmopolitan justice
	Recognize environmental citizen responsibility in terms of unavoidable political contestation between adversaries (non-enemies)
List F: General objectives	
	To be a participatory citizen and promoter (initiator) of development
	To be a responsible citizen who acts responsibly in the community
	To be a cooperative citizen and concerned about social justice

List G: Specific objectives	
	Build relevant (suitable) scientific knowledge for addressing societal issues
	Identify the values of nature according to cultures, as well as the cultural elements supporting environmental sustainability
	Determine the roles of the economy in structuring power relations (domination)
List H: Types of discussions conducted	
	End result is the teacher's point of view
	End result is consensus (agreement) between the different points of view
	Defense of opposing perspectives (which remain in dispute)
List I: Types of actions carried out by pupils or students	
	The activities are presented separately
	The activities are continued in a club
	The activities are carried out with a commitment to a common project with the local community

Table A1.3. *Help list*

Appendix 2

Report on Political Elements in the SDG 2030 Agenda and in the Contents of "Education for 2030 SDGs"

Dimensions and criteria		Examples of indicators
Environmental collective action	*Latent group*	– "[…] substantially increasing recycling and safe reuse globally" (Target 6.3 in the list of proposed Sustainable Development Goal indicators[1]) – "[…] sanitation-related activities and programs, including water harvesting, desalination, water efficiency, wastewater treatment, recycling and reuse technologies" (Target 6.a in the list of proposed Sustainable Development Goal indicators) – "[…] substantially reduce waste generation through prevention, reduction, recycling and reuse" (Target 12.5 in the list of proposed Sustainable Development Goal indicators)
Ecological citizenship	*Liberal*	– "[…] have equal rights to economic resources, as well as access to basic services, ownership and control over land and other forms of property, inheritance, natural resources […]" (Target 1.4 in the list of proposed Sustainable Development Goal indicators) – "rights to economic resources, as well as

1 Available at: https://unstats.un.org/unsd/statcom/47th-session/documents/2016-2-IAEG-SDGs-F.pdf.

<table>
<tr><th colspan="2">Dimensions and criteria</th><th>Examples of indicators</th></tr>
<tr><td>Ecological citizenship</td><td>Liberal</td><td>access to ownership and control over land and other forms of property, financial services, inheritance and natural resources […]" (Target 5.a in the list of proposed Sustainable Development Goal indicators)</td></tr>
<tr><td rowspan="2">Deliberation</td><td>Environmental technocracy</td><td>– "[…] ability to adapt to the adverse impacts of climate change […]" (Indicator 13.2.1 in the list of proposed Sustainable Development Goal indicators)
– "[…] mitigation, adaptation, impact reduction and early warning into primary, secondary and tertiary curricula" (Indicator 13.3.1 in the list of proposed Sustainable Development Goal indicators)
– "[…] implement adaptation, mitigation and technology transfer […]" (Indicator 13.3.2 in the list of proposed Sustainable Development Goal indicators)</td></tr>
<tr><td>Ecological deliberation</td><td>– "Strengthen the implementation of the World Health Organization Framework Convention […]" (Target 3.a in the list of proposed Sustainable Development Goal indicators)</td></tr>
<tr><td rowspan="2">Environmental literacy</td><td>Elementary</td><td>– "[…] appreciation of cultural diversity […]" (Target 4.7 in the list of proposed Sustainable Development Goal indicators)</td></tr>
<tr><td>Functional</td><td>– "[…] Increase scientific knowledge, develop research capacity […]" (Target 14.a in the list of proposed Sustainable Development Goal indicators)
– "[…] mobilize and share knowledge, expertise […]" (Target 17.16 in the list of proposed Sustainable Development Goal indicators)</td></tr>
</table>

Table A2.1. *The political potential of EDIs in 2030 SDGs*

Dimensions and criteria		Examples of indicators
	Latent group	– "[…] adopt daily water-saving habits" – "[…] the recovery of water, its desalination, water efficiency, wastewater treatment, recycling reuse technologies […]" – "[…] make responsible consumer choices in favor of […]" – "[…] buy sustainably harvested seafood products, for example, products with an ecological label"
Environmental collective action	*Intermediate group*	– "The student is able to claim and publicly support […]" – "[…] running a campaign to raise awareness about […]" – "[…] the possibility of mobilization in view of […]" – "[…] consider volunteering […]" – "Holding an information stand in town, for example on World Peace Day […]" – "Planning and running an awareness campaign for […]" – "[…] denounce all forms of discrimination […]" – "Celebration of the International Day for […]" – "[…] management of an awareness campaign […]" – "The student is able to influence public policy […]" – "Campaign for energy savings […]" – "The student is capable of defending […]" – "planning, implementing and evaluating strategies to address inequalities […]" – "planning a political campaign or raising awareness aimed at […]" – "The student is able to make connections with community groups both locally and online […]" – "[…] to speak out in an organized way for or against decisions that […]" – "[…] promote approaches […]" – "The student is able to act in favor

Dimensions and criteria		Examples of indicators
Environmental collective action	*Intermediate group*	of those threatened [...]" – "Earth Day Celebration (April 22nd) and/or World Environment Day (June 5)" – "[...] associate with others who can help him promote [...]" – "Celebration of the International Day of Peace (September 21)"
Ecological citizenship	*Liberal*	– "[...] rights of access to economic resources, access to basic services, ownership and control of land and other property and natural resources [...]" – "[...] the right to land, property and goods and to natural resources"
	Post-cosmopolitan	– "[...] reduce your individual water footprint [...]" – "Establishment of an action plan for the local community to reduce energy [...]"
Deliberation	*Environmental technocracy*	– "[...] water and the green economy"
	Ecological	– "[...] negotiating the rights of different groups on the basis of shared values and ethical principles" – "[...] the need to find compromises in order to design improved and sustainable systems" – "[...] to work for the application and extension of the provisions of the Convention on International Trade in Endangered Species of Wild Fauna and Flora"
	Elementary	– "demonstrate empathy and solidarity with regard to [...]"
	Functional	– "The student understands the concepts of extreme poverty and relative poverty [...]" – "The student knows [...]" – "The student knows the causes and effects of [...]" – "The student knows that [...]"
		– "[...] capable of critical reflection on normative assumptions and practices" – "The student is capable of showing awareness of questions linked to [...]"

Dimensions and criteria		Examples of indicators
Environmental literacy	*Operational*	– "The student is conscious of his experience and personal biases regarding [...]" – "The student is able to critically reflect on his own role in maintaining structures [...]" – "The student is capable of planning, executing, assessing and reproducing activities [...]" – "Conducting a project based on a study with a topic [...]" – "The student is able to reflect on his own values and to be interested in values, attitudes and strategies different from his own in matters of [...]" – "The student is able to draw a global vision of what is [...]" – "The student is able to suggest ways to resolve any conflicts [...]" – "The student is able to increase teaching others about the importance of [...]" – "The student is able to recognize and question [...]" – "The student is able to identify in his/her culture and in his/her country the possibilities of more ecological approaches [...]" – "The student knows the historical reasons for the different forms [...]" – "The student feels responsible for the environmental and social consequences of his/her personal lifestyle" – "The student is able to determine whether his/her private and professional activities are non-hazardous for the climate and, if not, reassess them" – "[...] criticize the human/nature opposition and reflect on the fact that human beings are part of nature and not removed from it"

Table A2.2. *The political potential of EDIs in "Education for 2030 SDGs"*

Dimensions and criteria		Examples of contents
Disciplinary cognitive socialization (ecoliteracy)	*Technical*	– "The learner understands that water is part of many different complex global interrelationships and systems" (p. 22[2]) – "The learner understands the concept of Integrated Water Resources Management (IWRM) and other strategies for ensuring the availability and sustainable management of water and sanitation, including flood and drought risk management" (p. 22) – "The learner knows about different energy resources – renewable and non-renewable – and their respective advantages and disadvantages including environmental impacts, health issues, usage, safety and energy security, and their share in the energy mix at the local, national and global level" (p. 24) – "The learner knows about harmful impacts of unsustainable energy production, understands how renewable energy technologies can help to drive sustainable development and understands the need for new and innovative technologies and especially technology transfer in collaborations between countries" (p. 24) – "The learner understands the concepts of sustained, inclusive and sustainable economic growth, full and productive employment, and decent work, including the advancement of gender parity and equality, and knows about alternative economic models and indicators" (p. 26) – "The learner understands how innovation, entrepreneurship and new job creation can contribute to decent work and a sustainability-driven economy and to the decoupling of economic growth from the impacts of natural hazards and environmental degradation" (p. 26) – "The learner understands the concepts of sustainable infrastructure and industrialization and society's needs for a systemic approach to their development" (p. 28)

2 The page numbers refer to the contents of "Education for SDGs" (UNESCO 2017). Available at: https://unesdoc.unesco.org/ark:/48223/pf0000247444.

Dimensions and criteria		Examples of contents
Disciplinary cognitive socialization (ecoliteracy)	*Technical*	– "The learner can define the term resilience in the context of infrastructure and spatial planning, understanding key concepts such as modularity and diversity, and apply it to their local community and nationwide" (p. 28) – "The learner knows the basic principles of sustainable planning and building, and can identify opportunities for making their own area more sustainable and inclusive" (p. 32) – "The learner is able to evaluate and compare the sustainability of their and other settlements' systems in meeting their needs particularly in the areas of food, energy, transport, water, safety, waste treatment, inclusion and accessibility, education, integration of green spaces and disaster risk reduction" (p. 32) – "The learner understands production and consumption patterns and value chains and the interrelatedness of production and consumption (supply and demand, toxics, CO_2 emissions, waste generation, health, working conditions, poverty, etc.)" (p. 34) – "The learner understands the greenhouse effect as a natural phenomenon caused by an insulating layer of greenhouse gases" (p. 36) – "The learner understands the current climate change as an anthropogenic phenomenon resulting from increased greenhouse gas emissions" (p. 36) – "The learner knows which human activities – on a global, national, local and individual level – contribute most to climate change" (p. 36) – "The learner knows about the main ecological, social, cultural and economic consequences of climate change locally, nationally and globally and understands how these can themselves become catalyzing, reinforcing factors for climate change" (p. 36) – "The learner knows about prevention, mitigation and adaptation strategies at different levels (global to individual) and for different contexts and their connections with disaster response and disaster risk reduction" (p. 36) – "The learner understands basic marine ecology, ecosystems, predator–prey relationships, etc." (p. 38) – "The learner understands the connection of many

Dimensions and criteria		Examples of contents
Disciplinary cognitive socialization (ecoliteracy)	*Technical*	people to the sea and the life it holds, including the sea's role as a provider of food, jobs and exciting opportunities" (p. 38) – "The learner knows the basic premise of climate change and the role of the oceans in moderating our climate" (p. 38) – "The learner understands threats to ocean systems such as pollution and overfishing and recognizes and can explain the relative fragility of many ocean ecosystems including coral reefs and hypoxic dead zones" (p. 38) – "The learner knows about opportunities for the sustainable use of living marine resources" (p. 38) – "The learner understands basic ecology with reference to local and global ecosystems, identifying local species and understanding the measure of biodiversity" (p. 40) – "The learner understands the manifold threats posed to biodiversity, including habitat loss, deforestation, fragmentation, overexploitation and invasive species, and can relate these threats to their local biodiversity" (p. 40) – "The learner is able to classify the ecosystem services of the local ecosystems including supporting, provisioning, regulating and cultural services and ecosystems services for disaster risk reduction" (p. 40) – "The learner understands the slow regeneration of soil and the multiple threats that are destroying and removing it much faster than it can replenish itself, such as poor farming or forestry practice" (p. 40) – "The learner understands that realistic conservation strategies work outside pure nature reserves to also improve legislation, restore degraded habitats and soils, connect wildlife corridors, sustainable agriculture and forestry, and redress humanity's relationship to wildlife" (p. 40)
	Cultural	– "[...] to identify opportunities in their own culture and nation [...]" (p. 28)
	Critical	– "The learner knows the main drivers and root causes [...]" (p. 14)
Political socialization (citizenship)	*Adaptive*	– "Plan an awareness or political campaign [...]" (p. 31)
	Democratic-	– "The learner is able to take on critically their role as

Dimensions and criteria		Examples of contents
	critical	an active global citizen" (p. 14)
Critical cognitive socialization (deliberation)	*Consensus*	– "Have interfaith dialogues in schools and college campuses about [...]" (p. 43) – "[...] simulation games related to global conference negotiations [...]" (p. 45)
Democratic socialization (action regime)	*Minimalist*	– "Develop an enquiry-based project" (p. 13, p. 45) "Organize excursions and field trips [...]" (p. 15, p. 21, p. 25, p. 31, p. 41) – "Set up an information stand in the city [...]" (p. 17) – "Perform role plays" (p. 35, p. 37, p. 39, p. 43) "Organize an excursion [...]" (p. 43)
	Intermediate	– "Plan and run a student company selling fair trade products" (p. 13)
	Maximalist	– "Develop partnerships between schools and universities in different regions of the world (South and North; South and South)" (p. 13, p. 19) – "Develop school partnerships between schools in regions with abundance or scarcity of water" (p. 23) – "Develop partnerships or global web-based distance education experiences between schools, universities or other institutions in different regions of the world (South and North; South and South" (p. 45)

Table A2.3. *Political learning and socialization in "Education for 2030 SDGs"*

Appendix 3

Report on political elements in the Tunisian Curriculum

Levels	Metathemes and themes
1	None
2	*Sustainable development* Rational management of ecosystems: – *Objectives*: to identify the factors of damage to the ecosystem; propose appropriate solutions for the preservation of the environment; show the importance of recycling material in the functioning of the ecosystem. – *Content*: towards a rational management of the ecosystem, concept of sustainable development; negative actions of humans; destruction of plant cover; extension of urbanism; desertification; pollution; soil salinization; soil erosion; positive actions; reforestation; sand dune stabilization; wastewater treatment; protection of fauna and flora; national parks and nature reserves. – *Possible activities*: field observations and other information (survey conducted by students, Internet research, documents, etc.), recognizing the damage to the environment resulting from certain human activities; reflecting on a fundamental problem facing humankind, namely how to exploit the ecosystem without destroying it; proposing solutions for safeguarding or restoring the ecosystem and protection of the environment, as part of a sustainable development strategy; carrying out a project (waste recycling, biodiversity, sand dune stabilization, reforestation, school gardens, etc.).
3	*Sustainable development* – *Objectives*: to adopt healthy eating habits. – *Content*: food and sustainable development: - GMOs - organic farming

Levels	Metathemes and themes
3	– *Possible activities*: promote the traditional food of the region, presenting various traditional dishes and mentioning their ingredients to highlight their nutritional values and health benefits. Point out the harmful effects of quick snacks ("fast food", fried food, etc.) which are often harmful; define organic agriculture and cite the virtues of food produced by this agricultural practice; point out the existence of genetically modified organisms (GMOs) to improve plant quality and productivity and to fight against certain diseases (tobacco mosaic virus). The possible risks of their consumption should be discussed; the topic of food and sustainable development can be dealt with by the student in the form of a project.
4	*Sustainable development* Section 1: concept of sustainable development: – *Objectives*: to identify development as a process; show that growth is the economic basis for development and that development supports growth; show that the concept of "development" has evolved; define the concept of sustainable development. – *Content:* A) development and growth; B) development as an evolving concept. – *Additional indications*: show that the notion of development has evolved to integrate the human and environmental dimensions; show that this notion also takes into account the rational inter- and intra-generational dimension. Section 2: the components of sustainable development: – *Objectives*: to present material capital, human capital, social capital and natural capital; identify human development from the elements that compose it. Section 3: human development indicators: – *Objectives:* to show that the Human Development Index (HDI) makes it possible to rank countries and compare their level of human development; identify other indicators to assess the level of human development. – *Content*: A) the HDI; B) other human development indicators. – *Additional indications*: note that the HDI is a composite indicator; use statistical data to identify inequalities in human development; refer to the gender-specific human development participation and the human poverty indicator.

Table A3.1. *Collected EDIs in secondary education requirements*

<table>
<tr><td colspan="2">Dates: February 11, 13 and 14, 2019</td><td>Place: Bir El Hafey High School – Sidi Bouzid – Tunisia</td></tr>
<tr><td colspan="3">EDIs (metatheme): Sustainable development</td></tr>
<tr><td colspan="3">Themes: Natural resource management</td></tr>
<tr><td colspan="3">Contents evoked in processing the EDIs</td></tr>
<tr><td>Environmental collective action</td><td>Latent group</td><td>Humans can produce what they need while respecting the balance of the ecosystem</td></tr>
<tr><td>Environmental citizenship</td><td>Liberal</td><td>The environment offers sustainable development, which in turn offers a pleasant living environment for all</td></tr>
<tr><td>Environmental literacy</td><td>Elementary</td><td>Ecosystem components: biodiversity and natural resources</td></tr>
<tr><td>Learning of ecoliteracy</td><td>Technical</td><td>To ensure sustainable development, human development must be ensured according to the components of the HDI by optimally meeting the needs of current and future generations and by safeguarding the environment</td></tr>
<tr><td>Learning of citizenship</td><td>Individualist</td><td>Promotion of development</td></tr>
<tr><td>Learning in action plans</td><td>Minimalist</td><td>Inter-comprehension between stakeholders is supposed to be instantaneous</td></tr>
</table>

Table A3.2. *Curriculum elements produced in secondary level education: direct observation*

<table>
<tr><th>Groups</th><th>Identifiers</th><th>Dates</th><th>Duration</th><th>Course of events</th></tr>
<tr><td>Teachers</td><td>Te_2</td><td>First contact: November 11, 2018
Interview: March 10, 2019</td><td>46 minutes</td><td>Individual direct</td></tr>
<tr><td rowspan="2">Students</td><td>St_1</td><td>First contact: February 14, 2019
Interview: February 18, 2019</td><td>32 minutes</td><td>Individual direct</td></tr>
<tr><td>St_2</td><td>First contact: February 14, 2019
Interview: February 18, 2019</td><td>35 minutes</td><td>Individual direct</td></tr>
</table>

Table A3.3. *Interviews: characterization*

Te_2
General information
Te_2 holds a master's degree in economics. He has been teaching economics in high schools for 15 years. *Te_2* considers the importance of the issue of sustainable development as a fundamental issue in the curriculum of 4th grade Economics and Management. The contents of this program are articulated through the notions of development, economic growth and globalization.
EDI themes involved
"Of course we need to have an idea about the management of natural resources to be able to talk about conserving them and fighting against the depletion and overexploitation of these resources and environmental damage. The student should lean towards thinking that these resources are essential for production and that future generations also have the right to exploit them. All this is in fact related to the concept of the environment as a natural capital that the students will encounter in management with the notion of the business environment as a resource for the business which includes several variables. Yes, the student must know that good management of natural resources is necessary to ensure the development of present generations and to give future generations the possibility of development. I think that the topic of economic growth is very important to teach sustainable development; it is fundamental even to fight against the costs of growth. The student must also know that without economic growth, sustainable development is impossible, and in the other sense, sustainable development ensures the sustainability of economic growth, i.e. sustainable development supports long-term economic growth. In fact, the objective of sustainable development is to meet the basic needs of the population."
Contents evoked in processing the EDIs
Environmental literacy "For the elementary components of the natural and social systems here it is clear that the natural and social pillars are considered as a starting point and this is important in the content of the curricula. Also, for the types of interactions between man and nature it is obligatory to go through this idea. Nature provides the natural resources to ensure the productive capacities required to satisfy basic needs, but man must also respect nature and the environment to ensure the sustainability of its development." *Environmental deliberations mentioned* "No, we don't mention these things in the content on sustainable development, except for a mere reference to the Brundtland report, but it's only a reference." *Environmental actions* "No, we don't even talk about clean-up measures. We talk about the negative effects of pollution on the environment but we do not look for solutions to avoid them." *Ecological citizenship (behaviors mentioned)* "Here we sometimes give examples. I remember that I mentioned the example of the claims of citizens in reaction to oil mill waste or factory waste in the region of Gabes."

Pedagogical aspects in processing the EDIs
Learning of citizenship (behaviors encouraged, general objectives) "Here I imagine that these are the objectives of the program. Already in the general objectives of these programs the student must explore his environment." *Learning of ecoliteracy* "For example, when we talk about human development that involves the means of human well-being. But we don't talk about models of development. We talk about the components of the development index without calculating it. The notion of economic growth with basic needs are essential concepts for building the notion of sustainable development which includes the notion of improving living standards." *Deliberative learning* "No. The discussion does not focus on the notion of sustainable development itself. I don't think the student has the background to get into a discussion. It's actually little notions that he's trying to put together to come up with the idea of sustainable development. Usually the student doesn't discuss this side, nor the notion itself. I don't think there's any scope for discussion." *Learning in action plans* "The activity of the students consisted in reading documents from the school textbook and answering the questions noted, which were oriented towards the objectives of constructing the notions of development and sustainable development."
St_1
General information
St_1 is a student enrolled in the 4th year of Economics and Management in a high school in the governorate of Sidi Bouzid (Tunisia). St_1 considers the importance of the question of sustainable development in that it allows him to enrich knowledge on the environment with a scientific vocabulary.
EDI themes involved
"Consumption of products that do not harm the environment"
Contents evoked in processing the EDIs
Environmental literacy "Climate change through energy use can cause pollution. This pollution has negative effects because it can cause disease. Man is an agent of pollution." *Environmental deliberations mentioned* "No, we don't have any examples of discussions." *Environmental actions* "No, we haven't talked about actions of this type, but I know that you can recycle paper and cardboard and plastics to produce bottles, for example, and I found this on the Internet." *Ecological citizenship (behaviors mentioned)* "When you protect the environment, you get a clean environment. This is a human right, such as the right to life and the right to health."

Pedagogical aspects in processing the EDIs
Learning of citizenship (behaviors encouraged, general objectives) "The voluntary commitment of the individual makes it possible to achieve development; the State, through its political and economic power, can intervene through laws to encourage this commitment." *Learning of ecoliteracy* "Sustainable development can ensure the well-being of the individual. The Human Development Index is a measure of progress towards well-being. Sustainable development cannot be achieved without economic growth." *Deliberative learning* "No, we didn't discuss with different points of view." *Learning in a collective action plan* "We did written activities from the textbook and we answered the questions asked of us."
St_2
General information
St_2 is a student enrolled in the 4th year of Economics and Management in a high school in the governorate of Sidi Bouzid (Tunisia). St_2 considers the importance of the issue of sustainable development in relation to her interest in natural resources, human, nature and wealth creation in protecting the environment.
EDI themes involved
"The management of natural resources"
Content evoked in processing the EDIs
Environmental literacy "Human activity, be it production or consumption, generates pollution such as the discharge of household waste, which can cause water pollution by wastewater. The overexploitation by man of natural resources in industry pollutes the soil and the atmosphere and can cause diseases." *Environmental deliberations mentioned* "None." *Environmental actions* "No, we did not mention any such action." *Ecological citizenship (behaviors mentioned)* "Countries must intervene to ensure that companies are regulated in their activities. The industrial zones must be far away from people's living environments."
Pedagogical aspects in processing the EDIs
Learning of citizenship (behaviors encouraged, general objectives) "To awaken a sense of responsibility and solidarity on the persistence of poverty. Participation in improving the living environment and above all in reducing pollution and its effects." *Learning of ecoliteracy* "Human development provides the means for well-being and health, which are human rights. It ensures conditions favorable to the human condition, like a healthy environment." *Deliberative learning* "No. No discussion." *Learning in a collective action plan* "We made notes on what the teacher said, having read a document from the book, and responded to the questions asked."

Table A3.4. *Interviews: summaries*

Te_2	St_1	St_2	**List A: Sustainable development themes**
X		X	Management of natural resources
	X		Consumption of products that do not harm (endanger) the environment
			Environmental problems as a consequence of power relations (domination)
			Collective ownership of production: a perspective for environmental sustainability
			Domination of nature and women by men as a root cause of environmental problems
Te_2	**St_1**	**St_2**	**List B: Environmental knowledge mentioned**
X			Elementary components of natural and social systems (living components, non-living components, etc.)
X	X	X	Types and examples of interactions between human and nature
			Appreciation of nature and society
			Empathy (benevolence, sympathy) towards nature and society
			Ecological, economic, geographic, political, cultural and educational processes
			The impact of beliefs and values on environmental issues
			Cultural values and historical perspectives in dealing with environmental issues
			Environmental awareness and sensitivity
Te_2	**St_1**	**St_2**	**List C: Environmental discussions raised**
			Adaptation to irreversibly engaged environmental dynamics
			Consensus (agreements) and conventions developed through international conferences and declarations
			Dialogues involving experts and citizens in direct experiences and local knowledge
Te_2	**St_1**	**St_2**	**List D: Environmental actions mentioned**
			Recycling of waste
			Purchase of ecological products
			Membership of environmental associations
			Attending gatherings and signing petitions (requests, complaints) in favor of environmental causes

Te_2	St_1	St_2	**List E: Environmental behaviors mentioned**
X	X	X	Claiming (demanding, claiming, requesting) rights to a healthy environment
			Recognizing the duties of participation in challenges (disputes) against any destructive aspect of development
			Recognizing environmental responsibility as a requirement of cosmopolitan justice
			Recognizing environmental citizen responsibility in terms of unavoidable political contestation between adversaries (non-enemies)
Te_2	**St_1**	**St_2**	**List F: General objectives**
X	X	X	Being a participatory citizen and promoter (initiator) of development
			Being a responsible citizen who acts responsibly in the community
			Being a cooperative citizen and being concerned about social justice
Te_2	**St_1**	**St_2**	**List G: Specific objectives**
X	X	X	Building relevant (suitable) scientific knowledge for addressing societal issues
			Identifying the values of nature according to cultures, as well as the cultural elements supporting environmental sustainability
			Determining the roles of the economy in structuring power relations (domination)
Te_2	**St_1**	**St_2**	**List H: Types of discussions conducted**
			End result is a teacher's point of view
			Achieving consensus (agreement) between the different points of view
			Defense of opposing perspectives (which remain in dispute)
Te_2	**St_1**	**St_2**	**List I: Types of actions carried out by pupils or students**
X	X	X	The activities are presented separately
			The activities are undertaken in a club
			The activities are carried out with a commitment to a common project with the local community

Table A3.5. *Interviews: help lists*

<table>
<tr><th>Semesters</th><th>Metathemes and themes</th></tr>
<tr><td>1</td><td>None</td></tr>
<tr><td>2</td><td>None</td></tr>
<tr><td>3</td><td>Evolution of the Earth and the living world, biodiversity and conservation biology
Environmental ethics
Values and ethics
– Instrumental value
- Goods and services
- Scientific, socio-economic and cultural values
– Aesthetic and recreational value (ecotourism)
– Ethical value
Sustainable development
– Biodiversity and sustainable development: climatology and environment, cartography, remote sensing and geographic information system
Environmental politics
Climate change and environmental impact
– Global risks: air pollution, global warming, ozone, greenhouse effect
– Water-related risks: floods, drought and desertification
– Risks related to air dynamics: air pollution, strong winds, cyclones, tornadoes
– Climate, epidemics and emerging diseases
– Impact of climate change on biodiversity</td></tr>
<tr><td>4</td><td>1) Bioethics/biosafety
2) Geomorphology and landscape – Geo-resources: water, soil
Concept of layout
Environmental politics
– Hydraulic installations (dams, aqueducts, sewerage and drainage systems, treatment plants, etc.)
– Development and protection of the natural environment (protection of coasts, fighting against erosion and desertification, quarries, deposits, landfill sites, etc.)
– Urban planning and quality of life in an urban environment
– Measures and means of soil protection
– Impacts of mineral and energy resource transformation and recovery processes on air quality (cement plants, oil refineries, phosphate treatment plants, etc.)
– Impacts of oil spills on terrestrial environments and marine ecosystems</td></tr>
</table>

<table>
<tr><th>Semesters</th><th>Metathemes and themes</th></tr>
<tr><td>4</td><td>3) Pollution, pollutants, environmental technologies
Environmental technologies and management
Pollution and environmental consequences
– Nature, origin, diversity and classification of pollutants
– Air pollution
– Soil pollution
– Water pollution
– Pollution by solid waste
– Nuclear pollution
– Pollutants and health
– Water treatment techniques
– Solid waste treatment (air emission treatment)
– Environmental biotechnology
– Preventive fight against pollution (renewable energies, biodegradable materials)
– Quality and environmental standards: discharge standards in the receiving environment, ISO certification standards
4) Quality, standards, environmental and metrology
Environmental politics
– Environmental legislation
– Labels, Ecolabel, Ecotex, organic production
– International conventions
– Biodiversity regulatory framework
– Conservation in situ
5) Protected areas policy
6) Nature reserves and protected areas: nomenclature, diversity, distribution, management and functions
7) National parks and biosphere reserves
8) Reintroduction and reinforcement of natural populations
9) Participatory approach to biodiversity conservation
– Ex-situ conservation
10) Botanical gardens
11) Zoological parks
12) Gene banks</td></tr>
</table>

Table A3.6. *Collected EDIs in 2009 higher education curricula*

Semesters	Metathemes and themes
1	None
2	*Ecology and environment* Objectives: the program provides basic training on the ecology and pollution present in the world and in Tunisia, as well as the impact of this natural and essentially anthropic pollution on ecosystems. The program also provides important knowledge relating to environmental protection through the application of international conventions and legal and regulatory measures applied in Tunisia. The objectives are as follows: – to provide students with scientific knowledge about ecosystems and the economic interests they can provide to humans – to introduce students to rigorous and critical scientific access to pollution and remediation issues – to establish a scientific basis for the actions necessary to protect and improve the conservation and sustainable use of ecosystems Course program Introduction 1) Ecology and the environment: definition 2) Humans and the environment – Human's relationship with the environment: history – Human's impact on the environment – Demography (evolution of the world population) – Population and resources (renewable/non-renewable) – Consumption and overconsumption – Ecological footprint – Sustainable development 3) Notion of the ecological system: ecosystem – Biodiversity and its geographical distribution – The ecological organization of biodiversity: biomes and ecosystems – Ecosystem benefits (values and use) 4) Ecosystem damage – Introduction – Origin of the damage Natural causes Anthropogenic causes Point source pollution Household waste Industrial waste Livestock effluents Diffuse pollution Chemical fertilizers Pesticides

Semesters	Metathemes and themes
2	Atmospheric emissions Acid rain The extractive industry (hydrocarbons, nuclear and mining) Overexploitation (overfishing, hunting, gathering) Deforestation Urban planning 5) Some vulnerable ecosystems in Tunisia 6) Consequences of pollution - On water resources - On the ground - On biodiversity - On the biology and behavior of living beings - On the deterioration of the landscape and heritage - On the deterioration of the ozone layer - Greenhouse effect - Global changes - On human health - On economic and socio-economic aspects (the main beneficiaries of ecosystems will be discussed here) 7) Pollution: management and control - Solid waste management and treatment (including landfilling, recycling, etc.) - Effluent treatment - Renewable energy - Natural reserves -Awareness-raising and associative activities (being responsible, ecological without overdoing it, buying ecological, biodegradable, non-toxic objects, etc.) - Environmental ethics 8) Legal and institutional measures for the protection of the environment in Tunisia - Application of international conventions - The RAMSAR Convention - The Convention on Biological Diversity (CBD) - The OSPAR Convention - The United Nations Convention to Combat Desertification (UNCCD) - The Barcelona Convention (1976) as amended - The United Nations Framework Convention on Climate Change (UNFCCC) - Legal and regulatory measures relating to environmental protection in Tunisia

Semesters	Metathemes and themes
2	- Creation of specific organizations - *Agence nationale de protection de l'environnement* – ANPE (1988) - *Office national d'assainissement* – ONAS (1974), restructured in 1993 - *Agence de protection et d'aménagement du littoral* – APAL (1995) - *Banque nationale de Gènes* – BNG (2003) - *Agence nationale de gestion des déchets* – ANGED (2005) - Implementation of legislative and regulatory texts related to environmental protection - Maritime public domain - Water and soil conservation - National emergency response plan for marine pollution events - Waste and the control of its management and disposal - Air quality Tutorial program – Food production and environmental protection: agroecosystems, comparison with natural ecosystems, global needs, issues specific to Tunisia, improvement of agricultural yield, crop treatment, impact on health, solutions (integrated pest management, organic agriculture, permaculture, etc.) – Screening of a documentary on an environmental issue + reflective questionnaire – Figures relating to the measurement of environmental parameters (microbiological, physico-chemical, etc.) concerning, for example, treated effluents (data before and after treatment), conclusion on the effectiveness of the treatment, discussion on the type of treatment according to the nature of the effluent, environmental consequences, concepts of standards and monitoring/control – Presentation by an environmental specialist (teacher, researcher, expert, association, etc.) – Seminar: presentation of topics Practical program – Ecological footprint: individual calculation of the ecological footprint following a pre-established question + discussion of the results, inter-student comparison with the ecological footprint of different countries – Visits to some vulnerable ecosystems: lagoons of Ghar El Melh, Bizerte and others; sampling of fauna and flora – Analysis of the output sampling, identifying species (based on determination keys), carrying out specimen collection, evaluating biodiversity, comparing biodiversity with other equivalent but preserved ecosystems – Seminar: presentation of topics

<table>
<tr><th>Semesters</th><th>Metathemes and themes</th></tr>
<tr><td>2</td><td>In groups, the students, following the bibliography, develop critical analysis in the general public concerning a current pollution problem and the measures taken to protect ecosystems (citation of texts of conventions, laws, decrees, regulations, etc.). They present their presentation orally and are thus evaluated on a piece of synthesis work, which will be done in groups (three at the most)</td></tr>
<tr><td>3</td><td>Animal biology/biodiversity and sustainable development
Objectives: to learn about the diversity and bio-ecology of different zoological groups belonging to the Deuterostomians. This information allows the student to expand on the biological knowledge acquired during L1 and to have a broad idea of the whole living animal world and the distinctive features that differentiate them. The student is also expected to understand the kinship relationships (phylogeny) between different groups of vertebrates
Biodiversity and conservation biology
Introduction: Notion of biodiversity
Chapter 1: Scales of biodiversity
– Genetic
– Specific
– Ecological
Chapter 2: Values and ethics
– Instrumental value
- Goods and services
- Scientific, socio-economic and cultural values
– Aesthetic and recreational values (ecotourism)
– Ethical values
Chapter 3: Characteristics of the geographical distribution of biodiversity (cosmopolitan, endemic, rare species, etc.).
Chapter 4: Dynamics of biodiversity renewal
Chapter 5: Anthropogenic disturbances of biodiversity
– Exploitation and overexploitation
– Depletion and extinction
– Introductions of non-native species and interactions with native species
– Development, fragmentation, transformation of and damage to habitats
– Pollution and environmental degradation
– Impact of climate change (global effects)
Chapter 6: Biodiversity assessment (the interest of inventories, the techniques used)
Chapter 7: Biodiversity and sustainable development
Chapter 8: Biodiversity and the regulatory framework
Chapter 9: Conservation biology</td></tr>
</table>

Semesters	Metathemes and themes
3	1) Notion of conservation biology 2) *In situ* – Protected areas policy - Nature reserves and protected areas: nomenclature, diversity, distribution, management and functions - National parks and biosphere reserves - Reintroduction and reinforcement of natural populations - Participatory approach to biodiversity conservation 3) *Ex-situ* conservation – Botanical gardens – Zoological parks – Gene banks
4	*Climatology/geo-resources* Climate change and environmental impact 1) Global risks: air pollution, global warming, ozone, greenhouse effect 2) Water-related risks: floods, drought and desertification 3) Risks related to air dynamics: atmospheric pollution, strong winds, cyclones, tornadoes 4) Climate, epidemics and emerging diseases *Pollution/ecotoxicology/environmental technologies* Objectives: – To master the fundamental knowledge on the treatment of different types of waste from various sectors of human activity – To understand the principles of environmental technologies and the potentialities of their application – To acquire know-how in the treatment of discharge and waste as well as environmental protection Pollution and environmental consequences – Nature, origin, diversity and classification of pollutants – Air pollution – Soil pollution – Water pollution – Pollution by solid waste – Nuclear pollution – Pollutants and health – Water treatment techniques – Solid waste treatment (air emission treatment) – Environmental biotechnology – Preventive fight against pollution (renewable energies, biodegradable materials)

Table A3.7. *Collected EDIs in the 2015 higher education curricula (restructured in 2016 and 2017)*

Date: December 15, 2018		**Place: ISSBAT – Tunis – Tunisia**
EDIs (metatheme): Sustainable development		
Themes: Natural resource management		
Contents evoked in processing the EDIs		
Environmental collective action	*Latent group*	Efforts to preserve natural resources for environmental purposes
	Intermediate group	Membership of environmental organizations is mentioned
	Post-cosmopolitan	Ecological footprint as a requirement to reduce the consumption of environmental goods
Deliberation	*Technocracy*	Specialists in environmental management develop management plans that are like decrees: these specialists are environmental physicians
Environmental literacy	*Elementary*	Ecosystem components Human–nature interactions
	Functional	Environmental problem analysis skills
	Operational	Skills in assessing the impacts of human activities on the environment and developing assessment tools and environmental management plans
Pedagogical aspects		
Ecoliteracy	*Technical*	Ecosystem dynamics and quality following a restoration or operational development
	Cultural	The protection of species of "cultural interest" is mentioned; for example, the craft of bangle-making in several regions of Tunisia
Citizenship	*Adaptive*	Adopt a participatory approach to environmental and social management plans
Action plans	*Minimalist*	Inter-comprehension between stakeholders as supposedly instantaneous

<table>
<tr><th colspan="2">Date: April 11, 2019</th><th>Place: ISSBAT – Tunis – Tunisia</th></tr>
<tr><th colspan="3">EDIs (metatheme): Environmental politics and changes</th></tr>
<tr><th colspan="3">Subjects: Pollution</th></tr>
<tr><th colspan="3">Contents evoked in processing the EDIs</th></tr>
<tr><td>Environmental collective action</td><td>Latent group</td><td>Efforts to preserve natural resources for environmental purposes</td></tr>
<tr><td>Deliberation</td><td>Environmental technocracy</td><td>Specialists in environmental management establish management plans like environmental physicians</td></tr>
<tr><td rowspan="2">Environmental literacy</td><td>Elementary</td><td>Ecosystem components
Human–nature interactions</td></tr>
<tr><td>Functional</td><td>Environmental problem analysis skills</td></tr>
<tr><th colspan="3">Pedagogical aspects</th></tr>
<tr><td>Ecoliteracy</td><td>Technical</td><td>Knowledge on the organization and functioning of ecosystems</td></tr>
<tr><td>Citizenship</td><td>Adaptive</td><td>Adopt a participatory approach to environmental and social management plans</td></tr>
<tr><td>Action plans</td><td>Minimalist</td><td>Inter-comprehension between stakeholders is supposed to be instantaneous</td></tr>
</table>

Table A3.8. *Elements of the produced curriculum of the environmental protection degree: direct observation*

Groups	Identifiers	Dates	Duration	Course of events
Teachers	Te_1	– First contact: September 14, 2018 – Interview: January 08, 2019 and April 16, 2019	44 minutes + 4 minutes (= 48 minutes)	Individual via telephone
Students	St_1	– First contact: December 15, 2018 – Interview: January 05, 2019	38 minutes	Individual via telephone

Groups	Identifiers	Dates	Duration	Course of events
	St_2	– First contact: December 15, 2018 – Interview: January 06, 2019	38 minutes	Individual via telephone
	St_3	– First contact: December 15, 2018 – Interview: January 06, 2019	35 minutes	Individual via telephone
	St_4	– First contact: April 11, 2019 – Interview: April 14, 2019	32 minutes	Individual via telephone
	St_5	– First contact: April 11, 2019 – Interview: April 14, 2019	35 minutes	Individual via telephone
	St_6	– First contact: April 11, 2019 – Interview: April 14, 2019	31 minutes	Individual via telephone

Table A3.9. *Interviews: characterization*

Te_1
General information
Te_1 is a lecturer at the University of Tunis El Manar (Tunis). He holds a PhD and a postdoctoral degree in biology. His field of expertise is ecology. He has 14 years of experience in Tunisian higher education. *Te_1* considers that sustainable development plays a minor role in the education of Tunisian students and has not taken on the scale it deserves. It is always linked to other concepts such as those of biodiversity, conservation biology and environmental management, and it is mainly at the terminal level of the environmental protection degree or at the master's level that this issue is addressed.
EDI themes involved
Sustainable development primarily concerns the management of natural resources and the consumption of non-hazardous products. "In my courses, I focus on resource management, and I have a module called wildlife management that I teach for the students of the GBR course. Even the consumption of

products, I don't put too much emphasis on that. I deal with this issue in relation to environmental themes such as anthropogenic activities, which students are introduced to in their first year. They study anthropization, pollution and global changes. This is important because students receive an introduction to this theme. Also, as far as sustainable development is concerned, I propose deepening the other concepts associated with it, such as those of biodiversity and the management of bioresources."

"For the ecology and environment module, I can summarize it in three points: what is ecology, the definition of pollution and a little about the notion of sustainable development at the end. In fact, it prepares students for the second-year modules. We just deal with the definitions to familiarize them with the jargon of ecology and the environment and everything related to pollution. It should be understood that ecology and environmental science are different but complementary. Generally, the focus is on notions of global ecology and global changes such as eutrophication and acid rain. We define terms such as 'greenhouse gases', 'ozone layer', 'aquatic pollution', 'biological pollution' which are related to what is now called global changes, looking mainly at the origins of pollution and its categories and impacts."

Contents evoked in processing the EDIs

Environmental literacy

"First of all, there are the elemental components, biotic and abiotic composts, and that's part of biodiversity or biodiversity ecology. Secondly, the types of interactions between man and nature, because it is man who really manages this stock of resources, so we need to know these interactions between man and nature. We need to study global changes, pollution. That is to say, how man influences the stability of these bioresources. Thirdly, the evaluation of the degradation of the state of nature, degraded or moderately degraded. In very few cases I deal with cultural values. Concerning the impact of beliefs and other types of knowledge I avoid them because I think that the students themselves are not ready to deal with these issues and there is no point in doing so. As I see it, the course is 80 percent technical knowledge. We train the students to be good technicians, and I support the idea of strengthening the technical side without including other points of view from women and others. What I see and also what they impose on us are these technical axes more so than a social relationship with sustainable development and a distant vision. We look under our feet and we try to make them learn technical terms."

Contents evoked in processing the EDIs

Environmental deliberations mentioned

"There are international agreements and conventions and that's already required by the program. In Tunisia we have Ichkeul, which is a biosphere reserve. We evoke what is called participatory ecology. The human population living in Ichkeul must adapt to the dynamics of its environment. One cannot foresee a management plan for Ichkeul without foreseeing a plan that integrates mankind. The ecosystem is a changing unit in space and time and even in the international conventions automatically man is part of its ecosystem. Even in a park there is a part that allows human life."

Environmental actions

"I insist on membership of environmental associations because of their importance and also because it is a source of employment for students by helping them find jobs. In fact, recycling waste, purchasing ecological products, all three can be considered environmental management methods."

Ecological citizenship (behaviors mentioned)

"For example, the ecological footprint, we're told that to maintain human food supplies at the current rate we would need 4 planets. That is to say, we have to be aware of these global problems. But we don't talk about the behavior of political protesters. We talk about the fair ecological footprint only to justify the reasons for which the international conventions have been developed. In fact, this question brings me to the slogan: we think globally and act locally. That's what I try to make my students understand, above all else."

Pedagogical aspects in processing the EDIs

Learning of citizenship (behaviors encouraged, general objectives)

"The general objectives are set for the entire learning program by targeting technical training. I encourage my students to participate in associations, to be active in society. The students are taught that they are environmental physicians. I push them to be active, essentially so that they can find work after university education."

Learning of ecoliteracy

"We are in the process of training technicians. The emphasis is on the management of bioresources. What interests us most is ecological, that is, the ecological functions of the environment are water, air and soil, which are sensitive to disturbances. Biodiversity is defined as bioresources that can be managed. In fact, we are teaching classical ecology or general ecology. We're not dealing with issues of modern ecology such as landscape ecology, for example. But really, it's a bit restricted to technical terms. In fact, we teach more physics and chemistry than environmental or ecological ideas."

Pedagogical aspects in processing the EDIs

Deliberative learning

"There was no discussion. In fact, the students did not get the training or the skills that enable them to be involved in such a discussion. Usually students move on to the teacher's point of view. They do not have an attitude towards environmental safety or the conservation of environmental matrices."

Learning in action plans

"The students didn't actually do anything. In fact, I know that there was a small project that existed before but the students dropped it for several reasons."

St_1

General information

St_1 2nd year of the applied degree in environmental protection at ISSBAT (Tunis).

St_1 considers the importance of the issue of sustainable development insofar as it affects natural resources, humankind and nature.

EDI themes involved

"For example, energy management such as renewable energy, solar energy and water. The other themes relate to the issue of sustainable development but I really can't find any examples."

Contents evoked in processing the EDIs

Environmental literacy

"Since man went from being a predator to a mutualist, there was a cooperative relationship between man and the other components of nature."

Environmental deliberations mentioned

"That is to say, when it comes to environmental problems, how human beings adapt to sustainably maintain biological resources."

Environmental actions

"For example, the manufacture of environmentally friendly means of transport and cars that do not pollute the air. Buying products that have the least environmental impact, i.e. that do not cause environmental damage."

Ecological citizenship (behaviors mentioned)

"For example, the right to clean air, because companies contribute to global warming with air pollution, deforestation and water pollution; that's why we need the right to protect the environment."

Pedagogical aspects in processing the EDIs

Citizenship learning (behaviors encouraged, general objectives)

"For example, we must participate in all environmental fields to improve our environment and be an ecological and environmental doctor like a doctor for human beings."

Learning of ecoliteracy

"For example, the societal question of pollution in the environment or that of the overexploitation of biodiversity through sampling and the calculation of indices relating to physicochemical parameters such as the salinity of soils and seas."

Deliberative learning

"We did not have a discussion. In fact, we were guided by the teacher who told us about treating our environment well, having very precise guidelines, knowing the factors that lead to the bad development of environmental phenomena and treating them well like doctors."

Learning in a collective action plan

"We listened carefully to the teacher."

St_2

General information

St_2 has a bachelor's degree in mathematics. He is enrolled in the 2nd year applied degree in environmental protection at ISSBAT (Tunis).

St_2 considers the importance of the question of development in its impact on natural resources that are being exhausted.

EDI themes involved

"In the management of natural resources, we have solar energy, harnessed by panels, wind energy and hydraulic energy, which are renewable energies that we can use."

Contents evoked in processing the EDIs
Environmental literacy "The interactions between man and nature, such as hunting and fishing, have been well studied. Several countries such as Kenya, Costa Rica and Nepal exploit nature by way of tourist activities such as ecotourism." *Environmental deliberations mentioned* "The example of the consensus developed in the COP meetings." *Environmental actions mentioned* "Membership of the World Wildlife Fund and Greenpeace has focused on special interest species as well as key species in biological terms such as pandas, elephants and seals. They are in the process of protecting these species."
Contents evoked in processing the EDIs
Ecological citizenship (behaviors mentioned) "We talked about hunters who claim the right to a clean environment."
Pedagogical aspects in processing the EDIs
Learning of citizenship (behaviors encouraged, general objectives) "In fact, it is our specialty which is the protection of the environment bioresources. The teacher encourages us to participate and to be promoters of development. The teacher encourages us to participate and promote development." *Learning of ecoliteracy* "There is the problem of pesticides that must be avoided because they damage the soil and the biodiversity of beneficial organisms, such as earthworms, and the problem of protecting biodiversity by controlling the specific and ecological diversity to avoid the dysfunction of ecosystems." *Deliberative learning* "In fact, we did not have a discussion. The teacher was mainly concerned with the principles of biodiversity conservation and more precisely the 7 principles of conservation biology." *Learning in a collective action plan* "We took notes on the information presented by the teacher."
St_3
General information
St_3 has a bachelor's degree in experimental sciences. He is enrolled in the 2nd year of the applied degree in environmental protection at ISSBAT (Tunis). *St_3* considers the importance of the issue of development as a means of conserving natural resources for present and future generations.
EDI themes involved
The sustainable development topic is about natural resource management "For example, in the plant world, algae are capable of producing lipids and biofuels, which we can draw on when the stock of fossil fuels runs out."

Contents evoked in processing the EDIs
Environmental literacy "Man acts in a direct and indirect way on the environment, for example when he overfishes or overhunts. In doing so he depletes a whole stock of game fauna and fish resources. There is also the conversion of land and other projects to build bridges or to meet food needs."
Contents evoked in processing the EDIs
Environmental deliberations mentioned "For example, among the international conferences that we have talked about, there is the COP to look for solutions to environmental problems." *Environmental actions mentioned* "For example how people deal with waste by following steps and studying the impact of projects to minimize waste and its effects on the environment." *Ecological citizenship: evoked behaviors* "We have spoken of the ANPE as an organization that can intervene against facilities that are harmful to the environment and the surrounding area by damaging them. Also, when highways crossing forests are planned, people can exert pressure."
Pedagogical aspects in processing the EDIs
Learning of citizenship (behaviors encouraged, general objectives) "We can be protectors of the environment and nature and we can participate in impact studies to prevent or minimize the effects on the ecosystem." *Learning of ecoliteracy* "For example, on the problem of damage to forests, the impact study of projects helps to prevent them from being damaged. These impacts must be identified by using sampling methods to calculate biodiversity indices and draw a diagram of it." *Deliberative learning* "During this session we did not have a discussion. We were guided by the teacher insofar as we are concerned with the conservation of natural resources as stocks are depleted to ensure the maintenance and sustainable use of biological resources for humanity." *Learning in a collective action plan* "We were writing down the information presented by our teacher, who does his best to make us understand the concepts in the session. He provides us with examples for each idea."
St_4
General information
St_4 has a bachelor's degree in experimental sciences. He is enrolled in the 1st year of the common core curriculum in life and environmental sciences at ISSBAT (Tunis). The teaching unit "ecology and environment" is his choice of major for the "environmental protection" degree.

General information
St_4 attaches great importance to the study of environmental issues since it helps to protect the environment, preserve the future of humanity and raise awareness of the importance of this preservation for survival.
EDI themes involved
"Scientific study of global environmental changes (ecological modernization)"
Contents evoked in processing the EDIs
Environmental literacy "We looked at the components of natural systems such as water, soil and air, species and biodiversity. Also, we looked at the consequences of pollution on animals and humans, for example, diseases caused by air pollution such as respiratory disorders." *Environmental deliberations mentioned* "For example, in Morocco, there is an environmental code. In Tunisia, too, a code is being discussed and it will soon see the light of day. This type of code requires asking for permission from environmental experts before doing construction work to see if it affects bioresources." *Environmental actions* "For example, instead of buying products treated with pesticides that are toxic to the soil, people buy organic products such as vegetables from fields where farmers use natural animal waste as fertilizer." *Ecological citizenship (behaviors mentioned)* "In Tunisia, in the region of Gabes, people there claim and demand their right to an unpolluted environment but they did not protest to stop work in factories which pollute the atmosphere with the toxic gases they release."
Pedagogical aspects in processing the EDIs
Learning of citizenship (behaviors encouraged, general objectives) "To be a citizen who does not litter in the streets and makes people aware of the consequences of pollution and the destruction of environmental resources such as soil, water and air, especially by plastics which are difficult to degrade." *Learning of ecoliteracy* "The causes and consequences of pollution; for example, the pollution of waste water not treated according to the required standards and used for irrigation causes parasites to enter the human food chain."
Pedagogical aspects in processing the EDIs
Deliberative learning "No, because it's our first time studying a subject like this, so we can't discuss what we don't know." *Learning in a collective action plan* "We were studying this optional subject and taking notes."

St_5
General information
St₅ has a bachelor's degree in experimental sciences. He is enrolled in the 1st year core curriculum with a specialization in life and environmental sciences at ISSBAT (Tunis). The unit "ecology and environment" is his choice of major for the "environmental protection" degree. *St₅* thinks that the study of environmental issues is very important because we must know and be aware of the consequences of our actions on the environment if we do not want to live in a destroyed environment.
EDI themes involved
"Scientific study of global environmental changes (ecological modernization)"
Contents evoked in processing the EDIs
Environmental literacy "In the introduction of this material we saw the composition of ecosystems. In the other lessons we have seen that man is linked to nature because it ensures man's survival. It is a source of food and through photosynthesis it provides oxygen. Through his activities, man uses this richness but throws the waste into the seas and the atmosphere." *Environmental deliberations mentioned* "For example, we talked about the environmental codes that are applied in France and Morocco, and it is already under discussion for Tunisia." *Environmental actions* "We talked about buying green products. The use of pesticides and chemical fertilizers is harmful to the soil and groundwater and there are farmers who use natural fertilizers that are not harmful and improve soil fertility." *Ecological citizenship (behaviors mentioned)* "We talked about the case of the industry in Gabes which causes several diseases in the inhabitants of that city. The people who suffer claim their right to have an environment that is not polluted but they have not blocked these industries."
Pedagogical aspects in processing the EDIs
Learning of citizenship (behaviors encouraged, general objectives) "You have to participate, be active, do activities and push young people to take action to protect the environment as environmental physicians." *Learning of ecoliteracy* "Treating water by skipping chemical treatment steps is dangerous. Parasites can escape during the biological treatment of wastewater, which poses a health hazard to consumers of products irrigated by this water." *Deliberative learning* "We didn't talk because we missed so many sessions." *Learning in a collective action plan* "We studied this subject by listening to the teacher, noted down the most important remarks and asked questions about difficult words."

St_6
General information
St_6 has a bachelor's degree in experimental sciences. He is enrolled in the 1st year core curriculum with specialization in life and environmental sciences at ISSBAT (Tunis). The unit "ecology and environment" is his choice of major for the "environmental protection" degree. *St_6* considers that environmental issues are essential in scientific fields because their study improves knowledge about the environment.
EDI themes involved
"Scientific study of global environmental change (ecological modernization)"
Contents evoked in processing the EDIs
Environmental literacy "The influence of the use of toxic products by man which affect the functioning of nature." *Environmental deliberations mentioned* "Climate change discussions are about international agreements." *Environmental actions* "There are people who campaign to recycle waste before throwing it into the environment, which poses a danger to the life of aquatic animals." *Ecological citizenship (behaviors mentioned)* "In the Gabes regions people demand a reduction in atmospheric pollution."
Pedagogical aspects in processing the EDIs
Learning of citizenship (behaviors encouraged, general objectives) "To be a responsible citizen is to be able to seek solutions to protect planet Earth with an awareness of the danger that affects this planet by holding awareness campaigns on this danger." *Learning of ecoliteracy* "The reactions between gases in the atmosphere cause the greenhouse effect and damage to the ozone layer, especially in the North Pole where the reactions occur more." *Deliberative learning* "No, we didn't have a debate with different points of view." *Learning in a collective action plan* "We listened to the teacher and took notes."

Table A3.10. *Interviews: summaries*

Te_1	St_1	St_2	St_3	**List A: Sustainable development themes**
X	X	X	X	Management of natural resources
X				Consumption of products that do not harm (endanger) the environment
				Environmental problems as a consequence of power relations (domination)
				Collective ownership of production: a perspective for environmental sustainability
				Domination of nature and women by men as a root cause of environmental problems
Te_1	**St_4**	**St_5**	**St_6**	**List A': EDI themes**
X	X	X	X	Scientific study of global environmental changes (ecological modernization)
		X		Green growth
	X			Green economy
				Environmental justice
	X			Environmental services for human societies
				Ethical pragmatism (environmental values dependent on the situation)
				Management of natural resources
				Consumption of products that do not harm the environment
				Environmental problems as a consequence of power relations
				Domination of nature and women by men as the root cause of environmental problems
				Consumption
				Consumer and food producer engagement
				Technological innovations for energy transition
				Decentralization of energy production
				Adaptive management of fossil energy resources

Te_1	**St_1**	**St_2**	**St_3**	**St_4**	**St_5**	**St_6**	**List B: Environmental knowledge mentioned**
X				X	X		Elementary components of natural and social systems (living components, non-living components, etc.)
X	X	X	X	X	X	X	Types and examples of interactions between human and nature
							Appreciation of nature and society
							Empathy (benevolence, sympathy) towards nature and society
							Ecological, economic, geographic, political, cultural and educational processes
							The impact of beliefs and values on environmental issues
							Cultural values and historical perspectives in dealing with environmental issues
							Environmental awareness and sensitivity
Te_1	**St_1**	**St_2**	**St_3**	**St_4**	**St_5**	**St_6**	**List C: Environmental discussions raised**
X	X						Adaptation to irreversibly engaged environmental dynamics
X		X	X	X	X	X	Consensus (agreements) and conventions developed at conferences and international declarations
							Dialogues involving experts and citizens in direct experiences and local knowledge

Te_1	St_1	St_2	St_3	St_4	St_5	St_6	**List D: Environmental actions mentioned**
X	X		X			X	Recycling of waste
X	X			X	X		Purchasing of ecological products
X		X					Membership of environmental associations
							Attending gatherings and signing petitions (requests, complaints) in favor of environmental causes
Te_1	**St_1**	**St_2**	**St_3**	**St_4**	**St_5**	**St_6**	**List E: Environmental behaviors mentioned**
	X	X	X	X	X	X	Claiming (demanding, claiming, requesting) rights to a healthy environment
							Recognizing the duties of participation in challenges (disputes) against any destructive aspect of development
X							Recognizing environmental responsibility as a duty stemming from cosmopolitan justice to reduce the ecological footprint
							Recognizing environmental citizen responsibility in terms of unavoidable political disputes between adversaries (non-enemies)
Te_1	**St_1**	**St_2**	**St_3**	**St_4**	**St_5**	**St_6**	**List F: General objectives**
X	X	X	X	X	X	X	Being a participatory citizen and promoter (initiator) of development
				X		X	Being a responsible citizen who acts responsibly in the community

Te_1	St_1	St_2	St_3	St_4	St_5	St_6	**List F: General objectives**
							Being a cooperative citizen and being concerned about social justice
Te_1	**St_1**	**St_2**	**St_3**	**St_4**	**St_5**	**St_6**	**List G: Specific objectives**
X	X	X	X	X	X	X	Building relevant (suitable) scientific knowledge to address societal issues
							Identifying the values of nature according to cultures, as well as the cultural elements supporting environmental sustainability
							Determining the roles of the economy in structuring relationships of power (domination)
Te_1	**St_1**	**St_2**	**St_3**	**St_4**	**St_5**	**St_6**	**List H: Types of discussions conducted**
							End result is the teacher's point of view
							Achieving consensus (agreement) between the different points of view
							Defending opposing perspectives (which remain in dispute)
Te_1	**St_1**	**St_2**	**St_3**	**St_4**	**St_5**	**St_6**	**List I: type of actions carried out by pupils or students**
X	X	X	X	X	X	X	The activities are presented separately
							The activities are undertaken in a club
							The activities are carried out with a commitment to a common project with the local community

Table A3.11. *Interviews: help lists*

Glossary

Agonistic (democracy): the agonistic conception of democracy requires the recognition of the contingent character of the articulations of the political realm with the economic realm that determine the specific configuration of a society at a given moment. The agonistic approach recognizes that society is always politically instituted and that the terrain on which political actions take place is always the result of previous social practices that are not neutral. This conception therefore does not accept the possibility of non-conflictual democratic politics. The latter reduces politics to a neutral set of techniques and procedures. By proposing a theoretical return to the conception of opposition that is removed from any type of conflict and establishment of consensus between "enemies", agonistic democracy rehabilitates conflict in politics by making it one of its tools. It is therefore with the aid of "agonistic democracy" that we can envisage a political system in which pluralism finds a form of expression whereby "enemies" become legitimate addressees who are recognized as having the right to defend their points of view within a common space.

Anti-political: the expression of a paradox of political thought where political actors affirm their capacity for political action that allows for a determination, once and for all, of the best way for humans to live together. Such political action is supposed to end the need for politics. It is indeed a paradox in the sense that the anti-political is politics that aims to eliminate politics because it supposes that by providing definitive answers, it eliminates the need to ask new questions. It is a political theory that denies the need for political thought. Social and political history show that humans have tended to give in to the temptation of the anti-political. Indeed, for long periods of time during the two and a half millennia of Western political life, anti-politics was the dominant attitude of the population.

Capitalism: a social system in which the relationship between capital and wage labor is the central element in the organization and accumulation of capital. The latter is seen as the main social driving force. It is a concept central to Marxism. This concept is derived from Marx's critical analyses of capital. It is mainly rooted in political economy. There is a strong tendency among Marxists to favor the concept with or without second-order specifications such as "Fordist" or "informational" capitalism. Non-Marxists develop other similar concepts such as "industrial society", "modernity" or "network society".

Citizenship: the link between the individual, society and government. It is linked to questions of the individual's role as a member of a political system and whether the individual has a duty to act in the common interest of society. The concept of citizenship is developed in different social contexts such as migration, multiculturalism, refugee status and human rights in general. Currently, cosmopolitan citizenship is a major focus of recent theorizations of citizenship.

Democracy: the event of democracy in the ancient Greek cities is considered to be the beginning of the history of political thought. Democracy is based on the freedom of citizens to participate in the decisions that determine their lives. Historically, democratic political life has not been easy because it is based on freedom that can be felt as a burden and responsibility to legitimize choices that weigh heavily. The history of democracy has been in the form of a series of episodes, too brief and sometimes tragic because the freedom to choose involves the right to make mistakes. The history of political thought has kept alive the questions that have motivated humans to invent fairer ways of living together.

Device (educational, didactic or pedagogical): the idea of device, in the educational field, classically designates a strategic set of measures, diversified but coherent, for controlling an educational situation. The concept has been developed mainly in the field of adult education. According to Astolfi, a specialist in the didactics of disciplines, an educational device designates a reasoned and open construction with four dimensions:

– a projective dimension, since it is a question of organizing educational actions around an objective, which constitutes the heart of a voluntarist project;

– a strategic dimension makes it possible to coordinate a diversity of parameters of a heterogeneous nature (tasks proposed, time allocated, methods adopted, organization methods, institutional context, material resources, etc.);

– a dialogic dimension, linked to the knowledge of the learner as an autonomous subject (with his/her own representations as well as his/her cognitive and socio-affective orientations) and to the respect of the characteristics of the group in training;

– a tactical dimension, which allows adaptations to a learning history that is not predetermined.

Ecofeminism: a thought and practice that approaches the environmental issue from the categories of patriarchy, male domination, sexism and gender. Based on materialist philosophy, ecofeminism assumes that the environmental problem and the problem of techno-scientific modifications of nature do not lie in the alteration of a sacred order but in the rudimentary nature of current human intervention and complex systemic adaptations with a history of millions of years. In the face of neoliberal globalization, ecofeminists call for ecojustice.

Ecosocialism: a social analysis that assumes that capitalism attempts to detach social life from nature through gender and class divisions. Ecosocialist thinking draws primarily on the writings of Marx and Engels on the nature of human society and its relationship to the environment. Ecosocialists link inequality and environmental damage to the exploitation of people and the environment by capitalism. They advocate the need to change the material conditions and social structure of society to overcome both environmental crises and social injustice.

Emancipation: a practice that consists of the transition, through the self-determination of agents, from an unwanted source of determination to a desired and necessary source of determination. It articulates "knowing" and "doing" by embracing the dialectic of emancipation and freedom.

Feminism: a political movement of actors targeting the transformation of a social order by putting an end to male domination and the subordination of women. From the mid-1960s to the early 1980s, feminist theory was realistic, aiming at the critical analysis of the gap between women's real capacities and needs and those attributed to them by political ideologies. In the 1970s, feminists criticized misogyny and gender discrimination in the Western literature and psychoanalysis. They argued that the oppression of women affected both white and working class, minority and Third World women, and they distinguished "sex" as a physical and sexual difference (seen as enduring) from "gender" as a sense of identity (seen as a social construct).

Inference: a cognitive process whereby a conclusion is drawn from a set of premises. An inference rule is a model of argument, a linguistic construct consisting of a set of premises, a conclusion and an (often implicit) assertion that the conclusion is appropriately related to the premises. Arguments can be divided into deductive and non-deductive:

– deductive inference is considered to be directly justified on mainly empirical grounds;

– inductive inference is amplifying in the sense that the content of the conclusion goes beyond the content of the underlying causes;

– abductive inference is another mode of amplifying inference. It corresponds to the process of inferring the best explanation, which means that a hypothesis is acceptable if it is the best explanation of certain phenomena.

Marxism: a structuralist theory that links social events to the underlying structures of economic and political power and the flows of capital it allows. This theory assumes that global capitalism brings about unequal development in space and time. Marxist theorists trace the evolution of the capitalist system in terms of waves of accumulated capital, division of labor, crises and contradictions that offer alternatives to guide anti-capitalist movements.

Onto-epistemology: epistemology refers to the conditions of the possibility of knowledge. It encompasses the study of knowledge systems that have historically been privileged as legitimate means of seeing the world. Ontology is a term closely related to epistemology. It refers to beliefs about reality, existence, and notions of truth and being. Epistemologically positivist research, for example, is based on the belief in a reality that can be found, while postmodernist research questions the notion of reality, truth and universality. Thus, ontology and epistemology appear to be inextricably linked: all ontology is itself founded on an epistemology. Onto-epistemology is therefore the term used to emphasize the symbiotic relationship between epistemology and ontology.

Political (the): transformative social practices and struggles that become intentional. It mainly reveals the contingency of the social order. The political is not a subsystem of society but rather an intentional and collective act by which society determines its form as a collective subjectivity. It is a dynamic principle of the constitution of society. Through the political, society, which symbolically represents itself as a unit, is also divided by struggle.

Poststructuralism: a set of social theories that emerged from the 1970s onwards. These theories are based on doubts about the usefulness of seeking to explain all social events and phenomena as components or outcomes of a more general system, such as global capitalism. Poststructuralism draws on social constructivism (arguing that human development is socially situated and that knowledge is built through interaction with others) to advance a theory of knowledge with three characteristics:

– anti-foundationism, which maintains that there are non-questionable foundations for knowledge and that there are no general criteria for distinguishing truth from falsehood;

– anti-totalization, which accepts a variety of limited theories and truths;

– anti-utopianism, which assumes that there is no justification for accepting the great stories or narratives of human progress that suggest that history has a purpose.

Foucault was a key figure in the development of poststructuralism. He argued that power functions in a dispersed way in the daily practices of institutions and that it hides and works in discourse.

Theory: a set of propositions used to explain certain phenomena. Theories are, in the most general sense, unifying propositions about the unfolding of phenomena and events. These propositions can predict or re-shape perspectives and visions of the world. Additionally, theories can be developed to fundamentally change the vision of social action. The fundamental meaning of theory is generally centered on the idea of a developed understanding of a phenomenon.

References

Aguilar, O.M. and Krasny, M.E. (2011). Using the communities of practice framework to examine an after-school environmental education program for Hispanic youth. *Environmental Education Research*, 17, 217–233.

Albe, V. (2011). Finalités socio-éducatives de la culture scientifique. *Revue française de pédagogie*, 174, 119–138.

Altet, M. (1994). Comment interagissent enseignant et élèves en classe ? *Revue française de pédagogie*, 107, 123–139.

Altet, M. (1997). *Les pédagogies de l'apprentissage*. PUF, Paris.

Altet, M. (2002). Une démarche de recherche sur la pratique enseignante : l'analyse plurielle. *Revue française de pédagogie*, 138, 85–93.

Anadon, M. (2006). La recherche dite "qualitative" : de la dynamique de son évolution aux acquis indéniables et aux questionnements présents. *Recherches qualitatives*, 26(1), 5–31.

Ardoino, J. and Berger, G. (2010). Forme scolaire ou processus éducatif : oppositions et/ou complémentarité. *Nouvelle revue de psychosociologie*, 9, 121–129.

Audet, R. (2016). Transition as discours. *International Journal of Sustainable Development*, 19(4), 365–382.

Avelino, F. (2009). Empowerment and the challenge of applying transition management to ongoing projects. *Policy Sciences*, 42(4), 369–390.

Avelino, F. (2011). Power in transition: Empowering discourses on sustainability transitions. PhD Thesis, Erasmus University Rotterdam, Rotterdam.

Avelino, F. and Rotmans, J. (2011). A dynamic conceptualization of power for sustainability research. *Journal of Cleaner Production*, 19(8), 796–804.

Avelino, F. and Wittmayer, J. (2016). Shifting power relations in sustainability transitions: A multi-actor perspective. *Journal of Environmental Policy & Planning*, 18(5), 628–649.

Avelino, F., Grin, J., Pel, B., Jhagroe, S. (2016). The politics of sustainability transitions. *Journal of Environmental Policy & Planning*, 18(5), 557–567.

Bacon, M. and Sloam, J. (2010). John Dewey and democratic role of higher education in England. *Journal of Political Science Education*, 6, 336–352.

Ballet, J., Bazin, D., Pelenc, J. (2013). Justice environnementale et approche par les capabilités [Online]. Available at: https://halshs.archives-ouvertes.fr/halshs-01071203/document.

Baribeau, C. (2009). Analyse des données des entretiens de groupe. *Recherches qualitatives*, 28(1), 133–148.

Barthe, Y., de Blic, D., Heurtin, J., Lagneau, É., Lemieux, C., Linhardt, D., Trom, D. (2013). Sociologie pragmatique : mode d'emploi. *Politix*, 103(3), 175–204.

Barthes, A. and Alpe, Y. (2018). Les "éducations à", une remise en cause de la forme scolaire ? *Carrefours de l'éducation*, 45, 23–37.

Barthes, A. and Lange, J.-M. (2018). Développement durable, postures et responsabilité sociale des chercheurs en éducation. *Recherches en éducation*, 31, 92–109.

Barthes, A., Lange, J.-M., Tutiaux-Guillon, N. (2017). *Dictionnaire critique des enjeux et concepts des "éducations à"*. L'Harmattan, Paris.

Beau, R. and Larrère, C. (2018). *Penser l'Anthropocène*. Presses de Sciences Po, Paris.

Beckman, L. (2016). Power and future people's freedom: Intergenerational domination, climate change, and constitutionalism. *Journal of Political Power*, 9(2), 289–307.

Bérard, A., Simonneaux, J., Simonneaux, L. (2016). Les questions socialement vives vectrices d'un activisme agonistique. *DIRE*, 8.

Biesta, G. (2010). On the weakness of education. In *Philosophy of Education*, Kerdeman, D. (ed.). Philosophy of Education Society, Urbana.

Biesta, G. (2011). *Learning Democracy in School and Society: Education, Lifelong Learning and the Politics of Citizenship*. Sense Publishers, Rotterdam.

Biesta, G. (2014). Learning in public places: Civic learning for the twenty-first century. In *Civic Learning, Democratic Citizenship and the Public Sphere*, Biesta, G., De Bie, M., Wildemeersch, D. (eds). Springer, Dordrecht.

Bisault, J. (2011). Contribution à l'élaboration curriculaire d'une éducation scientifique à l'école primaire. HDR, École normale supérieure de Cachan, Cachan.

Blanchon, D., Moreau, S., Veyret, Y. (2009). Comprendre et construire la justice environnementale. *Annales de géographie*, 665–666, 35–60.

Blokker, P. (2014). "The political" in the "pragmatic sociology of critique": Reading Boltanski with Lefort and Castoriadis. In *The Spirit of Luc Boltanski Essays on the "Pragmatic Sociology of Critique"*, Susen, S. and Turner, B. (eds). Anthem Press, London.

Blowers, A. and Leroy, P. (1994). Power, politics and environmental inequality: A theoretical and empirical analysis of the process of "peripheralisation". *Environmental Politics*, 3(2), 197–228.

Bonneuil, C. and Fressoz, J.-B. (2013). *L'Évènement anthropocène, la terre, l'histoire et nous*. Le Seuil, Paris.

Booth, S. and Coveney, J. (2015). *Food Democracy*. Springer, Singapore.

Bouchez, J.-P. (2014). L'émergence des communautés de pratique pilotées. *L'Expansion Management Review*, 154, 121–130.

Boutaud, A. (2004). Le développement durable : penser le changement ou changer le pansement ? Bilan et analyse des outils d'évaluation des politiques publiques locales en matière de développement durable en France : de l'émergence d'un changement dans les modes de faire au défi d'un changement dans les modes de penser. PhD Thesis, École nationale des mines de Saint-Étienne/Université Jean Monnet, Saint-Étienne.

Brechet, J.P. and Schieb-Bienfait, N. (2009). Logique d'action et projet dans l'action collective. Réflexions théoriques comparées. In *XVIII*[e] *conférence de l'AIMS*. Grenoble, 2–5 June [Online]. Available at: https://hal.archives-ouvertes.fr/hal-00421180/document.

Brougère, G. and Bézille, H. (2007). De l'usage de la notion d'informel dans le champ de l'éducation. *Revue française de pédagogie*, 158, 117–160.

Caetano, A. (2014). Defining personal reflexivity: A critical reading of Archer's approach. *European Journal of Social Theory*, 18(1), 60–75.

Caetano, A. (2015). Reflexivity and social change: A critical discussion of reflexive modernization and individualization theses. *Portuguese Journal of Social Science*, 13(1), 93–109.

Carr, P.R. and Thésée, G. (2016). Éducation et démocratie : liens et lieux de la formation à la participation citoyenne. Communication dans le symposium sur l'éducation et la démocratie : former les citoyens de demain, université d'Ottawa les 21 et 22 avril 2016 [Online]. Available at: https://www.academia.edu/24657013/%C3%89ducation_et_d%C3%A9mocratie_liens_et_lieux_de_la_formation_%C3%A0_la_participation_citoyenne.

Carr, P.R. and Thésée, G. (2017). Seeking democracy inside, and outside, of education: Re-conceptualizing perceptions and experiences related to democracy and education. *Democracy and Education*, 25(2), 1–2.

Centemeri, L., Borja, J.-S., Gaudin, A. (2016). Politiques d'adaptation au changement climatique et injustices environnementales. Le pluralisme des relations à l'environnement dans la mise en forme de la contrainte adaptative [Online]. Available at: https://hal.archives-ouvertes.fr/hal-01388939/document.

Charlier, J.-E. and Panait, O.M. (2018). Resistances to global educational prescriptions in the global south: Theoretical considerations through Michel Foucault's lenses. *British Journal of Sociology of Education*, 39(3), 348–364.

Charlot, B. (2017). Formes et enjeux des recherches en éducation et formation. *Les sciences de l'éducation pour l'ère nouvelle*, 50, 17–30.

Chaumel, M. and La Branche, S. (2008). Inégalités écologiques : vers quelle définition ? *Espace populations sociétés*, 1, 101–110.

Clenet, J. (2007). Complexité de l'approche qualitative et légitimation scientifique pour une genèse des possibles : relier pragmatique, épistémique, et éthique. *Recherches qualitatives*, special issue 3, 59–75.

Code, J. (2018). Ecoliteracy: The trouble with reading [Online]. Available at: https://www.researchgate.net/publication/326551479_Ecoliteracy_The_Trouble_with_Reading.

Coenen-Huther, J. (2003). Le type idéal comme instrument de la recherche sociologique. *Revue française de sociologie*, 44, 531–547.

Coquidé, M. (2000). Le rapport expérimental au vivant. HDR, Université Paris-Sud, Paris.

Costa, D. (2013). Food sustainability transitions: What citizen-consumer role for the transition movement. Master's Thesis, University of Wageningen, Wageningen.

Cristol, D. (2017). Les communautés d'apprentissage : apprendre ensemble. *Savoirs*, 43, 10–55.

Dalton, R.J. (2014). Political citizenship: Mapping the terrain. In *Handbook of Political Citizenship and Social Movements*, Heijden, H.A. (ed.). University of Amsterdam, Amsterdam.

Dany, L. (2016). Analyse qualitative du contenu des représentations sociales. In *Les représentations sociales*, Lo Monaco, G., Delouvée, S., Rateau, P. (eds.). De Boeck, Brussels.

De Ketele, J.-M. and Roegiers, X. (2015). *Méthodologie du recueil d'informations : fondements des méthodes d'observation, de questionnaire, d'interview et d'étude de documents*. De Boeck, Brussels.

Descarpentries, J. (2018). L'éducation pour la santé durable comme levier de transformation sociale. *Educations*, 2(1).

Descola, P. (2019). *Une écologie des relations*. CNRS/De Vive Voix, Paris.

Dimick, A.S. (2015). Supporting youth to develop environmental citizenship within/against a neoliberal context. *Environmental Education Research*, 21(3), 390–402.

Dobson, A. (2003). *Citizenship and the Environment*. Oxford University Press, Oxford.

Dobson, A. (2006). Ecological citizenship: A defence. *Environmental Politics*, 15(3), 447–451.

Dohou-Renaud, A. (2009). Le système de management environnemental comme moyen de contrôle de la déclinaison et de l'émergence des stratégies environnementales. PhD Thesis, Université de Poitiers, Poitiers.

Dozzi, J., Lennert, M., Wallenborn, G. (2008). Inégalités écologiques : analyse spatiale des impacts générés et subis par les ménages belges. *Espace populations sociétés*, 1.

Duit, A. (2010). Patterns of environmental collective action: Some cross-national findings. *Political Studies*, 59, 900–920.

Eastes, R.-E. (2013). Processus d'apprentissage, savoirs complexes et traitement de l'information : un modèle théorique à l'usage des praticiens entre sciences cognitives, Didactique et philosophie des sciences. PhD Thesis, Université de Paris 1 Panthéon-Sorbonne, Paris.

Faburel, G. (2008). Les inégalités environnementales comme inégalités de moyens des habitants et des acteurs territoriaux. *Espace populations sociétés*, 1, 111–126.

Felli, R. (2015). Environment, not planning: The neoliberal depoliticisation of environmental policy by means of emissions trading. *Environmental Politics*, 24(5), 641–660.

Finlayson, A., Markewitz, K., Frayret, J.-M. (2014). Postsecondary education in industrial ecology across the world. *Journal of Industrial Ecology*, 18(6), 931–941.

Fol, S. and Pflieger, G. (2010). Environmental justice in the US: Construction and uses of a flexible category. An application to transportation policies in the San Francisco area. *Justice Spatiale*, 2.

Forsyth, T. (2003). *Critical Political Ecology: The Politics of Environmental Science*. Routledge, London.

Fraenkel, B. and Mbodj-Pouye, A. (2010). Les new literacy studies, jalons historiques et perspectives actuelles. *Langage et société*, 133, 7–24.

Franc, S. (2014). Le sujet sous l'angle de l'éducation à la biodiversité : perspectives d'un apprentissage selon trois dimensions. *Éducation et socialisation*, 36.

Freedman, D. (2011). Embodying food studies: Unpacking the ways we become what we eat. In *Corpus: An Interdisciplinary Reader on Bodies and Knowledge*, Casper, M. and Currah, P. (eds). Palgrave-MacMillan, New York.

Freire, P. and Macedo, D. (1987). *Literacy: Reading the Word and the World*. Routledge/ Kegan Paul Ltd, London.

Fressoz, J.-B. (2012). *L'apocalypse joyeuse. Une histoire du risque technologique*. Le Seuil, Paris.

Gachkov, S. (2012). La politique et l'histoire dans la philosophie française face au socialisme réel dans l'après-guerre. Philosophy PhD Thesis, Université de Poitiers, Poitiers.

Gardin, J. (2012). *Justice ou décence environnementale ? Actes du colloque justice et injustices environnementales*. Presses universitaires de Paris Ouest, Nanterre.

Geels, F. (2014). Regime resistance against low-carbon transitions: Introducing politics and power into the multi-level perspective. *Theory, Culture and Society*, 31, 21–40.

Geels, F. and Schot, J. (2007). Typology of socio-technical transition pathways. *Research Policy*, 36, 399–417.

Giraldo, O.F. and Rosset, P.M. (2018). Agroecology as a territory in dispute: Between institutionality and social movements. *Journal of Peasant Studies*, 45(3), 545–564.

Gobert, J. (2008). Compensation territoriale, justice et inégalités environnementales aux États-Unis. *Espace populations sociétés*, 1.

Guerra, A. (2014). Problem based learning and sustainable engineering education: Challenges for 21st century. PhD Thesis, Aalborg University, Aalborg.

Hague, R. and Harrop, M. (2004). *Comparative Government and Politics: An Introduction*. Palgrave Macmillan, New York.

Håkansson, M. and Östman, L. (2018). The political dimension in ESE: The construction of a political moment model for analyzing bodily anchored political emotions in teaching and learning of the political dimension. *Environmental Education Research*, 25(4), 585–600.

Håkansson, M., Kronlid, D., Östman, L. (2017). Searching for the political dimension in education for sustainable development: Socially critical, social learning and radical democratic approaches. *Environmental Education Research*, 25(1), 6–32.

Hassanein, N. (2008). Locating food democracy: Theoretical and practical ingredients. *Journal of Hunger and Environmental Nutrition*, 3, 286–308.

Hess, D. (2014). Sustainability transitions: A political coalition perspective. *Research Policy*, 43(2), 278–283.

Hildreth, R.W. (2006). Teaching and learning democracy: An analysis of undergraduates' lived experiences of political engagement. *Journal of Political Science Education*, 2, 285–302.

Holden, M. and Scerri, A. (2015). Justification, compromise and test: Developing a pragmatic sociology of critique to understand the outcome of urban redevelopment. *Planning Theory*, 14(4), 360–383.

Hopwood, B., Mellor, M., O'Brien, G. (2005), Sustainable development: Mapping different approaches. *Sustainable Development*, 13, 38–52.

Howard, D. (2010). *The Primacy of the Political: A History of Political Thought from the Greeks to the French and American Revolutions*. Columbia University Press, New York.

Hsieh, H.F. and Shannon, S.E. (2005). Three approaches to qualitative content analysis. *Qualitative Health Research*, 15(9), 1277–1288.

Huckle, J. (2013). Eco-schooling and sustainability citizenship: Exploring issues raised by corporate sponsorship. *The Curriculum Journal*, 24(2), 206–223.

Hursh, D., Henderson, J., Greenwood, D. (2015). Environmental education in a neoliberal climate. *Environmental Education Research*, 21(3), 299–318.

Jagers, S.C. and Matti, S. (2010). Ecological citizens: Identifying values and beliefs that support. Individual environmental responsibility among Swedes. *Sustainability*, 2, 1055–1079.

Janner-Raimondi, M. (2017). Éducation à la responsabilité. In *Dictionnaire critique des enjeux et des concepts des "éducations à"*, Barthes, A., Lange, J.-M., Tutiaux-Guillon, N. (eds). L'Harmattan, Paris.

Jhagroe, S. (2016). Urban transition politics: How struggles for sustainability are (re)making urban spaces. PhD Thesis, Dutch research institute for transitions (DRIFT), Rotterdam.

Johnson, L. and Morris, P. (2010). Toward a framework for critical citizenship education. *The Curriculum Journal*, 12(1), 77–96.

Kanda, W., Sakao, T., Hjelm, O. (2016). Components of business concepts for the diffusion of large scaled environmental technology systems. *Journal of Cleaner Production*, 128, 156–167.

Kenis, A. (2016). Ecological citizenship and democracy: Communitarism versus agonistic perspectives. *Environmental Politics*, 25(6), 949–970.

Kenis, A. and Lievens, M. (2014). Searching for the political in environmental politics. *Environmental Politics*, 24(1), 531–548.

Kenis, A. and Lievens, M. (2017). Imagining the carbon neutral city: The (post)politics of time and space. *Environment and Planning A*, 49(8), 1762–1778.

Kenis, A. and Mathijs, E. (2014a). (De) politicising the local: The case of the transition towns movement in flanders (Belgium). *Journal of Rural Studies*, 34, 172–183.

Kenis, A. and Mathijs, E. (2014b). Climate change and post-politics: Repoliticizing the present by imagining the future? *Geoforum*, 52, 148–156.

Kenis, A., Bono, F., Mathijs, E. (2016). Unravelling the (post-) political in transition management: Interrogating pathways towards sustainable change. *Journal of Environmental Policy & Planning*, 18(5), 568–584.

Kluttz, J. and Walter, P. (2018). Conceptualizing learning in the climate justice movement. *Adult Education Quarterly*, 68(2), 91–107.

Kopnina, H. (2012). Education for sustainable development (ESD): The turn away from environment in environmental education. *Environmental Education Research*, 18(5), 699–717.

Krauz, A. (2014). Les villes en transition, l'ambition d'une alternative urbaine. Métropolitiques [Online]. Available at: http://www.metropolitiques.eu/Les-villes-en-transition-l.html.

Krief, N. and Zardet, V. (2013). Analyse de données qualitatives et recherche-intervention. *Recherches en Sciences de Gestion*, 95(2), 211–237.

Lange, J.-M. (2011). Éducation au développement durable : problématique éducative/ problèmes de didactique. HDR. École normale supérieure de Cachan, Cachan.

Lange, J.-M. (2013). Curriculum possible de l'éducation au développement durable : entre actions de participation et investigations multiréférentielles d'enjeux. *Éducation relative à l'environnement*, 11, 41–60.

Lange, J.-M. (2015). Éducation et engagement : la participation de l'École à relever les défis environnementaux et de développement. *Éducation relative à l'environnement : regards, recherches, réflexions*, 12, 105–125.

Lange, J.-M. and Martinand, J.-L. (2014). Principes d'élaboration et de structuration d'une éducation au développement durable scolaire. In *Développement durable, compétences 21, comprendre et développer les compétences collectives*, Brégeon, J. and Mauléon, F. (eds). ESKA, Paris.

Larrère, C. (2010). Les éthiques environnementales. *Natures sciences sociétés*, 18(4), 405–413.

Laurent, E. (2009). Écologie et inégalités. *Revue de l'OFCE*, 109, 33–57.

Lawhon, M. and Murphy, J. (2011). Socio-technical regimes and sustainability transitions: Insights from political ecology. *Progress in Human Geography*, 36(3), 354–378.

Lebeaume, J. (1999). Perspectives curriculaires en éducation technologique. HDR, Université Paris Sud, Paris.

Lebeaume, J. (2006). Les sciences et la technologie au collège. La question récurrente de leur unification ou de leur différenciation. In *La formation à l'enseignement des sciences et des technologies au secondaire dans le contexte des réformes par compétences*, Hasni, A., Lenoir, Y., Lebeaume, J. (eds). Presses de l'Université du Québec, Quebec.

Lebeaume, J. (2011). L'éducation technologique au collège : un enseignement pour la refondation du curriculum et les réorientations des disciplines. *Éducation et didactique*, 5(2), 7–22.

Lecours, A. (2002). L'approche néo-institutionnaliste en science politique : unité ou diversité ? *Politique et sociétés*, 21(3), 3–19.

Leenders, H. and Veugelers, W. (2009). Different perspectives on values and citizenship education. In *Global Values Education Teaching Democracy and Peace*, Zajda, J. and Daun, H. (eds). Springer Dordrecht Heidelberg, New York.

Legault, G.A. (2003). La médiation et l'éthique appliquée en réponse aux limites du droit. *Revue de droit*, 33, 153–193.

Lejeune, C. (2008). Au fil de l'interprétation. L'apport des registres aux logiciels d'analyse qualitative. *Revue suisse de sociologie*, 34(3), 593–603.

Lejeune, C. (2010). Montrer, calculer, explorer, analyser. Ce que l'informatique fait (faire) à l'analyse qualitative. *Recherches qualitatives*, special issue 9, 15–32.

Lenoir, Y., Esquivel, R., Froelich, A., Jean, V. (2013). Problématique et cadre de référence pour analyser les finalités éducatives scolaires chez les enseignants du primaire [Online]. Available at: http://www.usherbrooke.ca/crcie/fileadmin/sites/crcie/fichiers/ISEP-CI/4-ISEP-CI-Intro-Finalite__-VF.pdf.

Létourneau, A. (2010). Pour une éthique de l'environnement inspirée par le pragmatisme : l'exemple du développement durable. *Vertigo – la revue électronique en sciences de l'environnement*, 10(1).

Lhoste, Y. and Voisin, C. (2013). Repères pour l'enseignement de la biodiversité en classe de sciences. *Recherches en didactique des sciences et des technologies*, 7, 107–134.

Little, G. (2017). Connecting environmental humanities: Developing interdisciplinary collaborative method. *Humanities*, 6(4).

Loorbach, D., Frantzeskaki, N., Avelino, A. (2017). Sustainability transitions research: Transforming science and practice for societal change. *Annual Review of Environment and Resources*, 42(1), 599–626.

Lussault, M. (2018). Porter attention aux espaces de vie anthropocènes. Vers une théorie du *spatial care*. In *Penser l'Anthropocène*, Beau, R. and Larrère, C. (eds). Presses de Sciences Po, Paris.

MacGregor, S. (2014a). Only resist: Feminist ecological citizenship and the post-politics of climate change. *Hypatia*, 29(3), 617–633.

MacGregor, S. (2014b). Ecological citizenship. In *Handbook of Political Citizenship and Social Movements*, Heijden, H.A. (ed.). Edward Elgar Publishing Limited, Cheltenham.

Machin, A. (2012). Decisions, disagreement and responsibility: Toward an agonistic green citizenship. *Environmental Politics*, 21(6), 847–863.

Machin, A. (2014). Ends, means, beginnings: Environmental technocracy, ecological deliberation or embodied disagreement? *Ethical Perspectives*, 21(1), 47–72.

Maeseele, P. (2015). Beyond the post-political zeitgeist. In *The Routledge Handbook of Environment and Communication*, Hansen, A. and Cox, R. (eds). Routledge, New York.

Magrath, J. (2010). The justice of climate change: Voice from Africa. *Local Environment*, 15, 891–901.

March, J. and Olsen, J. (1984). The new institutionalism: Organizational factors in political life. *American Political Science Review*, 78(3), 734–749.

March, J. and Olsen, J. (2006). Elaborating the new institutionalism. In *The Oxford Handbook of Political Institutions*, Rhodes, R.A.W., Binder, S.A. and Rockman, B. (eds). Oxford University Press, Oxford.

Marpeau, J. (2013). *Le processus éducatif. La construction de la personne comme sujet responsable de ses actes*. Erès, Toulouse.

Martineau, S. (2005). L'instrumentation dans la collecte de données. *Recherches qualitatives*, Special edition 2, 5–17.

Martinez, M.-L. (2010). Approches anthropologiques de la co-construction d'identités écocitoyennes. In *Actes du congrès de l'Actualité de la recherche en éducation et en formation (AREF)* [Online]. Available at: https://plone.unige.ch/aref2010/symposiums-courts/coordinateurs-en-c/education-au-developpement-durable-et-territoires/Approche%20 anthropologique.pdf.

Martinez, M.-L. and Poydenot, F. (2009). Finalités, valeurs et identités pour fonder une éducation écocitoyenne. *Éducation relative à l'environnement : regards, recherches, réflexions*, 8, 57–74.

Mayo, P. (1995). Critical literacy and emancipator politics: The work of Paulo Freire. *International Journal of Educational Development*, 15(4), 363–379.

McBride, B.-B., Brewer, C.A., Berkowitz, A.R., Borrie, W.T. (2013). Environmental literacy, Ecological literacy, Ecoliteracy: What do we mean and how did we get here? *Ecosphere*, 4(5), 1–20.

McCarthy, J. (2013). We have never been post-political. *Capitalism Nature Socialism*, 24(1), 19–25.

Meadowcroft, J. (2009). What about the politics? Sustainable development, transition management and long term energy transitions. *Policy Sciences*, 42(4), 323–340.

Merriam, S.B. (1998). *Qualitative Research and Case Study Applications in Education*. Jossey-Bass, San Francisco.

Merriam, S.B. (2009). *Qualitative Research: A Guide to Design and Implementation. Revised and Expanded from Qualitative Research and Case Study. Applications in Education*. Jossey-Bass, San Francisco.

Millet, M. (2013). Les cadres cognitifs de la socialisation. HDR, Université de Poitiers, Poitiers.

Mokadem, M. (2018). Économie sociale et solidaire : vecteur du développement économique et social. *Bulletin du centre des études méditerranéennes et internationales* [Online]. Available at: http://www.cemi-tunis.org/medias/files/bulletin-cemi-02-fr.pdf.

Molette, P. (2009). De l'APD à tropes : comment un outil d'analyse de contenu peut évoluer en logiciel de classification sémantique généraliste [Online]. Available at: https://www.tropes.fr/PierreMolette-CommunicationColloquePsychoTarbesJuin2009.pdf.

Moore, S. (2012). Climate change and environmental citizenship: Transition to a post-consumerist future? PhD Thesis, University of Tasmania, Hobart.

Morin, O. (2013). Éducation à la citoyenneté et construction collaborative de raisonnements socio-scientifiques dans la perspective de la durabilité : pédagogie numérique pour une approche interculturelle de QSV environnementales. Université Toulouse le Mirail, Toulouse.

Morin, E. (2015). *Enseigner à vivre, manifeste pour changer l'éducation*. Actes Sud/Play Bac, Arles.

Morvan, A. (2011). Pour une éducation populaire politique à partir d'une recherche action en Bretagne. Education Sciences PhD Thesis, Université de Paris VIII-Vincennes-Saint-Denis, Paris.

Mucchielli, R. (2006). *L'analyse de contenu des documents et des communications*. ESF, Issy-les-Moulineaux.

Mukamurera, J., Lacourse, F., Couturier, Y. (2006). Des avancées en analyse qualitative : pour une transparence et une systématisation des pratiques. *Recherches qualitatives*, 26(1), 110–138.

Neal, S. (2013). Transition culture: Politics, localities and ruralities. *Journal of Rural Studies*, 32, 60–69.

ONU (2016). Rapport du groupe d'experts des nations unies et de l'extérieur chargé des indicateurs relatifs aux objectifs de développement durable (annexe III) [Online]. Available at: https://unstats.un.org/unsd/statcom/47th-session/documents/2016-2-IAEG-SDGs-F.pdf.

Orange, C. (2007). Quel milieu pour l'apprentissage par problématisation en sciences de la vie et de la Terre. *Éducation & didactique*, 1(2), 37–55.

Orange, C. and Orange Ravachol, D. (2017). Problématisations scientifiques fonctionnalistes et historiques en éducation relative à l'environnement et au développement durable : le cas de l'évolution climatique. *Formation et pratiques d'enseignement en question*, 22, 21–38.

Palier, B. and Surel, Y. (2005). Les "trois I" et l'analyse de l'État en action. *Revue française de science politique*, 55(1), 7–32.

Paredis, E. (2013). A winding road. Transition management, policy change and the search for sustainable development. PhD Thesis, University of Ghent, Ghent.

Pepermans, Y. and Maeseele, P. (2014). Democratic debate and mediated discourses on climate change: From consensus to de/politicization. *Environmental Communication*, 8(2), 216–232.

Pepermans, Y. and Maeseele, P. (2016). The politicization of climate change: Problem or solution? *WIREs Climate Change*, 7, 478–485.

Poussel, S. (2016). The democratic turn in Tunisia: Civic and political redefinition of canons of cultural diversity. *National and Ethnic Politics*, 22, 50–70.

Reed, M. (1996). Organizational theorizing: A historical contested terrain. In *Studying Organization*, Clegg, S.R. and Hardy, C. (eds). Sage, London.

Rees, W. (2008). Human nature, eco-footprints and environmental injustice. *Local Environment*, 13(8), 685–701.

Renting, H., Schermer, M., Rossi, A. (2012). Building food democracy: Exploring civic food networks and newly emerging forms of food citizenship. *International Journal of Sociology of Agriculture and Food*, 19(3), 289–307.

Riel-Salvatore, G. (2006). Gouvernance locale et démocratie participative : le projet de réaménagement de Benny Farm à Montréal. Master's Thesis, Université du Québec à Montréal, Montreal.

Robbins, P. (2012). *Political Ecology: A Critical Introduction*. Blackwell Publishing, Chichester.

Roberts, T. and Parks, B. (2007a). *A Climate of Injustice: Global Inequality, North-South Politics, and Climate Policy*. MIT Press, Cambridge.

Roberts, T. and Parks, B. (2007b). Feeling injustices: Globalization, ecologically unequal exchange and climate change. *Globalization*, 4(2), 193–2010.

Rockström, J., Steffen, W., Noone, K., Persson, Å. (2009a). Planetary boundaries: Exploring the safe operating space for humanity. *Ecology and Society*, 14(2), 32.

Rockström, J., Steffen, W., Noone, K., Persson, Å. (2009b). A safe operating space for humanity. *Nature*, 461, 472–475.

Roth, C.-E. (1992). Environmental literacy: Its roots, evolution and direction in 1990s [Online]. Available at: https://files.eric.ed.gov/fulltext/ED348235.pdf.

Rotmans, J. (2005). Societal innovation: Between dream and reality lies complexity [Online]. Available at: https://econpapers.repec.org/paper/emseuriar/7293.htm.

Sauvé, L. (2011). La prescription du développement durable en éducation : la troublante histoire d'une invasion barbare. In *Éducations, environnement et développement durable : pour une écocitoyenneté critique*, Bader, B. and Sauvé, L. (eds). Presses de l'Université de Laval, Montreal.

Scrase, I. and Smith, A. (2009). The (non-)politics of managing low carbon socio-technical transitions. *Environmental Politics*, 18(5), 707–726.

Seguin, L. (2015). Entre conflit et participation: Double apprentissage dans un mini-public et un mouvement de contestation. *Participations*, 13(3), 63–88.

Simonneaux, J. (2011). Les configurations didactiques des questions socialement vives économiques et sociales. HDR, Université d'Aix-Marseille, Marseille.

Simonneaux, J. (2013a). Les QSV : enjeux et leviers pour une éducation environnementale et citoyenne [Online]. Available at: http://www.grainelr.org/reseau-regional-education-sante-environnement/wakka.php?wiki=JourneeDeuxAgricultureAlimentation/download&file=Diaporama%20QSV.pdf.

Simonneaux, L. (2013b). Questions socialement vives and socio-scientific issues: New trends of research to meet the training needs of post-modern society. In *Actes du colloque ESERA, Topics and Trends in Current Sciences Education*, Bruguière, C., Tiberghien, A., Clement, P. (eds). Springer, Dordrecht.

Simonneaux, L. and Legardez, A. (2008). Efficacité de l'approche des questions socialement vives pour l'éducation à l'environnement et à la durabilité. In *Symposium au colloque Efficacité et équité en éducation*. Rennes [Online]. Available at: https://esup.espe-bretagne.fr/efficacite_et_equite_en_education/programme/symposium_legardez_lsimonneaux.pdf.

Simonneaux, L., Panissal, N., Brossais, E. (2013). Students' perception of risk about nanotechnology after an SAQ teaching strategy. *International Journal of Science Education*, 35, 2376–2406.

Slimani, M., Lange, J.-M., Azzouna, A. (2018). Le projet pédagogico-didactique de socialisation : perspective d'une socialisation démocratique pour l'enseignement-apprentissage des questions environnementales et de développement. *Éducation et socialisation*, 50.

Sloam, J. (2010). Youth, citizenship, and political science education: Questions for the discipline. *Journal of Political Science Education*, 6, 325–335.

Sloam, J. (2011). A pedagogy of engagement in higher education. Paper presented at the 2011 Annual Meeting of the American Political Science Association [Online]. Available at: https://papers.ssrn.com/sol3/papers.cfm?abstract_id=1910516.

Smith, C. and Bath, D. (2006). The role of the learning community in the development of discipline knowledge and generic graduate outcomes. *Higher Education*, 51(2), 259–286.

Smith, A. and Stirling, A. (2008). Social-ecological resilience and sociotechnical transitions: Critical issues for sustainability governance [Online]. Available at: centre.org/anewmanifesto/manifesto_2010/clusters/cluster7/Transitions_Working_Paper.pdf.

Smith, A. and Stirling, A. (2010). The politics of social-ecological resilience and sustainable socio-technical transitions. *Ecology and Society* [Online]. Available at: http://www.ecologyandsociety.org/vol15/iss1/art11/.

Stahelin, N., Accioly, I., Sánchez, C. (2015). The promise and peril of the state in neoliberal times: Implications for the critical environmental education movement in Brazil. *Environmental Education Research*, 21(3), 433–446.

Sund, L. (2016). Facing global sustainability issues: Teachers' experiences of their own practices in environmental and sustainability education. *Environmental Education Research*, 22(6), 788–805.

Sund, L. and Öhman, J. (2014). On the need to repoliticise environmental and sustainability education: Rethinking the postpolitical consensus. *Environmental Education Research*, 20(5), 639–659.

Swyngedouw, E. (2010). Impossible sustainability and the post-political condition. In *Making Strategies in Spatial Planning*, Cerretta, M., Concilio, G., Monno, V. (eds). Springer, Dordrecht.

Thésée, G., Carr, P., Potwora, F. (2015). Le rôle des enseignants dans l'éducation et la démocratie : impacts d'un projet de recherche sur la perception de futurs enseignants. *McGill Journal of Education*, 50, 363–387.

Theys, J. (2015). Le climat : une question de temps. *Natures sciences sociétés, Sup.*, 3, 1–2.

Touzard, H. (2006). Consultation, concertation, négociation : une courte note théorique. *Négociations*, 5, 69–74.

Twomey, P. and Gaziulusoy, I.A. (2014). Review of system innovation and transitions theories: Concepts and frameworks for understanding and enabling transitions to a low carbon built environment [Online]. Available at: https://www.researchgate.net/publication/306119135_Review_of_System_Innovation_and_Transitions_Theories_Concepts_and_frameworks_for_understanding_and_enabling_transitions_to_a_low_carbon_built_environment.

UNESCO (2006). Rapport mondial de suivi sur l'éducation pour tous [Online]. Available at: http://www.unesco.org/education/GMR2006/full/chap6_fr.pdf.

UNESCO (2017). L'éducation en vue des objectifs de développement durable : objectifs d'apprentissage [Online]. Available at: https://unesdoc.unesco.org/ark:/48223/pf0000247507.

Vachon, S. (2007). Green supply chain and the selection of environmental technologies. *International Journal of Production Research*, 45, 4357–4379.

Valkenburg, G. (2012). Sustainable technological citizenship. *European Journal of Social Theory*, 15(4), 471–487.

Vanoutrive, J., Derobertmasure, A., Friant, N. (2012). Analyse thématique et analyse propositionnelle : application à un corpus de témoignages concernant l'injustice scolaire. *Mesure et évaluation en éducation*, 35(2), 97–123.

Van Poeck, K. and Östman, L. (2017). Creating space for "the political" in environmental and sustainability education practice: A political move analysis of educators' actions. *Environmental Education Research*, 24(9), 1406–1423.

Van Poeck, K. and Vandenabeele, J. (2012). Learning from sustainable development: Education in the light of public issues. *Environmental Education Research*, 18(4), 541–552.

Van Poeck, K., Goeminne, G., Vandenabeele, J. (2014). Revisiting the democratic paradox of environmental and sustainability education: Sustainability issues as matters of concern. *Environmental Education Research*, 22(6), 806–826.

Vergnolle Mainar, C. (2008). Environnement et disciplines scolaires. *Natures Sciences Sociétés*, 16, 60–66.

Vergnolle Mainar, C. (2009). Les disciplines scolaires et leurs frontières : la géographie scolaire de l'environnement au développement durable. HDR, Université Paris 7, Paris.

Vergnolle Mainar, C. (2011). *La géographie dans l'enseignement, une discipline en dialogue*. Presses universitaires de Rennes, Rennes.

Vernin, Z. (2017). Justice environnementale et mouvements sociaux en Tunisie. Association internationale de techniciens, experts et chercheurs (AITEC) [Online]. Available at: http://aitec.reseau-ipam.org/IMG/pdf/justice-environnementale-et-mouvements-sociaux-en-tunisie_aitec_12_4_2017.pdf.

Veugelers, W. (2007). Creating critical-democratic citizenship education: Empowering humanity and democracy in Dutch education. *Compare: A Journal of Comparative Education*, 37(1), 105–19.

Veugelers, W., de Groot, I., Llomovatte, S., Naidorf, J. (2017). Higher education, educational policy and citizenship development. *Education and Society*, 35(1), 27–42.

Vial, M. (2000). La recherche en sciences de l'éducation et la santé. *Spirales–Revue de recherche en éducation*, 25, 19–142.

Vincent, G. (2008). La socialisation démocratique contre la forme scolaire. *Éducation et francophonie*, 36(2), 47–62.

Vogler, G. (2016). Power between habitus and reflexivity–Introducing Margaret Archer to the power debate. *Journal of Political Power*, 9(1), 65–82.

Voß, J. and Bornemann, B. (2011). The politics of reflexive governance: Challenges for designing adaptive management and transition management. *Ecology and Society*, 16(2).

Voß, J.-P., Smith, A., Grin, J. (2009). Designing long-term policy: Rethinking transition management. *Policy Science*, 42, 275–302.

Wals, A.E.J. and Peters, M.A. (2018). Flowers of resistance. Citizen science, ecological democracy and the transgressive education paradigm. In *Sustainability Science*, König, A. and Ravetz, J. (eds). Routledge, London.

Westheimer, J. and Kahne, J. (2004). What kind of citizen? The politics of educating for democracy. *American Educational Research Journal*, 41, 237–269.

Wever, C. (2015). Cultivating critical learning: Critical food pedagogy in FoodShare's school grown program. Master's Thesis, York University, Toronto.

Wooltorton, S. (2006). Ecological literacy ''basic'' for a sustainable future. In *Proceedings of the Social Educator's Association of Australia (SEEAA) National Biennial Conference*. Brisbane [Online]. Available at: https://fr.scribd.com/document/231704587/Ecological-Literacy-Basic-for-a-Sustainable-Future.

Yamashita, L. (2016). Making visible the people who feed us: Education for critical food literacy through multicultural texts. *Journal of Agriculture, Food Systems, and Community Development*, 6(2), 269–281.

Yardley, L. (2008). Demonstrating validity in qualitative psychology. In *Qualitative Psychology*, Smith, J.A. (ed.). Sage, London.

Yardley, L. (2017). Demonstrating the validity of qualitative research. *The Journal of Positive Psychology*, 12, 295–296.

Yazan, B. (2015). Three approaches to case study methods in education: Yin, Merriam, and Stake. *The Qualitative Report*, 20(2), 134–152.

Zaccai, E. and Orban, A. (2017). Mobilisations écologiques actuelles, mobilisations des années 1960–1970 : quels parallèles ? *Développement durable et territoire*, 18(2).

Zeleznik, A. (2016). Is successful deliberation possible? Theories of deliberative democracy in relation to state, civil society and individuals. *Croatian Political Science Review*, 53(4), 33–50.

Zhang, W.H. and Alexander, S. (2017). Objectifs pour un développement durable–pour l'analyse et pour la planification en santé. *Revue de médecine périnatale*, 9(1), 3–6.

Index

H, I, J

K, L, M

N, O, P

Q, R, S

T, U, V

Other titles from

iSTE

in

Innovations in Learning Sciences

2020

BOUISSOU-BÉNAVAIL Christine
Educational Studies in the Light of the Feminine: Empowerment and Transformation

CHAMPOLLION Pierre
Territorialization of Education: Trend or Necessity
(Education Set – Volume 5)

PÉLISSIER Chrysta
Support in Education

2019

BRIANÇON Muriel
The Meaning of Otherness in Education: Stakes, Forms, Process, Thoughts and Transfers
(Education Set – Volume 3)

HAGÈGE Hélène
Education for Responsibility
(Education Set – Volume 4)

RINAUDO Jean-Luc
Telepresence in Training

2018

BARTHES Angela, CHAMPOLLION Pierre, ALPE Yves
Evolutions of the Complex Relationship Between Education and Territories
(Education Set – Volume 1)

LARINI Michel, BARTHES Angela
Quantitative and Statistical Data in Education: From Data Collection to Data Processing
(Education Set – Volume 2)

2015

POMEROL Jean-Charles, EPELBOIN Yves, THOURY Claire
MOOCs: Design, Use and Business Models

Printed and bound by CPI Group (UK) Ltd, Croydon, CR0 4YY

15/09/2026

14962354-0001